SERMONS

BY

JOHN KERSHAW

John Kershaw

SERMONS

BY

JOHN KERSHAW

With a short biography
by B. A. Ramsbottom

1995

Published by:
Gospel Standard Trust Publications,
12(b) Roundwood Lane,
Harpenden, Hertfordshire, AL5 3DD,
England

ISBN   1 897837 06 2

Printed and bound in Great Britain by:
Biddles Ltd,
Walnut Tree House,
Woodbridge Park,
Guildford, GU1 1DA

CONTENTS

A SHORT BIOGRAPHY OF
JOHN KERSHAW: 1792-1870

It was a surprise to us some time ago to see one of John Kershaw's sermons translated into Chinese. Surely it would have been an even greater surprise to the poor Lancashire weaver himself. Yet even in his own lifetime there must have been things that amazed him – his visits to London when the large London chapels were filled to capacity when he preached; the loving welcome received year by year in the home of the affluent Lady Lucy Smith; and his successful preaching tour in Scotland, when he was entertained by the Lord Provost of Edinburgh. But what cannot the grace of God do? And John Kershaw would have put the emphasis on free grace.

After his death his autobiography was widely circulated, and there have been various editions since. We are pleased that this is so again, another edition having been republished at the end of last year. In 1970 a beautifully illustrated biography of John Kershaw, *Waar Gij Uw Voetstap Zet*, was published in Holland.

For nearly 53 years John Kershaw was pastor at Hope Particular Baptist Chapel in Rochdale, Lancashire, where his ministry was abundantly blessed. God made him an able minister of the new testament. But the whole spirit of such men as John Kershaw and his friends was one of self-abasement. They wanted Christ to be everything, and themselves nothing. Very typical of this was John Kershaw's sermon at Manchester following the death of William Gadsby (1844). Towards 2,000 people crowded into the chapel. What would the preacher say? What text would be fitting for such an eminent man as Gadsby? At last the preacher announced his text: "Less than the least" (Eph. 3. 8). This was how William Gadsby wished to be remembered, and this is how John Kershaw would have us remember him.

I

The whole of John Kershaw's life was spent in the vicinity of Rochdale. The son of a shoemaker, William Kershaw, he was born on August 25th, 1792, at a small place called Healey, now part of Rochdale itself. His birthplace can still be seen. His father was a good man who brought him up in the fear of God and took him to the Independent chapel. He would read to his family from John Newton, or James Hervey, or Ralph Erskine's Gospel Sonnets. But young John wanted none of these things. "I was like a vicious horse, champing the bit, prancing with its feet, longing to be gone; for my heart was with my sinful companions."

As he grew older, cock fighting, card playing and Sabbath breaking were his delight, despite some pricks of conscience and his father's rod. As he says, "My neck was an iron sinew, and my brow brass" (Isa. 48. 4). As an old man he wrote:

"It has often humbled my soul to think that the Lord should ever have thoughts of love and mercy towards such a vile, guilty rebel as myself; and as the effect of that love pluck me as a brand out of the fire, stop me in my sinful course, and bring me with a broken heart and godly sorrow for sin to Jesus' feet" (John Kershaw's autobiography, 1994 edition, page 5).

But for months John went on in the ways of sin – yet "angry with the Lord because he kept wounding me in my spirit."

"But the set time to favour Zion was come. I was walking alone on the footpath in the field next to the chapel when the Lord arrested me. There came such a power and solemnity upon my mind as overwhelmed me. I stood still, trembling, and burst into a flood of tears. I felt the powerful hand of God had laid fast hold of my poor soul. Death, the day of judgment, and the realities of a vast and awful eternity oppressed my thoughts and harrowed up my feelings in a manner I can never describe" (page 13).

Very deep were his convictions, feeling the curse of a broken law. The sudden death of his schoolmaster made him tremble: "The death of my schoolmaster was overruled by the Lord, to cause me to feel the uncertainty of life, and that I had not a day to call my own. I wondered greatly how it would be with me in that awful hour when the dread summons was served upon me" (page 15).

Now the scene of his wickedness became the place of prayer. Often he would go to the corner of a field and kneel down in a dry pit where no one would see him – there was no place for privacy in his own home.

"A bird began to build her nest near me. Before the Lord laid hold on me, I used to go into the woods with my companions to seek for and rob and plunder them of their eggs and young; but my conscience was now made so tender I was afraid to harm the meanest thing that lived. I was cautious not to disturb her, and went to my devotions as quietly as I could. She became in consequence so familiar that she would sit upon her nest, whilst I lifted up my heart and eyes to him who openeth his hand, and supplieth the wants of every living thing. She brought forth her young at the appointed time, and I soon lost these unconscious witnesses of the distress of my soul. I mention this simple circumstance to show the effect the grace of God has upon the heart. I continued to resort to this place until the grass was cut in the adjoining meadows, and haytime came on, when it became too public, and I had to retire to some woods near at hand" (pages 17-18).

These woods are now known as Healey Dell, a well-known local beauty spot – still unspoiled though only about three miles from the centre of Rochdale.

Chapel attendance now became regular, sinful companions were forsaken, and a Bible carried about. The change was noticed by all. But pride began to work, and even after attending the Baptist Association Meetings at Rochdale, he was left to backslide and go to the Manchester races – to the great distress of the godly, and afterwards brought to the borders of despair himself.

For some weeks he was in a very unsettled state.

"The immortal principle of grace which, I trust, was implanted in my soul, would not let me be happy as formerly in the ways of sin, when my whole heart and soul delighted in joining the multitude to do evil" (page 25). In this condition, as the time for the Rochdale races drew near, he made a most dreadful, solemn vow – and yet found himself off to the races when the time came. But this was the last time, and he knew it. "I stand here a monument of God's mercy and grace; for had he marked my iniquity, and dealt with me according to my sin, I should have been cut down as a cumberer of the ground" (page 30).

II

A time of bondage, exercise and deep soul-concern followed. There were many sighs and groans, and he felt he could do nothing at all to save himself, or repent and believe.

But the time of deliverance was near. John Kershaw felt constrained to walk to Bacup (five or six miles away), where the venerable John Hirst (1736-1815) had been minister at the Particular Baptist chapel for many years. His text that day was Isaiah 45. 22: "Look unto me, and be ye saved, all the ends of the earth, for I am God, and there is none else."

"Under this sermon I was led to see the ability of Christ to save unto the uttermost the chief of sinners; that the law of God which they had broken, he had fulfilled for them; that he had redeemed them from the curse of the law, being made a curse for them, and finished the work his Father gave him to do; and that there was everything done by him, and treasured up in him, that I stood in need of.

"As I sat and heard these things opened up, such light, life and power attended the Word that I said within myself, 'I shall never forget what I have heard this day.'

"I went home rejoicing that there was a new and living way, whereby God could be just and save poor, guilty sinners. The name, blood and righteousness of Jesus Christ became precious to my soul; so that I could not forbear saying, 'This is the Christ and the salvation my soul stands in need of.'

"It did my soul good to see that the whole work was finished by Christ upon the cross, and that there was nothing left for me to do, as the ground of my acceptance with God" (page 35).

Now all was different. He read the Bible and heard the preaching with new eyes and new ears. Great love flowed out of his heart to God's people and God's house, to the Bible and the throne of grace. Often would he go to Bacup to hear Mr. Hirst, whom he dearly loved, and who took a great interest in him. John Hirst was one of the old Particular Baptist ministers, highly esteemed and respected, and whose ministry was much blessed. He had a large congregation of about 800 people. Unlike some, he contended that the gospel call and invitations are not universal, but to characters.

But still John waited "for a manifestation of my personal interest in his salvation by the remission of sins." During this time he was very tried on the doctrine of election till this was made plain to him.

III

About this time John Kershaw was invited to attend a baptizing service at the Town Meadows Particular Baptist chapel in Rochdale, and from that day became a decided Baptist in principle, believing it to be in complete accordance with the Word of God. Soon he left the Independents, where he never really profited spiritually, and attended Town Meadows. His soul clave to the godly here, and here he felt he would live and die. The ministry of Thomas Littlewood he found experimental and helpful.

It was about this time (May 1807) that William Gadsby first came over from Manchester to preach in Rochdale. But this sadly led to a division in the church. Good man as he was, Mr. Littlewood had heard false reports of Mr. Gadsby, forbade his members to hear him, and excommunicated those who did. But all this, under the mysterious providence of God, led to the establishing of Hope Chapel where for so many years John Kershaw was to be pastor. "God moves in a mysterious way his wonders to perform."

John Kershaw was fourteen at the time, and listened with great interest when Mr. Gadsby preached in a large meadow outside the town. He was greatly impressed. Soon those who had been excluded for going to hear Gadsby felt constrained to be formed into a church. In fact, a time had come in Lancashire, and in other parts of England, when the people of God were longing for preaching deeper, clearer and more profitable than what they had been accustomed to hear. And God had ordained John Kershaw to be such a preacher. Much of the Calvinism of the day had become very dry and legal; many were dissatisfied; so it was with delight that a man like Gadsby was welcomed of whom one of the oldest and most highly esteemed Rochdale Christians could say, "I was never so blessed in my soul under any minister before. He does not preach a new gospel. It is the old gospel brought forward in a way so blessedly calculated to meet the cases of the Lord's tried family."

John Kershaw was much helped personally in hearing William Gadsby, on one of his Rochdale visits, describe the marks of a child of God. Yet he was still tried and tempted by Satan, even on one occasion to take his own life until the Lord was "graciously pleased to break into my soul. My hard, stubborn heart began to soften, and my darkness to flee away, and I was blest with a contrite and humble spirit whilst confessing my sins before him, and had nearness of access in pleading with him for mercy on such a rebellious wretch" (page 60).

At last the day of liberty arrived. Very tried and tempted,

the words came powerfully to him: "O wretched man that I am, who shall deliver me from the body of this death?" The latter part of the chapter (Romans 7) flowed into his mind. Hastening home, he reached for the Bible to examine the chapter.

"I read it with such light, power and comfort as I had never felt before; so pleased and blest in my soul that I began to read the next chapter, commencing thus: 'There is, therefore, now no condemnation to them which are in Christ Jesus, who walk not after the flesh but after the Spirit.' As I read these precious words, their blessed contents were brought into my soul with power and glory. I saw and felt that I was in Christ Jesus, saved with an everlasting salvation. The burden of sin was removed, my conscience cleansed by an application of the precious blood of Jesus Christ. I felt the sealing testimony of the Holy Spirit of God that I stood complete and accepted in the Beloved. I read the chapter through with a joy I cannot describe. I now knew my election of God, and that no charge could ever be brought against me, because Christ had died for my sins, and was raised again from the dead for my justification; that he ever lived to make intercession for me, and would receive me into his kingdom of glory. The love of Christ was shed abroad in my heart; I saw and felt that nothing could separate me from the love of God, which is in Christ Jesus our Lord. How precious and glorious were the truths contained in this chapter to my soul on that memorable evening!" (pages 63-64.)

Now, with the love of Christ in his heart, John Kershaw longed to follow the Lord in his ordinances. The time came for the separated friends to be formed into a church, and others came forward to be baptized – six in all, and among them John Kershaw. He gave his testimony before the friends, and later also to William Gadsby, who interviewed him along with a London minister (possibly Jonathan Franklin). Mr. Gadsby asked him several questions on the doctrines of grace,

and his views on the ordinances. The last question was:
"John, you are very young, and you will be exposed to many
snares and temptations. Do you think you can stand your
ground, and not bring a reproach upon yourself and the cause
of God and truth?"

Perhaps the reply was surprising, "Yes, the Lord keeping
me and preserving me; as Paul said, 'I can do all things
through Christ which strengtheneth me,'" but William
Gadsby smiled his approval, and his friend said, "I am well
satisfied."

The baptizing took place in a stream, in a field, before
nearly 2,000 people, William Gadsby preaching. Later the
church was formed in a farmhouse, and the Lord's supper
administered.

Writing over fifty years later, John Kershaw commented:
"We have [since that time] had removed by death 170
members, many of whom have left a blessed testimony behind
them that they died in the Lord, and about the same number
remain as members."

Within the next two or three years they built a chapel,
calling it "Hope," and John Warburton (later of Trowbridge)
became their pastor.

IV

Some time after this John Kershaw became friendly with
a young lady, baptized at the same time, and eventually they
married. Working as a handloom weaver, and soon with a
growing family, he and his wife found many trials. Bread was
very dear in those days – the end of the Napoleonic Wars and
afterwards – and times were hard. Yet mercifully was he
supported and his every need supplied. Yet so poor were they
they hardly ever had meat; oatmeal, milk and potatoes was
their usual fare. Sometimes after a hard day's work, he went
supperless to bed. But friends and relatives were constrained
to help, and even John Kershaw's master once put a pound
note into his wife's hand.

On one occasion he was sweetly favoured with a special time of communion with God:

"My soul was so taken up with my dear Lord and Master that I could say of him as the church of old: My Beloved is white and ruddy, the chiefest amongst ten thousand, and the altogether lovely. His mouth is most sweet, in speaking peace and pardon to the guilty sinner. His blood I felt to be most precious, as my redemption price, and as a 'fountain opened for sin and for uncleanness.' He appeared glorious, as my lawfulfilling Righteousness. I felt I had a firm standing upon him as the Rock of my salvation, and that I was complete and accepted in him" (pages 80-81). And as he was on his knees, blessing and praising God, the power of the Lord came upon him, moving him to preach the gospel.

From this time there was increased life and light in prayer and in reading the Word. Sweetly did he feel the Lord had called him to preach, though feeling such "an obscure, illiterate, despised youth, in poverty and distress." At length the Lord sweetly assured him that he was to be a minister.

But the Lord was exercising the hearts of the people as well and at a church meeting, when John was absent, John Warburton (now pastor at Hope Chapel) told the church he knew he would have to preach, and every member felt the same. So it was arranged for him to preach (at the beginning of the year 1814).

His ministry was well received, being made a blessing to the people – though at first some would come, and seeing that it was only "young John in the pulpit," would return home.

Many were the journeys he now made on foot to preach, trudging miles over the bleak Lancashire moors after a hard week at work.* Many were the dangers. Once he almost

* When F. L. Rowell was pastor at Rochdale, on one occasion he and another minister attempted one of John Kershaw's regular journeys over the hills. When they arrived at their destination, they said that neither of them could have preached. And John Kershaw had to walk home again afterward!

perished in a snow drift; often he met with a gang of robbers, who later were hanged, but they never molested him.

It was not long before John Warburton left Rochdale to begin his long, honoured ministry at Trowbridge, Wiltshire. Now the hearts of the people were set on John Kershaw as their pastor, and eventually he was chosen – at the age of 24. There was a debt on the chapel, the congregation was small and poverty abounded – whilst the young family of the pastor was bitterly persecuted by ungodly neighbours. To make things worse, the old Town Meadows chapel appointed an eminent and learned man to be their minister, and enemies (and even friends) prophesied that this would be the end of both John Kershaw and his chapel – "a poor weaver for the minister, with a family of small children, a heavy chapel debt, but few members, small congregation, and those mostly poor"!

But from that time the Lord began to work. Many came over from the Town Meadows chapel, including the two old deacons who for years had been pillars there. On one day ten persons were baptized, and four received from the other church.

From that time both the church and congregation greatly increased – so that in 1848 the chapel had to be enlarged to hold over 700 persons.

V

Much might be written of John Kershaw's long, honoured pastorate at Hope Chapel, Rochdale. Here he was maintained, experiencing the blessing of the Lord, for nearly fifty-three years. Many were the remarkable testimonies of those who were blessed under his preaching – one a violent, vicious soldier who had been one of Napoleon's guards on the island of Elba; one the wicked neighbour who so cruelly persecuted his family; one a well-known author and respected churchman; and many others.

Over the years there were many calls to other churches – one from the Manchester church after Gadsby's death, one from the large Great Alie Street church in London. But none of these things moved him.

Perhaps the most celebrated occasion on which John Kershaw was called to minister was the death of William Gadsby in 1844. It was a weighty responsibility which lay on the shoulders of Gadsby's younger friend – the danger of saying too much; the fear of saying too little. But what an outstanding address was that which he gave to the assembled multitude (around 3,000) that gathered at the grave that snowy January day. He himself declared, "I have never experienced the feelings I did on this occasion." John Kershaw said a few things about Gadsby's life, his character as a Christian and as an inhabitant of Manchester, but especially he was enabled aptly and briefly to outline the glorious truths for which Gadsby stood and which he delighted to preach. A week or two later he preached his memorable funeral sermon in the chapel from Eph. 3. 8, dwelling on "less than the least." These occasions were truly "days of the Son of Man."

During these years there were many journeys, usually the northern ones undertaken on foot. Once a month for forty-nine years John Kershaw walked several miles over wild moors to preach to a number of gracious people in a loft over a row of cottages (Limey Leach) or in a room in a cotton mill (Cheesden Pasture).*

His annual visits to London were much appreciated, his first visit in 1832 being to collect money for the chapel debt.

Year by year he stayed at the mansion of Lady Lucy Smith, Wilford House, near Nottingham, and preached there. Lady Lucy had married the wealthy banker Henry Smith and delighted to entertain several godly ministers (including J. C. Philpot). She was the daughter of the Earl of Leven and Melville.

* Details of these interesting visits are given in an appendix I wrote for the recently published autobiography of John Kershaw. It was on one of these visits that he fell into Cheesden Brook on a snowy day and broke his arm.

Specially interesting was John Kershaw's visit to preach in Edinburgh in 1861, arranged by Lady Lucy who felt that Scotland stood in need of his type of preaching. How remarkable to find the Lancashire weaver entertained by the Lord Provost of Edinburgh! Some of the congregations he preached to were exceedingly large, especially in the Great Hall of the College of the Free Church of Scotland. It was a great pleasure to John Kershaw to meet that eminent man of God, Dr. John ("Rabbi") Duncan, who came to hear him, and the two felt a sweet affinity to each other.

But it was in his home town of Rochdale that he was specially known and loved.* His kindness and geniality endeared him to the people. How loving he was as a pastor! Two instances will illustrate this. On one occasion an old man, wishing to become a church member, was called to speak his testimony before the church. But the poor man was shut up and could not speak. Sadly he was requested to leave; but as he left, Mr. Kershaw called after him something to this effect: "But you don't love the Lord Jesus, do you?" Almost angrily the old man retorted, "I do that, and aboon (above) a bit." This broke the snare.

The other was when a young lady was to give her testimony. She was rather afraid, and feared she would not be able to speak. The pastor kindly said to her, "I have heard your experience, and it is all contained in – (such a hymn). If you are stuck, read that, and I can vouch that it is your own experience." But she was blessed with liberty and her testimony moved the people's hearts.

A. B. Taylor said of him:

"In many respects our brother was an amiable man. He was kind, affectionate and tender, even to a fault. He well knew how to seek for the life of God in a longing sinner's soul and, if there, seldom failed to find it, and would seek to

* When the writer taught at a school in Rochdale in the 1950s, he found that the name of "Particular Baptist" was still respected in the town.

comfort the spirit by bringing to the foreground the invitations and promises of the gospel" (page 358).

But not only among his own people, but in the town of Rochdale itself, John Kershaw was honoured. The people had watched him; they knew him and honoured him. It is said that the famous Victorian statesman, John Bright (a Rochdale man, a Member of Parliament and at one time in the cabinet) said he felt it an honour to walk through the streets of Rochdale with John Kershaw.

VI

What was it about John Kershaw's preaching that had such an effect, and that drew such crowds to hear him?

His preaching was very simple; he spoke from the heart to the heart. The trumpet gave no uncertain sound as he clearly set forth the doctrines of free and sovereign grace, insisting on a gracious experience of the truth. At times his preaching was enriched by some homely incident from his own life or some personal testimony to the truths he preached. At the bottom of it all was a good foundation – the clear, deep experience of both law and gospel he himself had, a knowledge of his own sin and depravity and the riches of God's grace in his dear Son. But the secret of all his success was the power of the Holy Spirit applying the truth to the hearts of his hearers.

It seems clear, also, that there was at this time a people being wrought upon by the Holy Spirit and being prepared for the preaching of men like Gadsby, Warburton and Kershaw, the early ministers connected with the *Gospel Standard* magazine. Their souls were hungry and thirsty. For so long had they been starved under what John Kershaw would have called a "yea and nay gospel." The cold, arid, legalistic strain that had come into much of the old Particular Baptist preaching did not suit them or meet their cases.

This is the reason why, on John Kershaw's first visit to London in 1832, he soon found the large Zoar Chapel, Great

Alie Street, overflowing with hearers who delighted in such a ministry.

Very telling is John Kershaw's own account of his first Sabbath there:

"After service, one of the deacons came into the vestry and said, 'You see, my dear friend, we have been very thinly attended this morning.'

"I replied, 'Yes.'

"He added, 'Mark my words. You are come here for four Lord's days, and before you have finished them you will see this chapel, which seats from seven to eight hundred people, filled from the pulpit door into the street. There is such a want of these great and precious truths being preached in this simple Bible style of language in this great city that there will be such a flocking to hear as will astonish you. The few that have been here this morning will go amongst their friends in all directions, and, like the woman of Samaria, say, "Come see a man which told me all things that ever I did."'

"I replied I could not think that would be the case, but in the evening I was surprised to see the increase of people.

"After service, the deacon came again with a smile upon his countenance, saying, 'You see we are greatly increased tonight. I have just been talking with a God-fearing man who has been hearing you, who can speak seven languages. I told him what I had said to you in the morning, and that you were slow of heart to believe it. And he declares I shall be a true prophet.'

"And so he was; for before the four Lord's days were over, numbers went away that could not get within the chapel doors" (pages 203-204).

A magazine called *The Silent Preacher* was published in London about this time. The Editor seems to have been very attracted to John Kershaw. "Mr. Kershaw is in town, and so I shall be hearing him the next four weeks," he would say (or words to that effect). The opinion he came to was this:

"He is a good-tempered, warm-hearted, zealous, determined and spiritual teacher of the people. There is no bitterness, no wrangling – no foolish, unbecoming expressions; no preaching of self; but beginning with the love and purpose of the Father, passing on to the perfect work of the Son, he comes to the Holy Spirit's teaching, leadings and actings in the consciences of the saints. Mr. Kershaw is, indeed, 'a workman that needeth not to be ashamed, *rightly* dividing the Word of truth.'"

A short summary of John Kershaw's theme and his manner of speaking he gives as follows:

"'As the body without the soul is dead, so that religion,' said he, 'which is not begun by the Person and the work of the Holy Ghost, that religion which is not completed by the Person and work of the Holy Ghost, is a religion that is dead, that is barren, and of no avail.' And when the good man uttered this sentence, the smile usual on his countenance was laid aside – he stood erect in the pulpit – he cast his eyes around upon his audience, and he spoke with all that vehemence and power which told us it came from his heart, and that he solemnly felt the truths he proclaimed. And so, again, on the following Sabbath morning, in the course of that truly gospel sermon which he delivered on justification, he said, 'I always like doctrine and experience to go hand in hand together, and then I am satisfied that *practice* will follow'" (*The Silent Preacher*, January 1842).

VII

John Kershaw was spared to reach the 50th anniversary of his pastorate at Rochdale – very remarkably in the church where he was baptized and the town where he had spent all his life. The Jubilee Services on March 6th, 1867, must have been a most interesting and remarkable occasion, over 800 people being present. Several ministers took part, and a presentation was made of a gold watch and chain together with £362.

At the close of the day, Mr. Kershaw remarked, "It has been a great day. The next great day will be my burial day." And so it proved.

At the time of the Jubilee John Kershaw seemed to be in his usual good health, but soon afterwards he noticeably began to fail. His constant prayer was that he might be upheld to the end.

Yet as late as April 1869 he set off once again for his southern visit, preaching in London as usual, and was away for three weeks. But on his return he seemed far from well. Having with difficulty preached on the Sabbath at Hope Chapel, he was then confined to bed, and thought much of his end; for some weeks he could not leave his room. Before the end of the summer, however, he did manage to get to chapel and at the end of the year, remarkably, he preached on December 12th from, "For to me to live is Christ, and to die is gain," and again from the same text the next week. Again, a week later, he preached from Genesis 49. 10. The word that day was made a great blessing to a minister present (George Chandler) as Mr. Kershaw spoke of Shiloh making peace by the blood of his cross. The last time he went into the pulpit was the first Lord's day of the new year 1870.

After this he began to sink. He died on January 11th, 1870, aged 77. Among his last words were:

> "Yes, I shall soon be landed
>   On yonder shores of bliss;
> There with my powers expanded,
>   Shall dwell where Jesus is" –

joyfully repeating the last line several times. The last words he spoke were: "God is faithful! God is faithful!"

On his gravestone (in the Rochdale cemetery) the words are written:

> "And while he pressed to seats of bliss,
>   He sang no other song but this:
>   'A sinner saved by grace.'"

What an apt summary of John Kershaw's life and witness!

VIII

Perhaps the writer may be permitted a personal word. One of his earliest memories is how his old grandfather would speak of when he was a boy and John Kershaw visited their home.   For years his own father, the cobbler, James Ramsbottom, made the boots in which Mr. Kershaw trudged so many miles to preach the gospel.

Many were the tales that were told of those far off days, the many godly souls who lived over the moors, but especially Mr. Kershaw's monthly visits (in winter, always when there was a full moon) when he preached in a very large loft over the cottages.

But one memory was specially cherished (and not just as a story, but as typical of John Kershaw). On one occasion Mr. Kershaw was preaching on the love of Christ and his heart waxed warm. Loudly exclaiming,

> "O for such love, let rocks and hills
>   Their lasting silence break;
>   And all harmonious human tongues
>   The Saviour's praises speak,"

forcefully he brought down his hand and smashed the oil lamp, leaving the congregation in darkness.   A child's memory! Obviously a little boy would remember this. But surely John Kershaw would have preferred to be remembered in this way to any other – speaking on his darling theme, the love of Christ to sinners.

B. A. Ramsbottom
1995

*   *   *   *

We specially thank Mr. David Oldham of Stamford for his help in locating so many of John Kershaw's sermons. There is a small volume of his sermons, published by Gospel Tidings in 1976; none of the ten sermons published there appear in the present volume.

The question has been noted: why do John Kershaw's sermons need editing?

Let us be clear. The only changes that have been made have been to modernize the punctuation, and divide into more paragraphs for easier reading – along with some obvious printing errors and one or two archaic Lancashire expressions. Also there are explanations of the background and footnotes concerning persons mentioned. There has been no attempt to interfere with the style. We have left unaltered such things as the rather untypical ending to one of the sermons, and the mention (surely a reporter's mistake?) of riding through Rochdale on horseback.

We strongly recommend the autobiography of John Kershaw, republished last year by Gospel Tidings Publications, and obtainable from Christian Bookshop, 21 Queen Street, Ossett, West Yorkshire WF5 8AS.

We also thank Mr. John Kingham and Mrs. Hazel Parish for all their help in preparing this book.

1. THE PRINCE OF PEACE

Part of a Sermon preached at Zoar Chapel, Great Alie Street, London, on May 2nd, 1841

Text: *"Him hath God exalted with his right hand to be a Prince and a Saviour, for to give repentance to Israel, and forgiveness of sins" (Acts 5. 31).*

You will recollect, my friends, that last Lord's day evening we considered these words, and on that occasion we confined ourselves to the first branch of the subject, namely, to the exaltation of Christ with the right hand of the Father. The next branch of the passage is that of his being exalted as a Prince: "Him hath God exalted with his right hand, to be a Prince." To my mind, that is a beautiful passage in which we have the Lord Jesus blessedly set forth in the ninth chapter of Isaiah, and the sixth verse: "For unto us a Child is born, unto us a Son is given: and the government shall be upon his shoulder, and his name shall be called Wonderful, Counsellor, the Mighty God, the Everlasting Father, the Prince of Peace." Look at this, beloved; he is here called "the Prince of Peace"; and it is our mercy as poor sinners to have such a Prince as the Lord Jesus Christ.

In the prophecy of Isaiah we also read of the covenant of peace: "The mountains shall depart, and the hills be removed, but my kindness shall not depart from thee, neither shall the covenant of my peace be removed." Now what is this covenant of peace? It is that of which David speaks as "ordered in all things and sure." And why is it here called the covenant of peace? Because it has Christ, the Prince of Peace, for its covenant Head.

Again, my friends, this covenant of peace not only speaks of Christ as its covenant Head, but it has also the blood of this blessed Prince of Peace as its sealing. "Now the God of peace, that brought again from the dead our Lord Jesus, that great Shepherd of the sheep, through the blood of the everlasting covenant"; so that Christ stands in covenant blood, and thereby this is a ratified, sealed and confirmed covenant. And our comfort is everlasting because it is founded upon the everlasting covenant: "Who has given us everlasting consolation," and a good hope through the grace of Jesus Christ, who is exalted as the Prince of this covenant.

No sooner had this Prince, according to the promise, made his appearance here on earth, born of a woman and under the law, and even while he lies in the stable, as the poor Babe of Bethlehem, wrapped in swaddling clothes and lying in a manger, than angels are despatched from heaven to give him a welcome becoming such a mighty Prince. The shepherds hear the song of the incarnation of the Prince of Peace, and it is this: "Glory to God in the highest, and on earth peace, good will towards men"; "For unto you is born this day, in the city of David, a Saviour, which is Christ the Lord."

Again, beloved, in referring to the Lord Jesus as thus exalted, whom God has exalted as a Prince, I must direct your attention to his character as the Prince of Peace, the Mediator between God and man. What does the Apostle Paul say of his character in that precious chapter of the second Epistle to the church at Ephesus? There he speaks of him as having made peace by his blood. There is a blessed clause in Christ's sermon on the mount, and fitting no one so well as himself; it is this, "Blessed are the peacemakers." Christ has made peace between a holy, just and righteous God and a fiery law, and poor, guilty, sinful, vile, rebellious man. "There is one God and one Mediator between God and man"; and that Mediator is Christ Jesus, the Prince of Peace. And how has he made peace? O my friends, he has made peace by shedding his own most precious blood; by dying the just for the unjust; by putting away sin by the sacrifice of himself; by being made a curse that we might enjoy the blessing. So that Christ Jesus, in his glorious Person, is the Prince of Peace through his atoning blood.

And he is our great Peacemaker; and him has God exalted, and lifted up as an ensign to the nations, that every
guilty, burdened and distressed soul might flee to him for rest.
Peace, my friends, is made for us, and is not made by ourselves;
for Christ, the Prince of Peace, *is* our peace, and has broken
down the middle wall of partition between Jew and Gentile by
blotting out the handwriting of ordinances, and by removing
every obstacle in our way to Jehovah the Father. In him (that
is, in Christ) mercy and truth have met together, righteousness and peace have kissed and embraced each other; in
him, and his glorious death, and blood shedding on Mount
Calvary. And, O my friends, where shall a poor, distressed
soul look for peace and joy and rest but in this blessed Jesus,
exalted at the Father's right hand as the Prince of Peace?

A great many people are for doing the work of this Prince
of Peace themselves. I recollect a minister visiting a poor
woman who knew something of the Lord Jesus Christ, and he
asked her, "Have you made your peace with God?" She
smiled, looked up at him, and said, "What! have I made peace
with God? O no!" "Then," said he, "it is time you did." "Ah!
but," said the poor woman, "my peace with God was made
eighteen hundred years before I was born." He asked her how
it was that her peace was made so long back. Why, my friends,
she had to turn preacher, and directed his attention to Christ,
the great Prince of Peace, who had made peace for her by the
shedding of his blood, whom God has exalted as "a Prince and
a Saviour, to give repentance to Israel and forgiveness of sins."

Now you shall hear the voice of the Prince of Peace; for he
is not only so in his glorious Person, and has made peace, but
he is also a Preacher of peace, and he has left his people his
peace as a legacy. In addressing his disconsolate disciples in
the fourteenth chapter of John, he says, "Let not your heart be
troubled: ye believe in God, believe also in me." He says in the
twenty-seventh verse, "Peace I leave with you, my peace I give
unto you: not as the world giveth, give I unto you. Let not

your heart be troubled, neither let it be afraid." When the peace of the Lord Jesus Christ is possessed by the soul of a poor sinner, O then there is a joy that is past all understanding. How blessed is the condition of the poor sinner when in the sweet enjoyment of this precious peace!

O then, let us see this very night how matters stand before the Lord. Are we at peace, or are we harassed under the oppression of sin, and sighing by reason of our evil hearts and the feeling of our numerous infirmities? Are we tormented by doubts and fears, perplexed with temptation, and know not what to do or whither to fly? O! let but the Prince of Peace speak to your troubled breast and say, "I have made peace for you, and am the peace of your eternal spirit" – O then your peace shall be eternal, for it speaks by the blood of Christ to your souls, and when that is possessed, there is rest and joy, which the world can neither give nor take away.

We have already seen that the peace of the Christian in Christ is gained by the shedding of the Saviour's blood. Now you will recollect that the night God brought the children of Israel out of Egypt, they killed the paschal lamb, and ate it with unleavened bread and bitter herbs. This was typical of Christ. Not a drop of the blood was to fall on the ground or be lost, but it was to be put into basins and sprinkled on the lintel and the door posts of the houses of Israel. And on that very night, when the children of Israel were in their habitations with their shoes on their feet, their loins girded and their staves in their hands, eating the paschal lamb with unleavened bread and bitter herbs – O! awful and solemn is the thought! – the angel of destruction is dispatched from heaven with the sword of divine vengeance in his hand, passes through the whole territory of Egypt, enters every habitation not sprinkled with the blood of the lamb, and all the first-born of Egypt, from the first-born of Pharaoh to that of the meanest peasant in the land, are cut off. But, O! see; there is peace and rest for the Israel of God. They have the certain assurance of safety and security; as their lintel and door-posts are sprinkled with the blood of the lamb, the destroying angel cannot enter their habitations.

I must pause on this point; it is one of great moment to man, to be thus sprinkled with the blood of Christ, the Prince of Peace. For then we have no cause to fear the flaming sword of divine justice. Having faith in him, we sit down as under the shadow of a great rock in a weary land. He is our refuge from the storm, and our covert from the tempest. There is no rest for a poor, guilty sinner but in Jesus Christ's atoning blood; but having our hope in him, we are as sure of heaven as if we were there already, for there is no condemnation to that soul that is in the Prince of Peace. No charge can be brought against God's elect, for Christ their Prince has died for them.

There is another circumstance to which I will refer, that of Rahab the harlot. She having hid the spies, the children of Israel made a covenant with her that her house should not be destroyed with the rest of the inhabitants of that devoted city, and the house was to be known by a scarlet line in the window, which should ensure her safety; so that this woman, and her kindred who were with her in the house, had peace while all the rest were in fear and consternation. When the children of Israel entered Jericho, the people fled in consternation. And why was this? Because the terror of the Lord God of Israel had fallen on them; as the woman said to the spies, their hearts were like water, because they had heard of the great things God had done for them by bringing them out of Egypt, dividing the waters of the Red Sea, giving famous cities into their hands; they trembled. But the woman trembled not, and all that were with her had peace and rest.

And so, my friends, will it be on the great judgment day, when Christ comes riding on the clouds of heaven, and the trumpet of the resurrection begins to sound. The enemies of God will then feel dread and consternation, and will say to the rocks and mountains, "Fall on us," but Jesus will be the Prince of Peace and glory of his people. All the church of God will claim him as their Elder Brother, and will stand with firmness and boldness and will lift up their heads in triumph, and cry, "I see him come! It is our Friend and Mediator, Saviour and Redeemer." And Jesus Christ, the Prince of Peace to his church and people, shall claim them as his own, while those who would not have him to reign over them shall be driven back into the shades of everlasting sorrow.

Hearken to the voice of this Prince, my friends, once more. He says, addressing his disconsolate people that are near and dear to him: "In the world ye shall have tribulation, but be of good cheer, I have overcome the world"; he says, "In me ye shall have peace." Now, flesh and blood do not like tribulation; you and I, planning to get on in the world, never form crooked plans, but smooth plans, and straight plans. But the Prince says, "In the world ye shall have tribulation," and, "It is not in man that walketh to direct his steps," but, "A good man's steps are ordered by the Lord," and he leads the blind through paths they have not known, and makes darkness light before them, and crooked things straight, and says he will never leave them or forsake them. But the misery of it is, that sometimes we are for doing the work of this Prince of Peace ourselves; we are for making the crooked things straight, and the rough places plain. But let us not attempt to do the work of the Prince, but leave him to do it, and let us only watch his hand. However thorny our paths may be, let us trust our affairs entirely to his guidance, for he is an able and a just Prince, and all power in heaven and earth is in his hands, and the crooked will soon be made straight, and the rough places plain.

The church of God in this world, my dear friends, is like a vessel on a boisterous sea, and the members of his church have to buffet with storms and tempests as they pass along, and sometimes they "reel too and fro and stagger like a drunken man"; but when we get a sight of the Lord, then there is a little peace and rest but not else. "Cast thy burden on the Lord, and he shall sustain thee," for he is our Pilot, and will steer the vessel safely into the haven of eternal peace.

It is indeed a mercy to be under the protecting care of this Prince of Peace, and through faith in him, the billows of life shall drop harmless at our feet, when ready to overwhelm us. Perhaps some of you may know something about the sea. In the eighth chapter of Luke, twenty-third verse, we find Christ had gone to sleep; he slept as a man, but as a God he slept not. "But as they sailed he fell asleep; and there came a storm of wind on the lake, and they were filled with water, and were in jeopardy; and they came to him, and awoke him, saying, Master, Master, we perish! Then he arose, and rebuked the wind and the raging of the water, and they ceased, and there was a calm." You see here, my friends, the disciples woke their Prince with terror and dismay. He arose with a countenance calm and serene, and with majesty and power on his brow. He goes on the deck, takes a survey; the wind roars, the storm increases and seems to threaten destruction every moment. The Prince speaks, "Be still!" The elements obey, the face of the waters is changed, and there is a calm.

O my friends, have we not often felt such a storm raging in our own bosoms? I do not know how you Londoners are, but with me there is often sad kicking within. We shall never have peace till we come to our Prince; and when we look to him with the eye of faith, we shall hear his heavenly voice saying, "Be still" – and all will be calm.

I have heard a circumstance related, but the truth of it I know not. It has afforded consolation to my mind, and I will give you the relation, since it illustrates the point we are now dwelling on. There was a ship out at sea which was overtaken by a storm. The vessel was in great peril, and the passengers at their wits' end, expecting every moment to be buried in the waves. Death, grief and destruction were in their countenances. One of them, with much surprise, observed a boy playing, and seeming quite indifferent and unconcerned. He said to the boy, "Why, how is this that you are so calm in such a storm, and the danger we are in of going to the bottom?" "O!" says the boy, with a smile, "I am not afraid, for my father is at the helm, and I look to him." O my friends, in every storm let us look to our Father in heaven. Every Christian is a vessel of mercy; Christ is the Pilot, he is at the helm, and will steer the vessel in safety through every storm, till we arrive at the haven of happiness as our eternal resting place.

Then observe again, my friends, Christ is not only called the "Prince of Peace," but also the "*Prince of Life.*" This appellation is given to him in a most solemn and striking manner by the Apostle Peter, at the time Peter was interrogated by the elders of the Jews in reference to the power and ability by which a lame man was healed. Peter disclaims all power in himself by which the cripple was restored, but ascribes all power to Christ. I will read you two or three verses from the 3rd of the Acts: "And when Peter saw it, he answered unto the people, Ye men of Israel, why marvel ye at this? or why look ye so earnestly on us, as though by our own power or holiness we had made this man to walk?" No, no, my brethren; there is no power in us. Then he goes on to say, "The God of Abraham, and of Isaac, and of Jacob, the God of our fathers, hath glorified his Son Jesus; whom ye delivered up, and denied him in the presence of Pilate, when he was determined to let him go. But ye denied the Holy One and the Just, and desired a murderer to be granted unto you" – then comes the verse to which I will direct your attention: "and killed the Prince of Life, whom God hath raised from the dead, whereof we are witnesses." Now, you see, Peter charged the death of our Lord Jesus Christ, the Prince of Peace, on the wicked Jews; he says, "But ye have killed the Prince of Life." What! killed the Prince of *Life?* What did they kill? Why, they killed the body of the Prince and no more, for that was all they could do. You see, then, they nailed him to the accursed tree, exhibited him as a spectacle to men, angels and devils. He died this shameful, ignominious death, was laid in the cold and silent grave for three days and nights, but saw no corruption. He has risen again, and is now exalted to the right hand of the Father in glorious majesty.

O, my friends, hearken to that voice of his in the chapter I read to you tonight (Revelation 1). It is the voice of our Prince, who suffered death that we might live. Our Prince says, to stimulate our souls from earth to heaven, "I am he that liveth, and was dead; and behold, I am alive for evermore." So our Prince is not a dead Prince. No, though he died, "the Just for the unjust," he is alive, and lives in the high court of heaven as the Prince of Life; and for this reason he says, "Behold, I am alive for evermore, and have the keys of hell and of death." Thus Jesus Christ was victorious over the grave, and is now exalted to the right hand of the Father, and is the Prince of Life as well as the Prince of Peace.

Now, my friends, this part of our subject is of vital importance. I have endeavoured to show you that the Lord Jesus Christ is the Prince of Life – that is, he is the life of his saints, church and people. Now, my brethren, I give you time to ponder this, and may it yield consolation to your souls. I say, the life of Christ is the life of every saint of the Most High God. I repeat it, that the Lord Jesus Christ is the Prince of Life, and the saints' God; and those who have this Prince for their life *will never die till their Prince dies*; and when will he die? O (blessed word), never; for it is written, "Thou art a Priest for ever after the order of Melchisedec," who was both Priest and King. Now, I speak not of the body of God's Son; no, his body died; but I speak of his spiritual life, the life of God in the soul; and the life of God in the soul is that of the Lord Jesus Christ. He is the Life of every one of his subjects.

Now, you shall have the testimony of the Apostle Paul, first, by way of doctrine, and also by way of experience.

Hearken to what he says to the church at Colosse, by way of doctrine: "For ye are dead, and your life is hid with Christ in God. When Christ, who is our Life, shall appear, then shall ye also appear with him in glory." So you see that Christ is here represented as the life of the mystical body, the church. Now hearken unto Paul in reference to his experience: "I am crucified with Christ, nevertheless I live"; that is, not as in former times I lived, a natural life, but I live now that life of grace which Christ gives. O my friends, may we all say, like Paul, "I am crucified with Christ, nevertheless I live; yet it is not I that live, but Christ, the Prince of Life and Glory, lives in me. My life is now by faith in the Son of God, who loved me, and gave himself for me."

O, cheer up, brethren, you that complain of hard hearts, tribulation, harassing doubts and fears. If you have the Lord Jesus Christ, you have the root of the matter in you. He is the light of life in your souls; they shall never die while he lives. Hear his gracious voice: "Blessed is the people that know the joyful sound." "Because I live, ye shall live also." He is the Head; there is no spiritual separation. He is the Head of the body, and the body is the church; and as the members of the natural body can only live by being united to the head, so Jesus Christ is the Head of spiritual life, and we live in him, by him, and through him. How do these things affect you, my friends? Do they not bear your soul up to Jesus Christ, now sitting at the right hand of God, but who reigns on earth as the Prince of the saints and the life of his people?

A subject of this Prince cannot live without prayer. He must pray; it brings in the food which nourishes his spiritual life. And this Prince is the life of prayer; and he is also the life of reading. There is no reading the Word of God with any comfort without Christ. And I well know by experience, my friends, that he is the life of preaching. I sat in the vestry quite faint before I came into the pulpit; I seemed like a post, and felt as if I had nothing to say. I said to myself, "What shall I say to this people?" But, O my friends, I have had a glimpse of the Prince! He has opened my lips and enabled me to preach to you. He is the life of preaching. No life in religion without the Prince. As the body without the soul is dead, so religion is dead without Christ. He is the Alpha and Omega, the beginning and the ending, the first and the last of it.

But I feel I must conclude; I have not bodily strength to go further. I will now just refer you to Revelation 1. 5. Christ is there called "*the Prince of the kings of the earth.*" You see, my friends, he is called a Prince – King over all crowned heads and potentates. They all hear his voice, for he is a great Prince over all the kings of the earth. What does this glorious Prince say? "By me kings reign, and princes decree justice." All things are in his hands. The nobles of the earth are subject unto him; he lifts up one and pulls down another. He is God omnipotent, triumphs over all, and he is the Prince of Peace, keeping them in perfect peace whose minds are stayed on him.

But, to conclude, my friends, do you know the Lord Jesus Christ? Do you know this Prince of Peace? Do you know the character of this Prince? It is often said, "As rich as a prince." So likewise he is very rich; none have so many honours as he. All blessings and treasures are at his disposal, and he is ready to give them to all who ask him. O, then, acknowledge him, receive him, remember him, come to him for mercy and consolation, and enjoy his peace in your souls for evermore. Amen.

2. CAVE ADULLAM

The Substance of a Sermon preached at Zoar Chapel, London, in April 1842

Text: *"And every one that was in distress, and every one that was in debt, and every one that was discontented, gathered themselves unto him, and he became a captain over them"* (1 Sam. 22. 2).

These words contain something more than a literal meaning of the circumstances which are mentioned. And the order in which they have been laid upon my mind is as follows:

I. In many respects, David was an eminent type of the Lord Jesus Christ.

II. The men that went down to the Cave of Adullam, and the circumstances in which they were placed, were typical of all who really go unto Christ for salvation.

I. The psalmist, the sweet singer of Israel, was an eminent, a soul-comforting type of our spiritual David, the Lord Jesus Christ. Two or three observations here must suffice. Notice, then, David was anointed of the Lord to be king of Israel and the ruler of the people. Samuel received a special command from God to go and anoint one of the sons of Jesse to be king of Israel in the room of Saul. Samuel at first feared to enter upon the execution of this command, from a contemplation of the consequences that might result therefrom; but he is commanded to leave all the consequences – not to study subsequent events, but to go and do as the Lord had bidden him. Accordingly he entered into the house of Jesse, and the Spirit of the Lord was to signify which was the man whom God had chosen and provided as king over Israel. Jesse's first-born was called; and the prophet, consulting his own feelings, said, "Surely this is the man, the anointed of the Lord." But the Lord said, "Nay, this is not the man; let him go. I know he has a fine outside appearance; but I also know what is in his heart." The child of God is very jealous and very fearful lest his religion should be only in his head, in an outward appearance and outward profession, and not in the

heart. Well, Jesse called a second, and a third, and indeed all
the sons which he had in the house, but none of them would
do. And Samuel began to say, "Why, how is this? The Lord
did indeed send me. Are these all the sons that thou hast,
Jesse?" "No," says the old man, "I have yet another, young
David, but it cannot be him; and behold he keepeth the
sheep." Now, mark, no sooner does Jesse make mention of the
name of David than the Holy Ghost stirs up the spirit of
Samuel, and he says, "Send for him." And when he came, the
Lord commanded Samuel to arise and anoint David in the
midst of all his brethren.

And the Lord Jesus Christ is the anointed of the Father.
All the prophets, and apostles, and ministers of God have a
measure of the Spirit, the anointing, the sanctifying, the
life-giving and soul-saving influences, powers and operations
of the blessed Spirit; but they have only a measure of the Spirit
given to them to profit withal. The apostle is speaking to the
church of the living God; and to every member of that church
he says, "A measure of the Spirit is given to profit withal"; not
to be rejected, but possessed to the eternal well-being of their
immortal souls. But unto the Lord Jesus Christ the Spirit is
given without measure; hence, quoting the words of the
prophet Isaiah, and applying them unto himself, he said, "The
Spirit of the Lord God is upon me, because he hath anointed
me to preach good tidings unto the meek," and so forth. And
having read this interesting portion of Scripture, he closed the
book, and said, "This day is this scripture fulfilled in me."

Yes, beloved, every branch of vital godliness, all spiritual
light and life, all humility of soul and tenderness of conscience,
all sighing and sorrowing, hungering and thirsting, pantings
of soul and exercise of faith; all these things are derived from
Christ. He is God's anointed, and in him it has pleased the
Father that all fulness should dwell, that out of his fulness we
should receive grace upon grace. Our Lord is very solemn on
this subject: and I feel the weight of his Word on my soul this

morning, where he says, "Without me ye can do nothing." The poor child of God says, "That is true, Lord; without thy grace I can do nothing – I am helpless and hopeless until thou speak unto and work within me." But I forbear to enlarge.

Notice, secondly, what was David's occupation and employment? He was a keeper of his father's sheep. And where was it that he kept his father's sheep? Why, in the wilderness. And he gave good proof that he was not an hireling but a good and faithful shepherd, for while he tended and watched his father's sheep, behold, a lion and a bear (not a dog, not merely a wolf – but a mad and a voracious lion and a blood-thirsty and determined bear) came and attacked the flock; and they took a lamb out of the flock. And how did the shepherd act? Did he forsake the flock? Was he appalled and frightened by these monsters of the forest? And did he leave the poor sheep to become their prey? No, he was a good shepherd! And he says, "And I went out after the lion, and I smote him, and I delivered the lamb out of his mouth."

O, beloved, do you not see a beauty in all this? Do you not behold it fulfilled in the antitype, the Lord Jesus Christ? The Father loved the sheep which he had chosen, and he gave them into the hands of his dear Son; not only to ransom them, but to preserve them, to gather, to lead, to watch over them, and to bring them home to glory. For where are the sheep? Thousands of them are still in the wilderness where that cur of hell, the devil, as a roaring lion is ever going about seeking whom he may devour, and whom John Bunyan calls a dog, that worries the sheep but never can destroy. O no, blessed be his precious name, his eyes are on the sheep, and on every foe that would dare to attack them. He is the good Shepherd, and says, "I know my sheep, and am known of mine, and none shall ever pluck them out of my hands." All the chosen sheep are in the hands of a triune Jehovah – the Father holds them by his eternal purpose – the Son holds them by his unchanging love – the Holy Spirit holds them by his quickening and sanctifying grace; so that they can never perish.

Thirdly, David was a man of sorrows and acquainted with grief. Time would fail me to speak of the numerous trials, afflictions, difficulties, ups and downs, losses and crosses which attended this man of God all through his pilgrimage. Many of the sorrowful exclamations which fell from his lips had especial reference not only to himself but also to his great antitype, the Lord Jesus Christ; and particularly that solemn description of his sorrow and agony of soul when he cried out, "Deep calleth unto deep at the noise of thy water-spouts; all thy waves and thy billows are gone over me." This was true as regarded David himself; but it had also a very especial reference to those heavy and overwhelming sorrows which the Lord Jesus Christ endured when he took our nature, suffered for and bore away his people's sins.

II. But I come secondly to notice the characters who fled to David in the Cave of Adullam. And I shall endeavour to take this up exactly in the order in which it stands in the text: "Every one that was in distress, and every one that was in debt, and every one that was discontented, fled unto him, and he became a captain over them."

First, then, it was every one that was in distress. And, I am sure, if we bring this to bear upon spiritual things, we shall find that there never was, nor that there ever will be, one poor sinner ever flying to the Lord Jesus Christ for pardon and salvation until he is brought into distress. And I think I might justify this assertion both from my own experience and from many portions of the Word of God.

I can remember the time when I was as careless and unconcerned about my soul, about Jesus Christ and about eternity as I could possibly be; and it was not until the blessed Spirit convinced me of my awful state as a guilty, wretched, helpless and miserable sinner, showed me the spirituality, immutability, justice and holiness of Jehovah's law, and thereby deeply afflicted me in my soul, that I began to desire to seek after a refuge or hiding-place from the wrath that is to come.

And how was it with the prodigal? When did he begin to think about returning to his father's house? Was it when his pocket was full of money, when he was revelling in wantonness and luxury, when he was wallowing in sin? No, no. It was when he came to himself. It was when his pockets were empty, when he was in a far country, when he had spent all his substance, when he had nothing left and no man gave unto him, and he felt the pinchings of hunger – yea, when he was ready to starve. *Then* he began to think about his father's house, and, said he, "I will arise, and I will go unto my father." And how did he go? Did he come pleading his goodness, saying, "Father, I am a dutiful son," and so on? O, no; he confessed that he was a poor, guilty, unworthy sinner: "Father, I have sinned," saith he, "against heaven and in thy sight, and am no more worthy to be called thy son; make me as one of thy hired servants." Well, it was the father's grace that had brought him, and, therefore, the father's grace, love, pity and compassion welcomed him. He ran, fell upon his neck, kissed him and said, "This my son was lost, but is found; was dead, but is alive again." But, you see, it was when he was in distress that he came home.

And so again, when was it the sons of Jacob thought of going down to Egypt to buy corn? Why, it was when there was a famine in the land. Ah, and with what deep humility did they come to Joseph! How they bowed down before him, and acknowledged his authority, his dignity and his ability to assist them. And how did Joseph receive them? O, mark the tenderness and compassion of his heart! When they bowed down before him, he remembered his brethren. They had said they would never have this man to reign over them, but God had ordained that they should; and therefore in a most wonderful manner he brought it about.

And just the same is it with the proud, haughty, ignorant, sinner. He cares no more about Christ and his salvation than as though he had no soul to be saved. But when the Lord the Spirit brings a famine into the sinner's soul, when a fiery law in his conscience consumes all his works and carnal hopes, then he is humbled, he is broken, and he cries out, "What must I do?" "Whither shall I flee?" And our spiritual David, in the Cave of Adullam, says, "Come unto me; come, sit under my shadow; I will comfort you, I will help you."

And, so, you see, it is every "one that is in distress." And not only distress in the first setting out, but all through the journey. I do not know how you good folks get on in London, but we find that one trouble comes so close upon the heels of another that we really begin to believe there is positive truth in the word of our Lord when he says, "In the world ye shall have tribulation." But in all our harassments and troubles we are enabled to gather ourselves unto the Lord Jesus Christ. He is our refuge. Underneath are the everlasting arms. And we find there is a sweetness in those words: "To whom coming, as unto a living stone."

"And every one that was in debt." I doubt not but this literally was the case. Every one had his creditor. But we are not to confine this characteristic to those debts which we may have contracted in a civil point of view. And where is the man that breathes under the canopy of heaven but is in debt to God, having violated a holy, just and righteous law? But, alas! how very few who are brought to see and really to feel, to confess and to acknowledge that they are poor debtors, guilty, helpless, bankrupt sinners! But all that are thus brought are most certainly the elect of God; God's finger is in their consciences; they are brought to God's book; their debts, their iniquities, are all laid open before them, and charged upon them; and they find them to be of greater weight than they can possibly bear. When this was the case with me, I went to God, with promises of amendment, saying, "Next week, I will be better; I will amend my ways, and turn unto the Lord." But God weighed me in the balance of the sanctuary; and I found that unless my debts were paid, and my guilt atoned for by another, I must eternally perish. There is one thing in God's Word which I have not been able fully to comprehend; and it is what is meant by the *fifty pence debtor*. I have travelled for the last twenty-eight years through many parts of our country, but I have never yet found the Christian man who said he was only a fifty-pence debtor; all have declared themselves to be five hundred pence debtors. But be that matter as it may; when they have been brought to feel that they have nothing wherewith to pay, he has frankly and freely forgiven them all.

Ah, we come now to a very precious part of the subject: and you know what it is before I mention it. What has our spiritual David done? Why he has settled the whole account for us. He has settled it most gloriously, most honourably, most justly and completely, so that there is no condemnation to them that are in Christ Jesus. Dr. Crisp has an expression, and I approve of it from the very bottom of my heart. He says, "Christ, the great paymaster of his people's debts." Yes, all their debts he has paid; not by instalments, for we have full redemption through him. "By one offering he hath perfected forever them that are sanctified." Here is the confidence of the church, the pillar on which the Church rests.

There is both a doctrinal and an experimental principle in this justification. First, nothing but the atoning blood of the Son of God can ever obtain justification for guilty sinners in the high court of heaven. But in an experimental point of view, nothing but the application of that blood to the conscience can testify that the debt is paid, or give the sinner peace.

(Mr. Kershaw then referred to the debt of love and gratitude which the vessels of mercy owe to a triune Jehovah for the great things done for and in them and proved that without renewed manifestations of these things to the soul, the believer was the most discontented man on earth.)

3. THE DESIRE OF THE RIGHTEOUS GRANTED

Preached at Zoar Chapel, Great Alie Street, London on November 24th, 1842

Text: *"The desire of the righteous shall be granted"* (Proverbs 10. 24).

I shall not take up any time, my friends, by way of introduction tonight, but shall come immediately to the words of the text. And I hope and trust the Lord will be graciously pleased to assist me,

    I.   Briefly to describe to you the *character* of "the righteous." And

    II.   To take into consideration, "the *desire* of the righteous," which, it is said, "shall be granted."

Now, in reference to the character of the righteous, I shall be very brief, as I intend to speak more at large, by the Lord's help, upon "the desire of the righteous," which is to be granted.

    I.   First, then, "the righteous." But where are we to find a righteous man among all the fallen sons and daughters of an apostate Adam? My friends, as we stand in relation to the first Adam, our federal head, there is not a just man or a righteous person to be found under the canopy of the whole heavens. It is said, "the Lord looked down from heaven upon the children of men, to see if there were any that did understand, that did seek God." It was the omniscient God, who beholds all things with one glance of his eye. The Lord looked down from heaven upon earth, to see if he could find any that did good, and sinned not. But what was the result? He could not find one; for there was not a just man that did good, and sinned not; all flesh had corrupted his way. There is none righteous in this sense, no, not one: our very nature is fallen, depraved and sunken; it is unclean; the whole head is sick, and the whole heart is faint; from the crown of the head to the sole of the foot there is nothing but wounds, bruises and putrefying sores. The carnal heart of man is enmity against God; it is not subject to his law, neither indeed can be; it is carnal, deceitful above all things, and desperately wicked. The depraved heart of man is a dark fountain of impurity; it follows us all through the wilderness, and produces a black stream of iniquity and depravity; so that the thoughts and imaginations of the children of men, arising from this impure source, are only evil, and that continually. The poison of asps is under his lips; and sin, that accursed thing which God hates, man rolls under his tongue as a sweet morsel: he lies down in it, like the sow that wallows in the mire. But to cut it short, it is said, "destruction and misery are in all their ways; the way of peace have they not known, and there is no fear of God before their eyes." My friends, this is the universal description of divine truth concerning the awful state into which we are all plunged through sin. And therefore it is impossible to find a righteous man among the whole fallen race of Adam, as they stand in relation to him as their original head.

But, before we move any farther in this solemn subject, I have an important question to ask; and my question is this: How many of us present do in reality, from painful experience in our very heart and soul, feel that this description of an unrighteous man, which God has given us in his sacred Word, is a true one? How many of us are there who have been made mournfully to feel that we are the very characters which God has described in the good Word of his grace? Now, beloved, while a natural man may assent and consent to these statements of divine truth, and acknowledge them in his judgment, yet he cannot have a feeling sense of it spiritually, and sigh and groan on account of it in his mind, and repent and abhor himself in the dust of self-abasement, unless he is born of the Spirit of God, and has been taught by him these solemn truths. And therefore, I would say to every one of you that do see and feel sin to be a daily plague and a daily burden, and which causes you to sigh and mourn and groan before the

Lord: depend upon it, where such is the case, it is a safe and certain evidence that the grace of God is in your heart, and that you have been convinced of sin by the power of the Holy Ghost.

Now there is one observation I must make on this part of my subject. There are many professors of religion who, so long as outward things are straight and external observances correct, and they are attending to their duties, they think all is well, and they are quite happy and comfortable; they do not feel the inward warfare and strife; they are all at peace within, and Satan never troubles them. But I would not give a straw for such a profession: for however the saint may walk circumspectly before his fellow-creatures and his brethren, he has daily to mourn over the body of sin and death which he carries about with him; he feels the plague of his sins; he is pestered with his carnal reasonings, the fires of lust, worldly-mindedness and inordinate affections; and these things make the dear saint of God sick at heart, and a torment at times to himself; so that he often stands amazed at the goodness and mercy of God, and wonders how it is that he bears with him, and does not cut him down as a cumberer of the ground. And my friends, if you are not the subject of these exercises of mind, your heart is not right in the sight of God, and you have not the evidences of the new birth. But where these feelings are experienced, such characters are manifestly those for whom Solomon prayed at the dedication of the temple: for while on that solemn occasion he asked for many things, under the Spirit's teaching, he was especially moved to pray for those that knew "the plague of their own heart."

Now they that know and feel this plague will have to pray against the workings of it, and to supplicate the Lord to enable them to use such weapons, as shall be mighty to the pulling down of the strongholds of sin and Satan, so that every thought and power of their souls may be brought into the obedience of Christ; because wherever the Lord's grace is deposited, it will be sure to work an inward struggling and fighting against sin and corruption. Now there are times and seasons when, by his grace, he does for a few moments so rise up for their help that they are enabled to tread upon these scorpions and adders, and crush them under their feet, and triumph over the power of their enemies; but this is only at the time when God lifts upon them the light of his countenance, and gives them to glory in the riches of his grace.

"Well," say you, "you go a strange way to make out a righteous man!" Beloved, it is *God's* way; for the Holy Spirit never made a man righteous until he first gave him to feel his unrighteousness. He turns him inside out and shows him that while he has a desire and a will, yet he has not the power of himself to perform that which is spiritually good; the will is present, but how to perform that which is good, he finds not. But still, our text says, "The desire of the righteous shall be granted."

Where, then, is the righteous man to be found? We have discovered him where he is unrighteous, sinful and polluted – but where is he to be found righteous? Then, if we want to find him in this character, we must look for him in the place where he is to be seen. Now as all light and heat comes from the sun; so all the righteousness and holiness which exists now, or ever has been seen in the world from the fall to the present time, is alone in the glorious Person of our Lord Jesus Christ; therefore the people of God are only righteous as they stand in him. Christ is their substitute, their holiness and their sanctification; and his name is "the Lord our Righteousness," for they stand complete and accepted in him the Beloved. But let us examine a few portions of God's blessed Word on this subject.

If we look at the birth of the immaculate Jesus, we behold that his very nature was perfect; for the angel said to Mary, "That holy thing which shall be born of thee shall be called the Son of God." And the "Child born," and the "Son given,"

was without spot or blemish; he was "holy, harmless, undefiled, and separate from sinners." Now look at the heart of our
Lord Jesus Christ; purity and perfection dwelt in him in all its
fulness; for all that the law required, he did. He loved the
Lord with all his heart, and with all his mind, and with all his
strength, and his neighbour as himself. Grace was poured into
his lips; yea, even his bitterest enemies were constrained to
say, that "never man spake like this Man;" so that all he did,
from the cradle to the cross, was but one continued act of
purity and rectitude.

Now observe, he is the covenant head of his church and
people; therefore all that he did was as their covenant head.
He did it not for himself, it was for his mystical body. He
wrought out his perfect robe of righteousness, and placed it to
the account of his beloved members; so that the glorious
righteousness and perfect obedience of the Redeemer is ours,
made ours by Jehovah the Father, and by covenant oath
secured to us; as saith the apostle, "Of Him are ye in Christ
Jesus, who of God is made unto us wisdom, righteousness,
sanctification, and redemption."

I might enlarge text upon text on this point, but for
brevity's sake, I forbear, and will bring it down to the experience and feeling of the heaven-born soul in the living family
taught of God. For however there may be differences among
the Lord's people upon minor things, yet upon soul matters
they are all brought to speak one and the same thing, being
taught by one and the same Spirit, and made partakers of one
and the same truth, "Well," says one, "what does the
heaven-born soul say – and every one who is taught the same
thing by the same Spirit, say?" Why, they say, "O Lord, all
our righteousnesses are as filthy rags; and we are all as an
unclean thing: we all do fade away as a leaf, and our iniquities
like the wind have taken us away." Then it is clear, my
friends, there is no righteousness in us.

But then, on the other side of the question, and it is the

language of the Bible, it is said, "The just shall live by faith."
And again, "Surely shall one say, in the Lord have I righteousness and strength." In him we have a garment of salvation, a robe of righteousness, a wedding garment; for surely,
certainly and of a truth shall one say, "In the Lord have I
righteousness and strength;" and "in him shall all the seed of
Israel be justified and shall glory."

Perhaps I have one here that cannot join in this mode of
expression, and who would give worlds to be able to say, "In
the Lord have *I* righteousness and strength." It may be, I say,
that there is such a precious soul here tonight, who cannot
make use of this language but would rather say, "O that I may
have righteousness and strength in the Lord. I am hungering
and thirsting after it; it is what my soul desires, and there is
nothing else that can satisfy me." Then, I would say, the
blessing of the Lord is upon such an one as thee; for it is said,
"Blessed are they that hunger and thirst after righteousness,
for they shall be filled." Therefore, the righteousness of the
saints is not found in themselves. No, Christ's righteousness
is imputed to them, and placed to their account – in it they are
clothed, and beheld spotless before the eyes of infinite purity;
as it is written, "Blessed are they whose iniquities are forgiven,
and whose sins are covered: blessed is the man unto whom the
Lord will not impute sin."

II. But leaving the character of the righteous, we will
now proceed to the latter part of the clause and consider a
little more at large, "the desire of the righteous," which the
text assures us "shall be granted." But there are two or three
observations of a brief prefatory nature which it is necessary
for us to make first, in order to do justice to a subject of so
much importance.us to make first, in order to do justice to a
subject of so much importance.

The first remark then I would make is this. In looking at
the "desire of the righteous," we must view it in a complexity
of character, as it is recorded in Solomon's Song, where the

question is asked, "What will ye see in the Shulamite? As it were the company of two armies." What will ye see in the dear child of God, made righteous in the righteousness of Christ, but two armies and two companies wrestling and fighting, the one against the other? What will ye discover in him, but flesh and spirit – the old man and the new man – nature and grace; and these in continual opposition and warfare against each other? "For the flesh lusteth against the Spirit, and the Spirit against the flesh; and these are contrary the one to the other: so that ye cannot do the things that ye would."

Now the old man in the believer has his desires; and they are sometimes very naughty desires. They are desires after the flesh, and frequently of a very depraved, carnal and corrupt kind. And the new man of grace, created in righteousness and true holiness, he has his desires also which are of the operation of the Spirit. Now there is a continual fighting and wrestling between these two opposing principles in every child of God. But is the old man of sin to have his desires gratified? Are the lusts of the heart to be fulfilled? Oh no! they are to be mortified and crucified: "Mortify therefore your members, which are upon the earth"; and, "They that are Christ's have crucified the flesh, with the affections and lusts." The desires of the flesh are to be kept under, to be subdued, to be put off; and no provision is to be made for the flesh for the satisfying of the lusts thereof.

Again. There are many fleshly prayers and tears which the people of God have; but they are not the desires which are to be granted, nor intended by the words of our text. Many of the desires presented in our petitions to the Lord spring up from the flesh, and he refuses to grant them; so that oftentimes "we have not, because we ask amiss, that we may consume it upon our lusts." And indeed, even when we have had our fleshly desires granted, it has seldom been for our good. We read of some to whom the Lord granted their desires, but "sent leanness into their souls." Therefore it is better to be denied those desires that arise from our flesh which, if granted, would prove injurious to our best interests, contrary to our true comforts, derogatory to God's glory, and wounding to the minds of our brethren; and be the means of affording mirth to the ungodly who would rejoice over our falls and backslidings from the Lord.from the flesh, and he refuses to grant them; so that oftentimes "we have not, because we ask amiss, that we may consume it upon our lusts." And indeed, even when we have had our fleshly desires granted, it has seldom been for our good. We read of some to whom the Lord granted their desires, but "sent leanness into their souls." Therefore it is better to be denied those desires that arise from our flesh, which, if granted, would prove injurious to our best interests, contrary to our true comforts, derogatory to God's glory, and wounding to the minds of our brethren, and be the means of affording mirth to the ungodly who would rejoice over our falls and backslidings from the Lord.

But "the desire of the righteous shall be granted." The desires, then, that arise from the new man of grace, and from the teachings of the blessed Spirit in the soul, as a Spirit of grace and supplication, are sure to be granted; because every desire that he works in a poor sinner is in accordance with his sacred Word, and is always connected with the good of the soul and the glory of the Lord. And it is well always to bring our desires to the Book of God, and search the Scriptures to see whether they agree with its blessed contents; for if they are not according to the testimony of truth, and agreeable to the teachings of his Spirit, it is evident they arise from the flesh. But if our desires are in harmony with his mind and will, then the same Spirit that wrote the word in the Bible is the Author of these spiritual desires that we feel in our hearts. And therefore you will see a disposition in the Lord's praying people to be made spiritual seekers after the truth. They have many spiritual desires; they hunger and thirst after the bread of life and the water of life. They are made to be spiritual watchers; for they get up on their watchtower, and there they plead the promises of mercy before the Lord, and put him in remembrance of his gracious declarations, how he has promised to satisfy the desire of the longing soul, and "fulfil the desire of them that fear him."

But now, having made these general observations, I hope the Lord will assist me to enter more at large into the nature of the desires of his people; and that he would be pleased to meet with us, and unfold his precious truth to us. And I would say, "Dear Lord! do bless us with thy Spirit, that our minds may be refreshed while further waiting on thee."

Now I take it for granted, believing it to be a truth, that I have many precious souls here tonight of those that are righteous as they stand in their covenant Head. And I ask you, my friends, who have no righteousness of your own, but are looking for it all in the Person of the Lord Jesus Christ, what is your chief desire before the Lord? What is it you desire above everything else? Now, when I am in my closet, the thought will come home to me sometimes, "What is thy petition, and what is thy request?" What is it I principally desire before a heart-searching God? There are many of you present, who no doubt can say, "The Lord has shown me my weakness, sinfulness, helplessness and wretchedness; and he has taught me that if ever I am saved, it must be by grace, through the redemption that is in Christ Jesus; and I believe that he is an able and an all-sufficient Saviour, and that he is the only Redeemer of his church and people." And then comes the heart-felt desire, and which has been my prayer for days and months, and is the earnest desire of every one of the Lord's quickened family, "O that I might have the testimony of the Holy Spirit bearing witness to my heart that Jesus Christ is *my* Saviour and *my* Redeemer."

But again. "The desire of the righteous shall be granted." Now then, there is another thing the soul wants to be satisfied about. He is desirous of knowing whether Jesus has loved him, and given himself for him; he wants to have a personal testimony of the love of Christ. He says, "What will it avail me that Jesus has loved patriarchs, prophets and apostles, if he has not loved me, and shed his precious blood for me. I want to know the Lord for myself, to feel satisfied that he is mine; to be enabled to say, without doubt and fear, and that from God's blessed testimony and unction in my soul, that I have redemption through his blood, the forgiveness of my sins according to the riches of his grace: and to use the language of Job as my own, 'I know that my Redeemer liveth!' I want to know that God is my heavenly Father, that Jesus is my Saviour, that the Spirit is my guide and teacher, and that heaven will be my eternal rest and home."

I would say to such a precious soul as this who has these desires, Cannot you give yourself these things? for there are many persons that say we are warranted to believe and rest upon the Scriptures and take God at his word. But this poor soul says, "If I could have made it clear to my mind and satisfactory to my conscience that I was washed in the blood of Jesus, and interested in the love of his heart, I should have convinced myself about it long ago. But I cannot do it, for God knows the earnest cries and desires which have gone up from my heart to him to make these things clear to my soul." And, my friends, I have often been at this work. I have tried and toiled to apply Christ's blood and grace to my conscience: but I have found I could no more do it than I could pluck out the sun and stars from the heavens. And indeed, if I had the power to do it, then I could accomplish the work of the Spirit of God. But it is not in the power of any creature; it is the work of God himself, and it is he alone that can do it, and he will perform it in his own time and way.

Now the Lord gives the desire first, and afterwards he satisfies the longing of the soul; he gives hungerings and thirstings after it. The desire may be long delayed, but nevertheless the fulfilment of it is sure, for "the vision is for an appointed time, but in the end it shall speak, and not lie; though it tarry, wait for it; because it will surely come."

There may be some poor, cast-down soul present, who has long been waiting at the footstool of mercy, anxiously desiring to know when the Lord will be pleased to grant him the desires of his heart by giving him an experimental knowledge and enjoyment of his personal interest in the redemption that is in Christ Jesus. And he may be ready to ask such a question as this, "How long shall I be kept in the place of waiting?" Now, beloved, I cannot answer thee as to time. It may be the Lord's will to exercise thy faith and patience, and to keep thee long at his blessed feet. But that the desire of thy soul shall be granted at the last, we have his own sacred testimony; and I am sure that when he fulfils the desire of your heart, you will be satisfied then that his time is the best. But here I would say that, during the time such a longing, panting, hungering and thirsting soul is seeking after a knowledge of these things, he will be sure to ply the means of God's grace; he will read his Word, attend the ordinances of his house and plead the promises of his grace. Nor will he be without some tokens of the Lord's favour. He will impart to him some gratification of his desires; he will have some little drawings out of heart after him, though he will never rest satisfied until he is possessed of the full enjoyment of that which his soul seeks after. The Lord's people have many wants and desires, and they are only happy as they are brought into an apprehension of his love, and as they feel Jesus precious to them.

I believe that the Lord has suffered many of his dear family, who do not feel an assurance of their interest in the blood and righteousness of Christ, to be greatly depressed in their feelings, and dark in their souls, and perplexed with doubts and fears, and that for ten, twenty, thirty and even forty years, wondering how it will be with them in their dying hour. But there is a blessed text for such in the epistle to the Hebrews, where it is said Christ came to "deliver them who through fear of death were all their life-time subject to bondage." Precious soul! those fears which distress thee, and the devil who worries thee, shall not follow thee to the other side of Jordan, but they shall leave thee there. Jesus will accompany thee through the cold stream of death, and land thy soul in immortal bliss and blessedness. Well then, "the desire of the righteous shall be granted;" but it must be in the Lord's own time and way.

But I observe again, secondly, "the desire of the righteous shall be granted." Now I would ask you, my friends, this important question: Next to the salvation of your soul, what is the chief desire of your heart, and your earnest petition before the Lord? I am satisfied, if the heart is right with God and under the influence of his blessed Spirit, and he is your guide and teacher, that next to the salvation of your soul, your fervent cry at the throne of grace will be something like this: "Dear Lord! while I am in the wilderness, keep me very humble, keep me solemn, keep me ever watchful, keep me growingly acquainted with a knowledge of my total dependence on thee and of my own utter insufficiency, keep me ever jealous of my own heart, and never let me trust to it and fall away from thee like poor Peter. Keep my conscience very tender by renewed applications of the blood of Jesus, and the bedewing influences of thy blessed Spirit. Let me have thy fear continually before my eyes, both in my going out and in my coming in, that my desire may be, 'Hold thou up my goings in thy way that my footsteps slip not.' O Lord! keep me, and I shall be well kept. Do thou enable me to stand my ground, and having done all to stand. Keep me in the 'footsteps of the flock,' in the 'narrow way,' and never let me wander away from thee. Thus, Lord, grant that the residue of my days may be devoted to thy honour and glory, that I may increasingly love thee and thy ways, that thine ordinances may be my delight, and that I may keep thy commandments and precepts, and glorify thee in body, soul and spirit, which are thine, until the time shall arrive when thou wilt come and receive me unto thyself, that where thou art, there I may be also."

Now, my friends, I make nothing of the religion of any man or woman if it does not produce effects like these; and God makes nothing of it either, unless there is an experimental feeling of these things in the soul. Many persons when they die want to go to heaven, but they do not want their time, and their affections and every power of their souls to be consecrated to the Lord's service while they are in this world. Wicked Balaam wanted to die the death of the righteous, but he did not desire to live the life which they live. But where the heart is right, and the affections are set upon Jesus and heavenly things, there will be a desire continually springing up in the soul to honour the Lord, and to glorify him in everything that they do, and to show forth the praises of that Redeemer, who lived a life of suffering for them here, and at last died the accursed death of the cross, that he might bring them to God; so that these things will be seen and manifested in their life and conversation, both in the world and in the church.

Now Jabez's prayer is very appropriate to this part of our subject. There is very little said about Jabez, but quite enough to satisfy every God-fearing man or woman that the grace of God was in his heart. He says, "O that thou wouldest bless me indeed, and enlarge my coast, and that thine hand might be with me; and that thou wouldest keep me from evil, that it may not grieve me." My friends, I do love Bible words; they have a great hold on my heart, for there are no words fit and suit me so well as what are to be found in this blessed Book. And therefore, "do now, dear Lord, increase our desires after thee, that we may have more experimental knowledge of, and a deeper acquaintance with thee; that we may be more devoted to thee, and live more to the honour and glory of thy great name, until that we have done with all things here below; and do enable us to lay ourselves down at thy blessed feet, and to count ourselves at the last nothing but unprofitable servants."

But again. We have the promise of a faithful, covenant-keeping God that "the desire of the righteous shall be granted." The Lord never puts a desire into the soul of one of his family to disappoint him. I know that "hope deferred maketh the heart sick, but when the desire cometh, it is a tree of life." It is true, the heart may be sick and faint while waiting for the fulfilment of the promise, but nevertheless it shall come at the time appointed; and when it has entered into the soul of the poor sinner, accompanied with the blessed influences of the divine Spirit, it will then be a "tree of life" to him, and he will glorify and praise God for the enjoyment of it. Therefore, "the desire of the righteous," sooner or later, "shall be granted."

We see this truth strikingly exhibited in one beautiful circumstance in the Scriptures. And what was that? It was in the case of Hannah, the wife of Elkanah. God had put a desire into her heart; and she went into the temple to pour out her supplications, and tell her sorrows before the Lord. His eye was upon her, and his ear open to her petition. He listened to her cry and answered it, for he gave her the desire of her soul. Beloved, the Lord knows all our desires. He is acquainted with all our secret sighs and groans. He knows our downsitting and uprising, and understandeth our thoughts afar off. But he says, "For all these things will I be enquired of by the house of Israel, that I may do it for them." But to return to Hannah. It appears that Eli thought that she was drunken; he, looking at her steadfastly with angry feelings, says to her, "How long wilt thou be drunken? put away thy wine from thee." "Ah!" says Hannah, "I have drunk neither wine nor strong drink: but I am a woman of a sorrowful spirit." My friends, I would that there were more of "a sorrowful spirit" among us. I want to feel more of it in myself, and discover more of it in others. "I am a woman of a sorrowful spirit," she says, "and have poured out my soul before the Lord." The

Spirit then immediately comes upon Eli and he says, "Thy request shall be given thee. Go in peace, and the God of Israel grant thee thy petition that thou hast asked of him." Here then the promise of the text is sweetly fulfilled, "The desire of the righteous shall be granted."

But again. There is another circumstance which we will notice, and which strikingly exhibits the fulfilment of the promise in our text. In the 18th chapter of Luke, the Lord introduces to us a parable in order to encourage us to make known our requests unto him by prayer and supplication, that he may give unto us the desire of our hearts. It is said, "And he spake a parable unto them to this end, that men ought always to pray, and not to faint; saying, there was in a city a judge, who feared not God neither regarded man: and there was a widow in that city." Ah! in that same city, there was a poor widow woman who had a cruel adversary, which she could not manage herself; and therefore she went to this un-just judge to tell him her sorrows, and to put her case into his hands. But he would not take any notice of her, nor her trouble, and ordered her to be put away from him. Never-theless, this poor woman went to him the second and the third day; and she continued knocking again and again at his door, and was not to be silenced, for she would not give it up nor be driven away until at last the unjust judge says within himself, "This woman troubles me; and though I fear not God nor regard man, yet because this widow wearies me with her continual coming, I will arise and avenge her speedily, that I may have done with her." And the Lord says, "Hear what the unjust judge saith!

And shall not God avenge his own elect which cry day and night unto him, though he bear long with them?" And shall not the covenant God of his people, who hath loved them with an everlasting love, and hath given up his dear Son as a sacrifice for them – shall he not avenge them speedily? And shall not a precious Christ, who has laid down his life as a ransom for them, and hath redeemed them from the curse of the law, out of the hands of law and justice, and ransomed them from the power of sin, death, hell and the grave, and hath given them his blessed Spirit, and put holy and heavenly desires in their hearts – shall he not avenge his own elect and arise up for their deliverance, who cry unto him day and night? Yea, he will avenge them speedily, though he appears to delay for their help! Would to God my cries went up more fervently day and night to a covenant God! Alas! there is very little real prayer arising from the heart unless we are brought into circumstances of trouble and sorrow. And may I not say, my friends, that unless we are passing through deep waters and fiery trials, our prayers become very formal and there is but little of real wrestling and crying to the Lord in them, so that when we come to look at these prayers and compare them with our own, we stand ashamed and humbled before the Lord on account of our half-heartedness and backwardness to call upon him, and feel that they are not the prayers that deserve his notice or his special regard. Therefore, may the Lord quicken our souls to call more upon him in sincerity and truth. O that we may be more humbled down under a sense of our own sinfulness, that we may plead and wrestle with him to arise for our help! But when the soul is in trouble, what does he say to it then? He says, "Call upon me in the day of trouble; I will deliver thee, and thou shalt glorify me."

Now the elect "cry unto him day and night;" yea, not only in the day but at night when they cannot sleep upon their beds. But someone may say, "What! cannot the Lord's elect always sleep upon their beds?" Why, I can say for myself, and I hope and trust I am one of the Lord's people, that I have had many sleepless nights; for, what with the darkness of my mind, a feeling sense of my own vileness and wretchedness, the temptations of Satan, the anxieties of life, with the cares of the church, these things have so harassed and plagued my soul at times that I have known what it is to have many tossings to and fro on my pillow upon my bed, and they have produced many sighs and groans and desires after the Lord that he would appear for me, and when none but himself can know.

And thus David cried out in the secret watches of the night. He wet his couch with tears, and he could find no rest until the Lord spoke peace again to him, saying, "O remember me with the favour which thou bearest unto thy people"; and, "Say unto my soul, I am thy salvation." Now, my friends, do you know anything of these exercises of mind? Then "shall not God avenge his own elect, which cry unto him day and night?" Yes, he will; for "the desire of the righteous shall be granted."

It just occurs to my mind that there may be a precious soul here tonight who is in some such state of mind as this: that after having had an enjoyment of peace and pardon in his conscience by an application of the blood of Jesus, and after having lived in the light of God's countenance and felt sweet rest and joy in his soul, he had thought that he should have gone on and continued in this state of feeling to the end of his days. But alas! there has come a weaning time with him; he has been drawn from the breast of sensible enjoyment in order that he may learn doctrine.

I can recollect the time well, when the weaning of my soul was a work of sore distress and great trouble to me. I was enveloped in darkness, and such a one as could be felt – a thick darkness wherein I could not see a hand's breadth before me – that everything which appeared good in me was gone, and nothing seemed to be left but what was full of evil – that I thought I should go back again into the world and that all my experience would end in delusion. And then, at this time my prayers became very short and more earnest; and, my friends, I am a lover of short prayers, for the wise man says, "Let your words be few, for God is in the heavens, and thou art upon the earth." But now, while in this state of mind, my prayers were very many in number, but of few words, and indeed they were made up principally of sighs and groans before the Lord, so that I could say, "Let the sighing of the prisoner come up before thee"; and "All my sighs and groans are with thee." And therefore, if there should be any child of God here present that has these pantings and longings, they are from the Lord, and they will ascend into the ears of the Lord of Hosts, and in his own time he will come down for your relief.

But I shall never forget the period and the occasion when he appeared for my deliverance. I was on my knees at the time. I can recollect the place well, and it is in my mind now, though it is more than two hundred miles away from this spot. He dropped these precious words, and applied them with such divine power to my soul, "The eyes of the Lord are on the righteous, and his ears are open to their cry," that I shall never forget the feelings which accompanied it. I said, "What, Lord! and has thine eye been upon me for good, and thine ear open to all my supplications and mournings before thee?" Yes; the blessed Spirit turned preacher, and there is no preacher like him. He brought the word home to me with such power, light, life and liberty that my soul arose from the dust, my bondage was gone, the fetters were all broken away, and I was full of peace and joy in my soul. And therefore I stand here this night as a living witness, to bear testimony to the faithfulness and truth of the blessed promise in our text, "The desire of the righteous shall be granted."

And now, may the Lord own these things to do good to his dear people, and his name shall have the praise. Amen.

4. A PROMISE FOR THE DAY OF TROUBLE

Preached at Gadsby's Yard, London, on November 27th, 1842

I arise before you this evening, my friends, with the words of Paul in my mind, where he says, "Brethren, pray for me, that a door of utterance may be given unto me, that I may make manifest the truth of the gospel," as it ought to be made, for if there be anything good it is of God; that we may have our eyes to the great Head of the church that he may command his blessing on us. The longer I live, the longer I have to do with my Master's work, for I see the need of his presence. In a particular manner the Lord brought to my remembrance tonight this passage: "Yea, I am with you alway, even to the end of the world." Now I trust he will be with me tonight.

The passage I have selected you will find recorded in Psalm 50. 15:

"Call upon me in the day of trouble; I will deliver thee, and thou shalt glorify me."

Man that is born of woman is of few days and full of trouble. Trouble is the legitimate offspring of sin. The psalmist David speaks in this wise: "The wicked are not troubled like other men." Who are these other men whose troubles are not like the troubles of the wicked? God's saints, the poor people of God. God's saints have troubles peculiar to themselves, such as mere men of the world are utter strangers to. Troubles have a very different effect on the minds of the men of the world to what they have on the minds of God's people. "The sorrow of the world worketh death." Some, in their calamities and under the power of the devil, have committed the awful crime of suicide. They sink to hell in the very act of breaking God's law: "Thou shalt do no murder."

Many of God's saints have been tempted to this sin. Many have been afraid to go into a dark place when alone. It has been powerfully brought to their mind; but the Lord was their keeper. He has said to the enemy, "Hitherto shalt thou come, and no further." Worldly trouble cometh even to them.

But the men of the world say, when they are overcome of sorrow and trouble, Sorrow must have drink; but it is only heaping coals on the fire and increasing their trouble. It is, as the Scripture expresses it, "a refuge of lies." God says, "Call upon me in the day of trouble"; like Hezekiah, who spread before the Lord the letter he had received from Sennacherib the king of Assyria.

There is trouble at this time, especially in the north, where I come from. I have seen many who have had recourse to other refuges. They have turned Chartists*. They have associated themselves with this class of men for the redress of their grievances. Yes, and they have even had recourse to the pike. But this is decidedly wrong, especially for those who love the Lord. It is their part to go to the Lord and spread their cause before him. He has said, "Cast thy burden on the Lord, and he shall sustain thee." They have a throne of grace to go to. God says, "Call upon me in the day of trouble, and I will hear thee."

For our edification, let us consider: there are some troubles peculiar in a religious point of view, or *soul troubles*, and there are *providential* trials and difficulties experienced in God's family.

Soul troubles. "Call upon me in the day of trouble." Some say religion begins its course in love and joy. I did not so learn Christ. It is contrary to the Word of God, contrary to the teaching of the Holy Spirit. When religion commences in the soul of the sinner, trouble commences also. Trouble assails the soul. The blessed Spirit wounds the soul of the sinner, and sorrow and distress is his portion. The blessed Spirit, in the very commencement, makes sin burdensome. Job says, "Thou makest me to possess the iniquities of my youth." The blessed Spirit discovers to the poor sinner the sin of his nature, his depravity, the carnality of his heart, and makes him sore distressed so that he cannot look up. There is a heaviness in

* The Chartists were a body who agitated for political reform between 1837 and 1848

his heart which makes the poor sinner to stoop. He is weary and heavy-laden, he is burdened. It is not pleasant to feel the burden of sin in the conscience; but the results are blessed. The sinner must first see and feel the malady before the cure can be effected. "The whole need not a physician, but they that are sick."

The curse of God seems to be upon them. David says, "The pains of hell gat hold upon me." The curse of the law gets hold on the conscience of a poor sinner; he finds sorrow and trouble. Bunyan, in his *Pilgrim's Progress*, calls it the Slough of Despond. The sinner is wretched and full of trouble. He is afraid of the very ground opening and swallowing him up, as it did in the case of Dathan and Abiram. He says, "Lord, how vile I am! how guilty! how polluted!" Here is soul trouble! Trouble indeed. This is the work of the Spirit in the conscience of the sinner. The Lord pulls down the sinner, but he brings him up again. The law brings him into bondage, but grace proclaims hope. It is a day of trouble to the sinner. When the soul is in these circumstances, how adapted is this exhortation to his case, "Call upon me in the day of trouble"! He cannot but call on him in sighs, in groans, in pantings, in breathings after God. His very heart and soul are going out to the Lord. To the Lord he cries, beseeching him to help and to have mercy on his soul. Again he hears the following declaration, just adapted to meet his case, "I will look down from heaven, from the height of my sanctuary." What for? "To hear the groaning of the prisoner." How it enters into the very case and feelings of the poor sinner when he is shut up in soul trouble!

David says, "I am shut up." Here is a poor destitute sinner; he cries unto the Lord. What does the Lord say? "To this man will I look, even to him that is poor and of a contrite spirit, and trembleth at my Word." The sould, therefore, is calling upon him in the day of trouble, and in his own good time he will hear; he will come down to the help of the poor sinner. David saith in Psalm 40, "I waited patiently for the

Lord, and he inclined unto me and heard my cry. He brought me up also out of an horrible pit, out of the miry clay, and set my feet upon a rock, and established my goings." Yes, the Lord did something more to him than hearing him, or listening to his cry; he brought him up. He set his feet on the Rock of salvation, on the Rock of Ages, a sure foundation stone. God is represented in the Scriptures as a rock. The work of salvation is a perfect work. When the sinner feels that he has for his stand and his rock the holy God, he finds that with the more weight he presses the more firm he feels; he is then satisfied with his foundation. He finds that a new song is put into his mouth, even praise and thanksgiving. David called on the Lord in the day of trouble, and the Lord heard him, and delivered him from all his trouble. David glorified God; he blessed and praised the Lord for his goodness.

Have I a soul here in legal bondage, trying to do good on the ground of his own doings? The more you work, like the poor woman recorded in the Scriptures as having an issue of blood twelve years, you will like her grow worse. My friends, may God make you sick of yourselves. May that poor sinner see his weakness, his guilt, his condemnation. Though the soul be in bondage, yet there shall be a calling on the name of the Lord. God puts into the heart a cry for help. Not like the Pharisee, who said, in a proud self-righteous spirit, "God, I thank thee I am not as other men are." No; a sinner cries, like the poor publican, in broken accents, "Lord, have mercy upon me! O, Lord, what a miserable wretch I am! What a sinner I am! Lord, save me, or I perish." This cry never gets stale, my friends; the Lord will hear him. God leads the sinner to feel that the law is satisfied. He is brought out of bondage into the glorious liberty of the sons of God. One dear Christian (William Huntington) was nailing up some branches on the wall of his garden when the Lord broke in on his soul, and when in his employment he wanted his hoe, he could not collect his mind sufficiently to recollect, when he reached the tool-house, what it was that he wanted; so that he cried out, "My soul has got a holiday, and my poor body shall have one too." He sighed, and groaned, and cried to God; and in the day of his trouble the Lord came down, and gave him the witness of the Spirit, and he experienced the glorious liberty of the gospel.

I shall never forget the night when God made himself known to me, and showed me his loving heart. And really, friends, it is quite overcoming when such is the case, to think that he should ever show so great mercy to me, such a vile brat of hell. Some of your fine parsons, with bibs on and rings upon their fine turned-up fingers, would say, "You should not come with such language"; but such men know nothing at all about the matter. Our poet beautifully expresses it,

> "Hail! sovereign love, that first began
> The scheme to rescue fallen man;
> Hail! matchless, free, eternal grace,
> That gave my –

poor, wretched, guilty, hell-deserving

> – soul a hiding-place."

Israel was to keep in remembrance their being brought out of Egypt – the bringing them out of their trouble. O the soul trouble I had! O the wretchedness, the horror! But the Lord in his own due time manifested himself, and applied the pardoning love and blood of Christ to my heart. I felt more happy than an angel. "What! All my sins and iniquities gone!" I said. "Where is my sin?" I could not find a single sin. It was God's doing; he had put it all away. I said, "Where is it?" I felt indeed happy. Where is the devil at such times as these? The devil feels he cannot stand his ground before the King of kings and Lord of lords. The blessed soul is brought into the liberty of the sons of God: "Stand fast, therefore, in the liberty wherewith Christ hath made us free, and be not entangled again with the yoke of bondage."

The Lord says, "Call upon me." Now the precious soul begins to glorify the Lord. He feels him in his heart. When the soul is thus brought into the glorious liberty of the sons of God, he is astonished at the love of God, and he says, "Why does the Lord love me?" He finds that he is one of his blessed people. He wonders at the riches of God's grace, and he glorifies the Lord. He offers up praise for the great things God has done for him. He honours him who has brought his soul out of bondage into a large place. He rejoices in the God of his salvation, and yields him perfect obedience.

He glorifies the Lord Jesus Christ. He is at a loss to set forth his praise. He finds he cannot lift the dear Redeemer too much to the notice of others; he cannot glorify him enough. He wants to exalt him, to crown him Lord of all. His language is, "Bless the Lord, O my soul." Thus they glorify the dear Redeemer.

Why do they glorify the Eternal Spirit? Why, for convincing them of sin; for bringing down their proud and rebellious hearts; but more particularly for taking of the things of God and revealing them to their souls. They honour the Eternal Spirit as a glorious Person in the ever-blessed Trinity. They find their need of him, and that they could not do without his influences. They glorify a Triune Jehovah, – "the Three that bear record in heaven."

Now this is what generally takes place in the soul, in the experience of God's people, when the Lord has heard their prayers, when he has blessed them by the good Word of his grace, and his presence is sweet to them; then he is the fairest amongst ten thousand, and the altogether lovely. "This," the man says, "is just what I wanted; now I shall go on my way rejoicing. I shall never have such hardness, such misery as before." Some are for going to heaven in silver slippers, or in a carriage and four. Some are, like Peter, for building their tabernacles. They fancy they are never to go into the valley again. But days of trouble are not gone yet. We must be weaned; we must be taken from the breast. I have many fathers and mothers here tonight, and they know what it was with their children. There is a deal of trouble yet. And, like a weaned child, there is a deal of kicking and rebelling.

I wish to tell you respecting my own soul's experience, as being the case generally with others. There is a time of trouble comes on again, my friends. The beauty of the glory of the Redeemer seems to be obscured, and there is a cloud and darkness overshadows the mind of man, and a darkness which results in a hardness of heart. He cannot pray, he cannot feel at the time of offering up his prayer. He begins to feel he is moping in the dark. His words do not leave his mouth aright, or so readily as before. Like Job, he seeks God on the right hand and on the left. Trouble assails him. And when the child of God is in this state, Satan comes in to him as a flood, and suggests all manner of abominable wickedness. There is worldly-mindedness, too, creeps in, and all sorts of evil occur to his mind. He says, "Lord, I did not think I was so vile. I abhor myself." He is in soul trouble. There is a stirring up of his wicked nature.

Poor soul, let him turn to the Bible, to read that which has been his companion. It has before been found to be very precious to his soul; but, ah! it does not afford him now any comfort. When my soul was brought into gospel liberty, even the sight of the Word of God as lying on the shelf filled my soul with joy. When the soul is brought into this state of trouble, he looks to the Book, and he cannot think how it is he cannot extract one drop of comfort from it, nor one drop of honey. There is a feeling of heart-hardness. Yea, even, if the Bible and the daily journal lie on the table together, he takes up the latter in preference, and he says in the anguish of his soul, with Job, "O that it were with me as in months past, as in the days when God preserved me; when his candle shined upon my head, and when by his light I walked through darkness!" So that here is a looking back; and the Lord's commandment is, "Ponder the path of thy feet."

During my last visit a friend showed me a letter written by the departed Huntington, wherein he mentions having lately

visited many of the spots where the Lord had blessed him with
the enjoyment of real gospel liberty of soul. And it is not long
since that I had, when travelling on horseback to a place I had
to preach at, to pass by the wood (for I had no closet then, and
there being only one field near I had to resort to the woods)
where the dear Lord was pleased to break in upon my soul,
and set me at happy liberty. I had made two holes at the
bottom of the ditch with so frequently kneeling there. And,
my friends, it is good to look back. The Lord told Israel of old
to remember all the way the Lord had brought them. He told
them to remember how he had brought them safe through the
Red Sea.

When the soul that is in this trouble comes to hear the
minister preach, he comes and wishes to hear with the hearing
ear and understanding heart; but in vain does he begin to
enter into the subject; for the devil is busy in reminding him of
some project, or of something he has to do. I will relate to you
one instance of a good woman who was a clothes dealer. Late
one Saturday night a man called to buy a coat. After a deal of
bargaining, he discovered it was too little for him. A tailor
was called in, and not being able to settle how it was to be let
out, as it did not fit in the back and was too long, the coat was
left till Monday morning. Monday came, and with it came the
man and also the tailor. During the conversation the old
woman called out, "O! I have a better plan than you. I know
now how it must be let out; the devil told me all about it
yesterday morning during the sermon. I can tell you exactly
how to do it." This good woman was a member of the church
at Manchester, over which my old friend Gadsby is now
pastor, before he was settled there. She has been dead now
some time.

I merely relate this to show that Satan does harass and
perplex the minds of God's saints with secular objects, and by
distracting their imagination prevents them from deriving
good to their souls. The man does not hear the Word
preached as he used to do; he has got into soul trouble. His

feelings are not the same, and he blames the ministers of God, and makes them stand the brunt of all this. His soul is lean, and brought into darkness, wretchedness and bondage. The enemy thus taunts him: "Where is all thy religion now?" Like the Israelites who were carried away captives, they were in a state of trouble; they hanged their harps upon the willows, and were taunted by their enemies requiring songs and psalms, while in a situation of grief and despondency. They said to them, "You have songs of deliverance, of great goodness?" But, alas. They could only reply, "How can we sing the Lord's song in a strange land?" There was bondage here, my friends. God's saints are sometimes in this predicament. "Where is all thy religion now? Thou hast the form, but not the power!" Such is the language of the enemy, and they fear they are like the stony-ground hearers. The soul staggers. I was in this frame one time myself. I frequently said to myself, "O that I had never entered upon the course of religion. I am afraid I am only a deceiver!" The Lord says, "Who is among you that feareth the Lord? Let him trust in the name of the Lord." Even this declaration cannot be observed without spiritual influence. One of old was in something of this kind of strait, when he said, "My soul chooseth strangling, and death rather than life." We seem to have a hatred against everything, that is God-like, and even are tempted to curse God, and persuade ourselves that the Bible is false and the result of priestcraft. O how the saint striveth! There is inward groaning at the bottom of his soul.

God will come down to the help of this soul. He says, "Call upon me in the day of trouble." The page of inspiration says, "Be instant in season and out of season." Perhaps the person may say, I have no desire to call upon the name of the Lord; but God will give this desire. The Lord will come down to thy help in his own due time.

David saith, "My soul waiteth for the Lord, more than they that watch for the morning." David then, you see, had been in this state. He says, "Restore unto me the joy of thy salvation, and uphold me with thy free Spirit." Salvation is like a bulwark round the church of God; the joy may be lost for a time, but not the salvation. There is something in the case of the women at the time of Christ. They had enjoyed his presence and conversation, but when he was crucified they thought it was all over with them. They could not lie in their beds; they were up very early in the morning to look for him. They went to the sepulchre, and Mary cried, "They have taken away my Lord, and I know not where they have laid him." Their joy had for a time fled. The joy of the saints of God is when they have his presence with them, and when he manifests his love by the comfort he imparts to their souls. There is deliverance after deliverance in this vale of tears.

I have been myself in the state of bondage I have been describing for twelve months. I cried unto the Lord day after day. While in this state of mind, the passage, "The eyes of the Lord are upon the righteous," was powerfully impressed upon my soul. The blessed Spirit began to preach to my soul. He is the best preacher I have ever heard. My chains and fetters were broken off. I felt in my soul a sweet satisfaction of a change effected within me. Mr. Booth*, that good man, the author of *The Reign of Grace*, an excellent book, in speaking with his last gasp, tried to sing this beautiful verse, and died with it on his lips:

> "The gospel bears my spirit up;
> A faithful and unchanging God
> Lays the foundation of my hope,
> In oaths and promises and blood."

May God of his great goodness apply the Word to each of our consciences, and bless our souls. Amen.

---

* Abraham Booth (1734-1806), minister at Prescot Street, London.

5. THE POOR AND NEEDY IN GOD'S REMEMBRANCE

Preached at Zoar Chapel, Great Alie Street, London, on behalf of
The Aged Pilgrims' Friend Society,
on December 1st, 1842.

Text: *"But I am poor and needy; yet the Lord thinketh upon me"*
(Psalm 40. 17).

My friends, we are now met in the presence of a heart-searching and rein-trying God, who knows our state and condition, and is perfectly acquainted with the feelings and views we have of ourselves as sinners before him. And if one may speak for the rest, the state of our mind is fully expressed by David in the language of the text: "But I am poor and needy, yet the Lord thinketh upon me."

I am growingly persuaded, that among the great bulk of professors, it is but here and there one can be found who is experimentally brought to see and feel his real spiritual poverty and destitution in the sight of a just and holy God; for there are so many saying, either directly or indirectly, that they are rich and increased in goods and have need of nothing, whilst they are ignorant what poor, needy, miserable, wretched, helpless and guilty creatures they are in themselves.

Now I will tell you the difference between such as these and the heaven-born soul. Those that "are rich, and increased in goods" can read and pray and get comfort whenever they like. Outward things go on smoothly with them, and inwardly their souls are quiet and easy. They are spoken well of amongst others, and they are happy and comfortable in themselves. They are rich, and well satisfied, and are not in want of anything. But I look at them with feelings of grief and sorrow, and my soul sighs and groans over those who only have the form of religion but deny the power thereof. The devil will let such persons alone; he will not plague and harass them as he does the Lord's people. No, such are rocked in his cradle, they are in carnal security and fleshly ease. But if they leave the world with only such a profession as this, they will die in the dark, and their form of religion will drop off just like a mantle from the shoulders, and leave their souls naked at last to sink into hell in delusion and error, having only a form of godliness, but denying the power thereof; and therefore Paul says, "from such turn away."

But then, how does it fare with the dear child of God, the heaven-born soul, who in his very heart can adopt the language of the text as his own, and which is expressive of his inmost feelings: "But I am poor and needy"? Why, with him, as it respects the means of grace, reading the Scriptures, the use of prayer, the ministry of the Word and attending the ordinances of God's house, they neither are nor can be satisfied with anything short of realizing God's presence in the use of them. Someone will say, "Are they then against the use of means, and of assembling themselves together in the name of the Lord?" God forbid! they cannot be; for the exhortation is, "Forsake not the assembling of yourselves together, as the manner of some is, but exhort one another, and so much the more as ye see the day approaching." But, is the Christian satisfied when he has merely done his duty by attending to the means and ordinances of grace? O no! my friends, unless he enjoys something of the precious truths delivered, by the application of the Spirit to his soul, he is dissatisfied. He will go about sighing, groaning, mourning and praying unto the Lord that he would speak home some comfort and peace to him. It is not the *form* of religion that he wants, but it is the *power* of it that he pants after. He feels his deep poverty, weakness, helplessness and misery, and he desires the refreshings and renewings of the blessed Spirit that he may be enabled to enjoy something of the fulness and preciousness of that grace which is treasured up in the Person of Christ, as it is said, "And out of his fulness have all we received, and grace for grace."

The living soul, then, that knows the plague of his own heart, sees and feels his helplessness; he knows he is poor and needy, and does not need to be told of it. He knows he is miserable and wretched in himself, and that all his riches and happiness are in the Lord Jesus Christ. And if you are one of the Lord's family, the longer you live the more you will see and feel your poverty, weakness, helplessness and insufficiency. You will have greater discoveries of your misery and ruined state by the fall, which will cause you to sigh more and more on account of what you see and feel yourself to be before a heart-searching God. O what a mercy then it is that the Lord thinketh upon such an one as you. "But I am poor and needy, yet the Lord thinketh upon me."

The Lord does not think upon his people with thoughts of indignation; they are thoughts of love, thoughts of mercy, and thoughts of compassion. He says, "I know the thoughts that I think toward you, thoughts of peace, and not of evil, to give you an expected end." And therefore, David says, "Remember me, O Lord, with the favour that thou bearest unto thy people: O visit me with thy salvation!"

Our God is in the heavens, surrounded by angels and the spirits of just men made perfect, who are casting their crowns at his feet and unceasingly adoring him as the God of their salvation. And yet, though this is the case, he has as much regard for poor, destitute, weak, worthless and helpless worms, that are crawling about upon the face of the earth, sighing and groaning over the abominations that are committed in the land, and over the corruptions of their own hearts, as he has for the spirits of the glorified now before the throne. Yea, I had like to have said he has more regard for them; for the saint before the throne is as happy as it is possible for him to be, but the poor child of God, who is now in the wilderness, is surrounded with cares and sorrows. He is tempted by the devil, he feels the workings of his corrupt nature, he has to wade through darkness, he has to deplore

the hardness of his heart, and he has many discouragements
both from within and from without. But then, they have the
Lord himself as their great High Priest; and he sympathizes
with them in all the afflictions they have to pass through, for
he has such a special regard for them that he looks down from
heaven to watch over them, and to listen to their sighs and
groans. He has so much interest in them that "he ever liveth
to make intercession for them." His precious blood always
prevails on their behalf, for they are the mystic members of his
body and heirs of eternal glory; therefore he will arise for their
help and salvation, as it is said in the 12th Psalm, "For the
oppression of the poor, for the sighing of the needy, now will
I arise, saith the Lord; I will set him in safety from him that
puffeth at him." Bless the Lord, then, for the regard which he
has to the poor and needy soul. "But I am poor and needy, yet
the Lord thinketh upon me."

My friends, I would now in the *first* place make a few
remarks upon what David saith concerning himself, which is:
"But I am poor and needy."

And *secondly*, show that the Lord thinketh upon his poor
and needy people – "yet the Lord thinketh upon me."

I.   In the first place, let us notice what David saith of
himself, "But I am poor and needy." Now this could not mean
in a literal sense as to temporal prosperity, for David was a
king and possessed great personal wealth, insomuch that he
heaped up a great portion of his riches for his son Solomon to
build the temple with. But when he says that he is "poor and
needy," he means experimentally so, in the feelings of his soul,
the same as it is expressed by our Lord in his sermon on the
mount, where he says, "Blessed are the poor in spirit, for theirs
is the kingdom of heaven." It is a feeling sense of our poverty
and destitution before the Lord. But to state it clearly and
pointedly, I observe, in a literal point of view, that that person
is considered to be poor and needy who goes from hand to
mouth, who has no stock in hand, nor anything which he can

call his own. And just so it is with God's poor people. What have they in possession of their own that they can bring before the Lord? What have any of you, but poverty and wretchedness? St. Paul says, speaking of himself, "as having nothing, yet possessing all things." And therefore, if this is the state of our feelings, "having nothing," then that sweet invitation will suit us well: "Ho! every one that thirsteth, come ye to the waters, and he that hath no money; come ye, buy and eat; yea, come buy wine and milk, without money and without price." But if we have anything of our own to bring in our hand, God will surely send us empty away. I am so glad then, my friends, that it is all free, for those that come with money in their pockets to purchase it, he will have nothing to do with; but those that come empty, poor and wretched will find a welcome here. He will have those that are needy, lost and helpless, and in them he will magnify the freeness and fulness of his grace.

But whenever I speak of this subject, there is another thing which always comes into my mind – that I *have* something to bring before the Lord! Why, what have you to bring, then? Alas! I have a hard heart, a wandering mind and a barren soul, many failings and infirmities, with much short-coming and unprofitableness! But yet it is to such characters as these to whom our God will have respect, for he says in his Word, "If we confess our sins, he is faithful and just to forgive us our sins, and to cleanse us from all unrighteousness." Come then, poor sensible sinner, just as you are. Do not try to cover over your sin, but tumble it out just as you feel it; for mark what the Word of the Lord says, "To this man will I look, even to him that is poor, and of a contrite heart, and trembleth at my word." This is the way in which God's children come to him; they have to make hearty confessions of sin and iniquity, and are brought with many tears, groans and supplications to his feet; and it is in this way the Lord makes his work of grace manifest in the conscience.

"But I am poor and needy, yet the Lord thinketh upon

me." Now a person may not only be poor, and have nothing of his own, but may also be very deep in debt. There are many persons in this state; they have contracted very heavy debts and are without anything to pay them with. My friends, I have been very poor, and can recollect the time well when I used to reckon up what I owed when I went to bed at night, and that exhortation would follow me with such force, "Owe no man any thing," that I could scarcely get sleep or take any rest on account of it. And I make nothing of the religion of any man or woman who can be happy and indifferent while they are deep in debt.

Now, God's spiritual people are not only deep in debt, but in addition thereto, they are all bankrupts and utterly unable to pay their debts. All his saints are poor and needy; therefore our dear Lord said, "When they had nothing to pay," he frankly forgave them their debt. Our sins are like debts; and beloved, I have felt mine to be a very great and dark debt, for my sins have appeared to me more in number than the hairs upon mine head, or the sands upon the seashore innumerable; and while discovering this deep and dark debt, I have felt myself to be without one single farthing wherewith to pay it. But, my friends, I have several times quoted from this pulpit what Dr. Crisp* says in his writings (and which are good food for God's spiritual people), that "Jesus Christ is the Paymaster of all his people's debts." And, blessed be his name, he did not pay it by instalments; he paid it in full all at once. He gave his life a ransom for the church, and he has taken their sins completely away. There is no debt-book standing open against them to all eternity; law and justice are satisfied on their behalf, and there is no charge against them, for "there is no condemnation to them which are in Christ Jesus."

There are some persons who talk about being justified by the law of works, and performing certain works of super-erogation. But is the heaven-born soul satisfied with anything

* Tobias Crisp (1600-1642)

of this kind? No! he is satisfied with nothing short of that wherewith God is satisfied. And if you can find refuge in any other than the slaughtered Lamb of God, who shed his precious blood to redeem his people, you are not one of the poor and needy spoken of in the text.

But again. A person may be worse off and more wretched than being deep in debt. How is that? Why, he may not only be heavily in debt, but he may have been arrested and put into prison for the payment of it. Jesus says, "I was sick, and in prison." I merely mention this to show that a person in such a case is truly poor and needy. Now every one of God's saints, who are brought to rejoice in Christ Jesus and have no confidence in the flesh, and to whom he is truly precious, are brought to see and feel that they are not only deep in debt, but that they are sick and in prison also; and therefore they come with sighing and groaning before the Lord to pour out their case unto him. But what kind of sickness is it that they feel? Why, they are sick of sin, sick of self, sick of their vile hearts and evil thoughts, and sick of all that they say or do; they abhor themselves, and repent in dust and ashes, and often utter this cry, "But I am poor and needy."

My friends, do you know anything of these feelings? Some folks are satisfied with having a sound creed, with holding the doctrines of predestination, election and the final perseverance of the saints according to the letter of the Word, but can leave experimental things quite at rest. But a sound creed, a clear judgment and a talent to explain God's truth may do very well to live with, but they are not sufficient to die by. Good doctrines cannot do anyone good unless the heart is affected by them and they are reduced into personal experience in the soul. There are many persons who have the truth of the doctrine clear enough in the head, but know nothing of the vital power of it in the heart. Therefore we can never really value and feel the grace and power of God's truth until we are made sick of ourselves, and brought to understand our own weakness and insufficiency, and are driven out of self to take refuge alone in Jesus Christ; and thus experimentally made to know that we are among those described in the Word as "having nothing, and yet possessing all things." It is not every saint who is favoured like St. Paul to have the same measure of grace which he had, but still they are all brought to know that they have nothing in themselves and that they possess all things in Christ. This appears very strange to a natural man, but it is full of blessedness to the children of God: that while they have nothing in themselves, they possess all things in a covenant God, who hath given us all things that we stand in need of, both for time and eternity, in our Lord Jesus Christ, who is our "all and in all." Thus the Lord's people must be made to feel their deep poverty and destitution, and then they will cry out in the words of the text, "But I am poor and needy."

But now, having made these remarks in reference to the Lord's people considered as "poor," we will look at them under the description of being "needy" also. I know they are nearly synonymous, for those that are poor, are needy characters also; but yet, as David mourned over his state and circumstances, and could express himself better by using both the terms, "poor and needy," we will look at it for a minute or two. Some may be ready to say, "Well, what does the child of God need?" May I not rather reverse it, and say, "What is it he does *not* need?"

But here a large field opens to me on this part of my subject. God's poor and needy family see that they are lost and ruined, and that they can do nothing to save or help themselves. They see that the whole work must be commenced, carried on and completed by God himself; that he must be the author of every spiritual feeling they have; that he must save them with a present and an everlasting salvation. Therefore they feel that they need to be saved wholly and completely; that all their needs are treasured up in Christ; that

"Israel shall be saved in the Lord with an everlasting salvation"; that their "salvation is of the Lord," not partly of the Lord and partly of themselves; but that "salvation belongeth unto the Lord; his blessing is upon his people." The prophet Isaiah speaks solemnly on this subject. He says, speaking of Jesus, "Mine own arm brought salvation," not my arm along with that of others helping me. No, no! Many professors must put a helping hand to it; they will say, as we do in the north, "We must have a finger in the pie." They must be like Uzzah of old, putting forth their hand to prop up the ark. But the Lord will not have it so. His salvation is all of pure, free and sovereign grace and that man who attempts in any way to put his own works to it is offering an insult to God; for it is written, "By grace are ye saved through faith; and that not of yourselves, it is the gift of God; not of works, lest any man should boast."

Thus God's own people, who are born from above and taught of the Spirit, are poor and needy, lost and ruined, and they want to be wholly saved, completely saved and everlastingly saved. But this is an eternal salvation treasured up for them in Christ Jesus, and it is all of free, sovereign and discriminating mercy. Now all that the Lord requires the poor creature to do is what he enables him to perform by his blessed Spirit (and we bless his name for it), and that is to cast himself at the feet of the dear Redeemer as a poor, lost, needy and faulty sinner, and to count all his own doings as less than nothing and vanity. Such a poor soul as this will enter into his presence like one we read of in the blessed Word, who, when she entered into the presence of the king contrary to law, said, "If I perish, I perish." Just so it is with the sensible sinner; he is brought with a determination to perish at the feet of the Lord Jesus Christ. But the Holy Ghost never did nor ever will put such solemn feelings in the heart and conscience of the poor sinner and then disappoint him at the last. No, the Spirit will bring him to lie submissively at his feet, to cast his soul into the hands of a blessed Jesus, and will give him at length to see that he has a personal interest in his blood and righteousness, that he is saved in him with an everlasting salvation, and that all the fulness of grace to supply his needs is treasured up for him in his glorious person. Thus he discovers not only that he is lost and ruined, and stands in need of being saved from sin, the curse of the law, death, hell and the grave, but that he needs the power and grace of the Lord to keep and guide him all through the wilderness until at last he shall land his soul in immortal bliss and blessedness. The Lord must do it all; it is all of his own free grace from first to last; for "of him, and through him, and to him are all things, to whom be glory for ever and ever." He has done all the work, and therefore he alone shall have the praise.

But again. God's poor and needy family not only need saving, but they need washing also in the precious blood of the Lord Jesus Christ; and they will continue to feel their need of it as long as they remain here. Then it is clear, they do not get perfect in themselves and free from sin, as some persons assert. What! God's saints get perfect in the flesh, and free from Adam's sin and corruption? If that be the way in which they are led, I must say I have been out of it for more than thirty-five years. But Job says, "If I say I am perfect, my own mouth shall also prove me perverse," and God's truth would not be in me. For the more the Lord's people see an end of all perfection, and the more light and life they have in their souls, the deeper will be their discoveries of self, and the more will they be humbled in the dust, and see and feel their need of being washed and purged from the very sins of their nature in the precious blood of the Lamb.

Bless God, then, that we have such a fountain opened for us. It is not opened for good and self-righteous folks, for those that are without sin, but for those who feel and know what the guilt of sin is on the conscience; as it is said, "In that day there shall be a fountain opened to the house of David, and to the inhabitants of Jerusalem, for sin and for uncleanness." Well then, there is sin and uncleanness in the house of David and among the inhabitants of Jerusalem. And there are not any of those inhabitants here tonight but feel that there is sin and uncleanness in them, and who are crying out from time to time like the leper of old, "Unclean, unclean, unclean!" for "the whole head is sick, and the whole heart is faint." This is the case of many who are now present before the Lord; and they would sink into feelings of dismay were it not for the blood of Jesus, for his peace-speaking blood, and for his hell-conquering blood. And this is the glory of the church, and the triumph of the saints. What! cannot the Lord's people live without the blood of Jesus? No; it is the glory of the believer; it is the joy of his heart, and the boast of his soul. And all that he wants now is to feel renewed applications of it by the almighty power of the Holy Ghost. So that, my friends, we need continued washing from our sins in the precious blood of the Lamb.

I shall never forget hearing what a precious woman once said, when coming before the church to tell what God had done for her soul. While relating how the Lord had met with her and taught her what she was as a poor, lost, ruined sinner; and what an ungodly, vile, and wretched creature she saw herself to be, she said, "One night, after I had laid down, I was afraid to go to sleep lest I should fall into hell; but while I was praying on my bed, with my soul full of agony and near despair, these words dropped into my heart with a power that completely delivered me from my terror:

'Black, I to the fountain fly,
Wash me, Saviour, or I die.'"

You see she had a precious view of the value and efficacy of the blood of Christ, and she felt its power so sweet that she began to sing in her bed the triumphs of salvation. And therefore we have cause now to sing, "Unto him that loved us, and washed us from our sins in his own blood, and hath made us kings and

priests unto God and his Father, to him be glory and dominion for ever and ever."minion for ever and ever."

David felt his need of being washed in the precious blood
of the Lamb. And if you go to the 51st Psalm, he says, "Wash
me throughly from mine iniquities, and cleanse me from my
sin. Purge me with hyssop, and I shall be clean; wash me, and
I shall be whiter than snow." We need this washing as much
as he did; for though we may not have committed adultery, as
David did with the wife of Uriah, yet we have the same evil in
our hearts; and our dear Lord says, "He that looketh on a
woman to lust after her hath committed adultery already with
her in his heart." So that the abominable, carnal desires of the
flesh are that which worry the soul, and make it to feel as a
sink of iniquity. O, then, for fresh applications of the precious
blood of God's dear Son, which cleanses from this, as well as
from every other evil! And therefore, though we feel lust and
worldly-mindedness and wanderings of heart, yet there is a
sovereign remedy for it all in the blood of Jesus. "The whole
need not a physician, but they that are sick;" and, "The blood
of Jesus Christ cleanseth from all sin."

Now, I know persons generally do not like this plain way
of speaking. They will skim over these evils nicely and cover
them up smoothly; it is not pleasant to hear it. But God's
family want to know the true state of their case, to have it
probed to the bottom, and to see where their blessedness is,
that it is in Jesus Christ, and in him alone. Therefore nothing
but the precious blood of Christ can cleanse the conscience
from guilt and sin; but whenever it is applied with power, it
will remove the burdens that oppress the soul, and enable it to
praise the Lord with joyful lips.

But again. God's poor and needy family not only need
washing in the blood of Jesus, but they are all naked and
require clothing. The Lord strips his people of all their fig-leaf
garments and creature righteousness. He gives them to see
that all their righteousnesses are as filthy rags. He empties

them of all their self-sufficiency, and brings them into a state of poverty and destitution. And when they are brought to feel that they stand in need of a garment to clothe them from their nakedness and to cover them from condemnation, then he will reveal to them that there is no other righteousness that will do for them, or that they can stand in, but that of the Lord Jesus Christ. My soul rejoices in this robe of righteousness, for the poor sinner cannot stand in any garment of his own doing. He must lay it all aside, and come as a poor, destitute, naked sinner to the Lord Jesus Christ, and say, "Dear Lord, thy Word says thou hast wrought out and brought in an everlasting righteousness, a wedding-robe, and made it ours, and there is nothing else will satisfy my soul. I hunger and thirst after it, for it suits my state and circumstances." Bless the Lord, then, it is provided for such an one as thee; for the Holy Spirit would never give hungerings and thirstings after it unless he had intended to satisfy the desires of such a soul. He will clothe him in this glorious robe of righteousness, and give him to know that he shall shine in it for ever and ever, as it is written, "I will greatly rejoice in the Lord, my soul shall be joyful in my God; for he hath clothed me with the garments of salvation, he hath covered me with the robe of righteousness.

Now I might go on with this subject until midnight in this simple way. But I must now appeal to the conscience. Then, I say, do not you and I feel ourselves to be weak and worthless worms? Not merely weak, but weakness itself. And if we in reality feel ourselves to be poor, weak and helpless worms, do we not then need the Lord to strengthen us and to hold us up? Well, has he not promised to strengthen us with might by his Spirit in the inner man? And one good word from the Lord, under the bedewing influences of his Spirit, will enable these poor worms to thresh the mountains of sin and reduce them to a plain. Do you know anything, then, of having a word of comfort from the Lord? Newton sings,

> "O! I have seen the day,
> When, with a single word,
> God helping me to say
> My trust is in the Lord;
> My soul has quelled a thousand foes,
> Fearless of all that could oppose."

And so it is, my friends; if we have the God of Jacob, the Lord Jehovah, on our side, what shall we have to fear? And therefore, although we are poor and needy, and continually require the help of the Lord to enable us to stand, yet "he giveth power to the faint, and to them that have no might he increaseth strength." O that we may be kept every day and every hour growingly sensible of our own weakness and helplessness, and that our hearts may be ascending up to the Lord in the language of the church of old, where she so beautifully sings, "The Lord Jehovah is my strength and my song; he also is become my salvation."

But again, as poor and needy creatures, we need the Lord Jesus Christ as our Wonderful Counsellor: "He is wonderful in counsel, and excellent in working." Now when a person has a difficult case and needs advice, he will go to a lawyer and consult counsel; he will put his case into his hands, and the lawyer will manage the matter for him. I know with far too many it is not a very easy thing to get clear of them, when once you are in their hands; but when you can meet with an honest, upright lawyer, he is a very valuable man; and I do hope there are a few honest ones to be found. But I do not say these things with the intention of applying them to anyone. I simply refer to it as it serves to illustrate the case of our Lord Jesus Christ as our Wonderful Counsellor, and of us as his clients. And, therefore, let us follow the example of Hezekiah, and go to the Lord with our troubles, and pour out our complaints before him, and say as he did, "Lord, bow down thine ears, and hear; open thine eyes, and see" what they are going to do unto us, and help us to stand still, and watch thy hand in all things.

May we, then, be enabled to go to him continually, for the soul can never weary him; although we may be weary in going to him, he is never weary of hearing from us. He invites us to come again and again, and says, " Cast thy burden on the Lord, and he shall sustain thee." If we need wisdom, then let us ask it of him, who giveth liberally, and upbraideth not. Blessed be his name, he gives it all free; he manages all the intricacies of his dear family, and he will counsel them in every step which they take. Let us praise him for it, for he has promised to "guide us by his counsel, and afterward receive us to glory." So that, though we are poor and needy, yet we are encouraged to seek his direction every day and hour while we are travelling through the wilderness. And oftentimes when sitting, walking and riding, my heart is up to him that he would help me to trust in and commit my way more unto him, that he would direct and hold up my goings in his paths that my footsteps slip not; so that my desire is that the Lord would keep me in the narrow way while I am here, until I am out of the reach of sin, Satan and the world, and have done with all things that harass and oppress me. But I will not say any more on this point, but come to the last part of the subject, as the time is now nearly gone.

II. "But I am poor and needy, yet the Lord thinketh upon me." The Lord's family need his care, both in temporal and spiritual things. And I hope you have come here with the intention of giving something to his saints, as there is to be a collection made here tonight, on behalf of the Aged Pilgrims' Friend Society. Now God has left us many examples in the Word of his grace to show that he thinks upon the poor and needy.

You recollect when Elijah was in the wilderness, how the Lord thought upon him there. He sent ravens night and morning with bread to feed him, and he drank of the brook which he provided, and thanked God for his care of him. But alas! in a little while the brook dried up, and he must now

leave the place. Yet notwithstanding, the Lord thinks upon
him still. He had commanded a poor widow woman to sustain
him, who thought that she was near her end, for the devil and
unbelief had so wrought upon her mind that she went as she
thought for the last time, to gather up a few sticks to make a
fire to dress her handful of meal, that they might eat it and
then lie down and die. But God had sent the prophet to help
her. "What!" say you, "send the prophet to help her, and he
could not help himself?" O yes! the Lord's servant is to be
helped, and he is to help the poor woman too!

So when he came to the gate of the city, he beheld the
woman gathering up the sticks, and he said to her, "Fetch me,
I pray thee, a little water in a vessel that I may drink." And as
the woman was going to get the water, he called after her and
said, "Bring me also, I pray thee, a morsel of bread in thine
hand." The poor woman now turned round, with a countenance full of gloom and despondency, and said, "Man, I
have nothing to give; for to tell you the truth, I have just now
come out to gather up a few sticks to make the last meal for me
and my son, and then we are going to die." And now the
prophet said (for the Spirit of the Lord came upon him), "The
barrel of meal shall not waste, neither shall the cruse of oil fail,
until the day that the Lord send rain upon the earth." And
thus the prophet and the poor woman ate of it, and were
sustained until the time of rain, according to the word of the
Lord. Let us, therefore, likewise, think of God's poor and
needy, and see what we can do tonight to help them.

Do you not remember the case of another poor widow
woman, to whom the Lord sent the prophet Elisha in the time
of her distress? For he is a father to the fatherless, and a
husband to the widow. It appears that her husband was a
good man, and that he had died in debt. And, my friends, I
have heard many of God's praying people say that the great
desire of their soul was that they might be able to pay their
debts, and obey the apostle's exhortation, "Owe no man any

thing." And I have no doubt that this was his desire also. But nevertheless, it appears that he had died in debt, and the creditors had come, as was the custom in that country, to take away her sons to sell them as bond-slaves in order to procure money to pay the debt. And she came to Elisha and told him her case; and he said to her, "What shall I do for thee? What hast thou left in thy house?" I have no doubt she had sold all that she could towards paying it; for she was not like some fine folks, who must have plenty of plate and other fine things because it is respectable, regardless of whether they are able to pay their debts or not.

But he says to her, "What have you got?" She replied, "Thine handmaid hath not any thing in the house, save a pot of oil." Then he said, "Go, borrow thee vessels of all thy neighbours, even empty vessels, borrow not a few," which she did till no more could be found; and, according to the direction of the man of God, she poured out from the little pot of oil into all the vessels that she had borrowed, and the oil stayed not until they were all full. Then she went and sold it, and paid her debt, and lived upon the rest of the money. But mark, she paid her debt first, and afterwards kept the remainder to live with.

And here we may look at the Lord Jesus Christ as the great pot of heavenly oil, the merit of whose sacrifice never stayed till justice was fully satisfied, and he had cried out, "It is finished!" And also it points to the efficacy of his intercession, which will never cease until he has brought every one of those for whom he shed his precious blood to be with him in endless bliss and glory.

But now, as we are assembled in behalf of the poor and needy tonight, mere thinking about them will not do; we must have something more than this. It is not, "Be ye warmed, and be ye clothed," that will do; neither is it to give grudgingly, "for the Lord loveth a cheerful giver." Therefore I hope you will be able to give generously towards the support of the

Lord's aged poor. But, my friends, I cannot enlarge, as the time is gone. I would only say, that this Society is a most valuable one; that it has done a wonderful deal of good. Their finances are now straitened, and they are looking to you for some help and assistance. They have already gone beyond the limits of their funds, and they are prevented from doing much which they are desirous of, on account of the heaviness of their expenditure. I do hope and trust, therefore, that the Lord will enable you to give freely and cheerfully with a single eye to his glory, that what you do will be in the name of a disciple, and then you shall not lose a disciple's reward. So that when the King shall say, "For I was an hungred, and ye gave me meat; I was thirsty, and ye gave me drink; I was a stranger, and ye took me in; naked, and ye clothed me: I was sick, and ye visited me; I was in prison, and ye came unto me," though you may be ready to say, "Not so, Lord, no, no: when saw we thee so and so?" yet the King will answer and say, "Inasmuch as ye have done it unto one of the least of these my brethren, ye have done it unto me."

What then you do tonight, you will do for the Lord's poor and needy, the spiritual members of the mystical body of our Lord Jesus Christ. Therefore, give with a single eye to his glory and the good of his people; and then you will prove the truth of his Word, that "he that hath pity upon the poor lendeth unto the Lord, and that which he hath given him will he pay him again."

And now, may the Lord add his blessing to what has been said, and his name shall have the praise. Amen.

6. CHRIST'S SHEEP, AND THEIR MARKS

Notes of a Sermon preached on April 11th, 1843

Text: *"I give unto my sheep eternal life, and they shall never perish"* (John 10. 28).

The Holy Ghost, in the canon of Scripture, has borrowed a variety of metaphors from natural things to show us what Christ is to his people, and what his people are to him. Here he calls them "sheep," and himself the "Shepherd."

Jesus has received his sheep from his Father's hand as his portion, as the lot of his inheritance. He knows his sheep intimately and perfectly. When they are wandering on the mountains of the Adam fall, the shepherd has his eye upon them, and he seeks them out, and calls them to the rest of his flock, in his own time.

I.   The dead state the sheep of Christ are in with the rest of the world by the Adam fall.

All mankind, living in the loins of Adam, fell when he fell, their great federal head and representative: "As *in* Adam *all* die." We want no proof of this if we look around us. Not only the openly profane, but how many of the professing world are still "dead in trespasses and sins."

An outward form of religion serves as a cradle for the devil to rock the soul to the sleep of death. "There is death in the pot." The true sheep are living sheep and want living pasture. David was one, and he says in an ecstasy of joyful remembrance: "He leadeth me into green pastures, and beside the still waters."

II.   None can give life to the dead but Christ. "Thou hast given him power over all flesh, that he should give eternal life to as many as thou hast given him." He will never give eternal life to a goat, and never let one sheep pass through the world without it.

There are many kinds of life – vegetable life. Sometimes I see many beautiful flowers, but there is no savour, no smell, no life in them; they are artificial. Where is he that can give life to a blade of grass? There is none. There is the life of brutes; but none can give a worm life. There is our own natural life. What was Adam when he came from his Maker's hands? A lump of clay – no sense, no feeling. Did he leave it so? If he had it would soon have returned to its own dust again; but "he breathed into him the breath of life, and man *became* a living soul."

Sinners, dead in trespasses and sin, lie in sin as in a grave, and have no more power to rise than a dead carcase, and nothing but the sovereign power of Christ can effect it. This truth is borne out by the experience of every true Christian.

God's quickened family feel a great deal of deadness. My brother, cannot thou raise thy soul above this poor world, and fix thy soul on spiritual things? Oh no! your language is, "My soul cleaveth unto the dust: quicken thou me according to thy word"; and you are constrained to feel, "My springs are all in thee."

III. The evidences and marks of eternal life in the soul.

1. Before the sinner is quickened he can live in sin, and enjoy it as much as sin can give joy; but not so with the living soul. God has put his fear in his heart that he *cannot* sin against him (i.e. but with grief). 'Tis a burden. 'Tis bitter. God says, "Come out from among them, and be ye separate, and *touch not* the unclean thing." "What doest thou here, Elijah?"

The poor soul tries to defeat the Lord, and says, "Go away now. At a more convenient season I will send for thee"; but it is of no avail, for "he works in him to will and to do of his own good pleasure." I used to curse my father for taking me to the prayer-meeting, when I hated the Bible, and I do declare before God that I should have gone on to this day, and at last been damned but for the sovereign, almighty, electing love of Christ.

2. He begins to cry. God's living family often pray when they do not think they do; they mourn, they sink, and groan

till they seem full of sighs, and the devil cannot smother them.

3. They become as little children. What is it to become as a little child? Ezekiel describes it as a newborn babe cast out in a wilderness, unwatched, unwashed, unclothed. How weak! how helpless! how indigent! What can it do for itself? Nothing but cry and wait; and what can you do for yourselves more than this child? Can you wash yourselves, clothe yourselves, feed yourselves? "Except ye become as *little* children, ye shall not enter into the Kingdom of heaven."

4. Living souls are hungry and thirsty. A dead man neither hungers nor thirsts, but a quickened soul longs for the bread of heaven, for the means of grace, for gospel food. Before a sinner is made alive he can go on without the Bible; aye, the Bible is no book for a dead soul.

Here is an anecdote to show how living souls *must have the means of grace.* There was an old man in the north, and his name was Penderderry. This man had been what he called a churchman for seventy years, though the only time he had been to his parish church was when he was married, and when any of his children were christened. Now in the same village there were some of the Lord's living sheep, and they asked a good man to come and preach to them. Well, some of the neighbours asked this old churchman to go and hear, but, "No," said he, "I'll na gang near they dissenters." However, when the day came, one asked him as a favour to himself to go and hear; and at last the old man said, "Well, ye're a good naibor, and so to please *ye* I'll gang." He went, and the good man took for his text, "Thine arrows are sharp in the heart of the king's enemies, whereby the people fall under thee." (Psa. 45. 5).

The good man drew his bow at a venture, but the Lord directed the shaft. When the old churchman went home, he sat him down by the fire, and his head was down, and his wife said to him, "What's to do wi' ye?" The old man told her that he had heard things at the meeting that would not let him be easy. "Thou shalt gang na mare, thou shalt gang na mare," said his wife. The good man preached again, and the old churchman went again, and God wrought more upon him this time than he had before, and he went home and sat him down as before. Well, after he had sat some time, said he to his wife, "I would someone would rout me aut a Bible." His wife went into the loft and there found his old Bible, and wiping the dust off with her apron, brought it to her good man. Well, he read and read, and at last said, "Is this the right auld Bible we used to have?" "Aye, sure it is," said his wife; "we've got na ither." "I see how it is," said the old man. I see how it is, I've got nae een [new eyes]."

Quickened souls cannot live in the neglect of the means of grace.

In giving eternal life, Christ gives himself. Wherever life is in the soul, there Christ is: "When Christ, who *is* our life shall appear."

Renewed souls can only thrive on a living Saviour. O! soul, can you live on your studies? If so, you don't know what it is to feed on Christ. "Should do," "ought to do" and "will do" are the husks that the swine do eat; but whoso hungers and thirsts after righteousness will say, "There is bread enough in my Father's house (for Christ is there, and he is the true bread), and I cannot live on this swine's food."

5. The assurance given. I've no time to enter on this boundless part of the subject, but just ask how do matters stand between God and your soul? Are you alive? Can you be satisfied with outward forms, the swine's husks? If you can, there is no sign of life in you. But can you feed on Christ alone? Are you satisfied with nothing else? If so, Christ has given you, as one of his sheep, "eternal life, and you shall never perish."

7. THE ADDRESS AT THE GRAVE OF WILLIAM GADSBY

Given at Rusholme Cemetery, Manchester, on February 2nd, 1844

[In his autobiography, Mr. Kershaw writes:

On the morning of the funeral the friends flocked together from far and near, formed a procession, and walked before the hearse, many hundreds of them four abreast. The hearse was followed by eleven mourning coaches and many other vehicles, and thousands of people lined the streets through which the mournful cortêge had to pass, vast numbers of whom were evidently affected. One of the friends who had been brought up under Mr. Gadsby's ministry left his carriage and walked by the wayside to hear what the people said, and the general tone was, "He was a good, great, honest, upright man, a friend to the poor, and would be greatly missed in the town, as well as in his own chapel."

As we got nearer to the cemetery the number of people greatly increased. It was recorded in the Manchester papers that three thousand persons surrounded the grave; and had it not been a snowy morning there is no doubt but many more would have been present. I had stood by the graves of many who had been members of churches, deacons and ministers, and seen their bodies lowered into their last resting-place until the trumpet shall be sounded and the dead shall be raised, but never experienced the feelings I did on this occasion. Several of my ministerial brethren and deacons of the different churches stood by me while I addressed the assembled multitude.]

As it hath pleased Almighty God to call the soul of this his ministering servant and our brother from the body, we commit the body to the ground, dust to dust and ashes to ashes, in sure and certain hope of a joyful resurrection from the dead at that eventful period when Christ, the great Judge of all, shall descend upon the clouds of heaven; when the trumpet shall be sounded, and the dead shall be raised; wher.

the body, which we now sow a corruptible body because of sin, must put on incorruption, and this mortal must put on immortality, and be fashioned like unto the glorious body of our Lord Jesus Christ; and the saying that is written be fully accomplished, both in reference to Christ and all his spiritual seed, the purchase of his precious blood, "DEATH IS SWAL-LOWED UP IN VICTORY."

What I have further to say concerning our departed brother is not to give praise and honour to him as one of the fallen sons of an apostate Adam. This would be decidedly hostile to what was the feeling of him who, while dwelling amongst us, so often exclaimed, "Not unto us, not unto us, but unto thy name be all the glory, for thy mercy and thy truth's sake." What I would say is to exalt the riches of God's grace that shone so brightly in him as a Christian and a minister of the everlasting gospel, and as a citizen of this great and populous town.

By nature, he was no better than the rest of his father's house. He was shapen in iniquity, and in sin did his mother conceive him. Like the rest of the people of God in their Adam-fallen state, he erred and strayed from God like a lost sheep, joining the multitude of the ungodly in the broad and downward way that leads to destruction. Dead in trespasses and sins, at enmity against God in his heart, he lifted up his puny hands and arms in hostility against the God in whose hand his breath was. He had his conversation amongst his ungodly companions in sin in the lusts of the flesh, fulfilling the desires of the flesh and of the mind, and was by nature one of the children of wrath, even as others. But, in apostolic language, we would exultingly exclaim, "But God, who is rich in mercy, for his great love wherewith he loved him, even when dead in sins, hath quickened him together with Christ."

It pleased the Lord, in the riches of his grace, to pluck him as a brand out of the fire, and to put his fear into his heart, which is as "a fountain of life to depart from the snares of death." Thus he was called by God's irresistible grace from amongst his ungodly companions in sin, out of the kingdom of Satan into the kingdom of God and his Christ, out of darkness into God's marvellous light. The Holy Ghost, whose prerogative it is to quicken the dead sinner and to convince his people of their sins and sinfulness, carried the law (by which is the knowledge of sin) with an almighty power into his soul. He died to all hope of being saved by works of righteousness done by himself. What divines have justly denominated "a law-work in the conscience" was very deep and powerful in him. He felt the thunderings of Mount Sinai in his soul, which made him tremble, fear and quake. He proved by heartfelt experience that Mount Sinai is no hiding place for a poor guilty sinner, and that all that the law could do for him was to curse and condemn him as a vile transgressor, as it is written, "Cursed is every one that continueth not in all things which are written in the book of the law to do them." His soul lay as in chains, shut up as in a prison. He felt himself sinking in the miry clay and the horrible pit of guilt and condemnation. He sighed, groaned, and cried mightily to the Lord for help and deliverance.

The Lord was graciously pleased to hear his cry, and to lift him up out of the horrible pit and miry clay, and to set his feet upon the Rock of salvation and establish his goings, and to put the new song of praise and thanksgiving into his mouth. The ever-blessed Spirit was graciously pleased to take the precious blood and love of Jesus and apply them with a divine and almighty power to his soul, and to seal peace and pardon in his conscience, and to lead him into the sweet enjoyment of the glorious liberty of the gospel wherewith Christ Jesus makes his people free. So that he rejoiced in Christ Jesus, putting no confidence in the flesh, and became determined to know nothing but Christ Jesus and him crucified as the Rock of his salvation, the ground and foundation of his hope.

Thus it pleased God, who separated him from his mother's womb, to call him by his grace, and to reveal his Son in him, that he might preach him among the heathen; for I fear not to say that, like Paul, he was a chosen vessel of mercy to bear the precious name of Jesus before Gentile sinners, as a minister of the everlasting gospel. Our departed brother received not his credentials from the heads of universities or academies, but from Christ, the great Head of the church, who has ascended up on high, and led captivity captive, and gives gifts unto men, some apostles, and some prophets, and some evangelists, and some pastors and teachers, for the perfecting of the saints, for the work of the ministry, for the edifying of the body of Christ. The Lord of the harvest, whose prerogative it is to send forth labourers into his vineyard, laid the work of the ministry upon his mind with such a great and solemn weight that he had no rest day or night. The greatness and importance of the work of an ambassador of King Jesus on the one hand, and his own unfitness and inability for such a great, solemn and important work on the other hand, had such an effect upon his mind that (as I have heard him say) he chose rather to die than to enter upon the work. But the Lord had ordained him for the work, and he must go forth; for he that wrought effectually in Peter to the apostleship of the circumcision, wrought mightily in him towards the Gentiles. It was with him as with Jeremiah. Though he said in his heart, "I will not make mention of the name of the Lord," the Word of the Lord was in his heart as a burning fire shut up in his bones; so that he was weary with forbearing and could not stay. Power from on high came upon him, and the friends with whom he was connected had it impressed upon their minds that he was ordained of God for the work of the ministry, and they gave him encouragement to speak in the name of the Lord amongst them. He did so, though with fear and trembling, the Lord working with him, confirming the good Word of his grace spoken by him in the souls of his people. Visible signs followed; sinners were converted to God, and saints were edified.

Thus began the ministerial labours of our departed brother in the midland counties of Warwickshire and Leicestershire, where doors were opened for him to preach the word of eternal life. A chapel was built for him at Hinckley, in Leicestersbire, where he laboured for several years, and the Lord greatly blessed his labours, as several who are still living can testify. But Hinckley, the small and obscure town of Hinckley (when compared with the large and populous town of Manchester), was not to be the place of his future destiny; but Manchester, and the populous counties of Lancashire and Yorkshire, was to be the place of his more extensive usefulness as a minister of the everlasting gospel. But, my dear friends, in the present unfavourable state of the weather, and as you have to stand exposed to its severity, being in danger of taking cold, I will not detain you in recapitulating the circumstances which led to his coming to Manchester. Suffice it to say that he watched the hand of the Lord, he saw the pillar of cloud move from Hinckley to Manchester and he followed it, and the Lord was with him to bless him.

The Baptist cause at St. George's Road in this town was very low at the time he first came to Manchester. The first Lord's day morning that he entered the pulpit, he had not more people than there were pews in the place. He preached the great truths of the gospel with the ability that God gives, and not man. The power of the Lord rested upon him and blessed the good Word of his grace spoken by him to the souls of the people. The doctrines he preached dropped into the souls of the people under the bedewing influence of the Holy Ghost, as the rain upon the thirsty ground, and his speech distilled as the dew. There was that power attended the Word to the souls of the people that they felt their hearts knit to the preacher for the truth's sake. During the intermission between the morning and afternoon service several of the friends (like the Samaritan woman that the Lord met with at Jacob's well, who went into the city and said, "Come, see a man which told me all things that ever I did") went among their friends and acquaintances, and said, "Come, and hear what a man the Lord has sent us to St. George's Road!" By these means the chapel was tolerably well filled in the afternoon, and in the evening it was crowded out. He abode with them three or four Sabbaths, and the Word of the Lord spoken by him ran and had free course and was glorified, so that the good old veterans connected with the place, whose souls are now in glory, said, "This is the man for us; arise, and anoint him!" They began to cry mightily to God to make a way for him to come amongst them, and they never rested till he was settled over them as their pastor†.

In the year 1805 he was placed over them in the Lord as their pastor, and the Lord has been graciously pleased to enable him to stand on Zion's walls, firm in the truth, in this town and neighbourhood and in many parts of this land for more than thirty-eight years.

† I have had a personal acquaintance with the greater part of those who were the honoured instruments in the hands of the Lord of bringing brother Gadsby to Manchester, and can testify that they were men and women fearing God. They loved the truth, and they esteemed their minister highly in love for the truth's sake, and through grace they stood fast in the truth and in their attachment to their dear pastor until the Lord took them home. Now they are all gone, with the exception of two or three.

The Lord's day but one after Mr. Gadsby's death, being the ordinance day, I broke bread to the people of his charge, and before I entered upon the solemn ordinance of the Lord's supper I made a few observations to the church, showing them how highly the Lord had favoured them in placing such a man over them, and continuing him among them so long, and crowning his labours amongst them in such an abundant manner; that instead of murmuring and repining that the Lord had taken him from the church militant to the church triumphant, they had abundant reason to be thankful that he had been spared so long, and to put the Lord in remembrance of his promise to give them another pastor after his own heart. I sincerely desired that the Lord would send them one that he would make as useful, faithful, honourable and exemplary as their late

The great and glorious truths of the gospel that he has so faithfully and ably defended, in the face of great opposition, are: the doctrine of the fall, Adam's great transgression, that "by the disobedience of one man sin entered into the world, and death by sin," for that "all have sinned, and come short of the glory of God"; for we were born in sin and conceived in iniquity. The whole head is sick, and the heart faint, and we are altogether as an unclean thing, sin, that accursed thing, which a holy God hates, being in our nature, in our hearts, in our thoughts, and in all our ways. I never heard a man who was so well qualified by the Lord to lay proud man in the dust and upon the dunghill as was our departed brother. He deeply felt the depravity of his own nature, and the plague of his own heart, and was well able to describe them, lifting up his voice like a trumpet to show the people their transgression, and the house of Jacob their sin, and pointing out their lost, ruined, weak, helpless, undone state and condition as vile trans-

pastor had been, and one whose labours might be crowned with as great a blessing.

There was a large number of members present. I inquired if there were any persons present who were members of the church when Mr. Gadsby was first settled amongst them. There was for a short time a solemn silence, the deacons looking round among the people. At length one of them said, "There is an old woman here that was a member of this church when Mr. Gadsby came, but she is deaf and did not hear you ask the question." The following Lord's day morning, when I went into the vestry, there sat a venerable looking old man of eighty years of age. He said, "Friend Kershaw, I was not able to attend last Lord's day, and I am told that at the ordinance you asked if there were any persons there that were members of the church when our late pastor, Mr. Gadsby, came, and that there was only one. I am come into the vestry to tell you that there are three of us in the church that were members when he came, two old women and myself. It was only a few days before our pastor was taken ill that we were talking things over, and that the time we had to stay here was very short as we were upon the threshold of a better country, with eternal glory before us, and as I am the older man, I expected to go first, but now he is gone and I am still left behind." – J. K.

gressors, and proving the impossibility of justification by their own righteousness.

He also ably contended for the doctrine of a Trinity of Persons in the Godhead, the Father, the Word and the Holy Ghost, unitedly engaged in the salvation and the glorification of the church; the everlasting and electing love of Jehovah the Father; the glorious person of Emmanuel our incarnate God, in his covenant engagement as the Mediator of the better covenant, established upon better promises; the incarnation of our Lord Jesus Christ, who came into the world to save the chief of sinners; the perfect obedience of Christ to the law, as the law-fulfilling righteousness of his people, imputed to them as the matter of their justification and acceptance before God; the great atonement made by the shedding of the precious blood of Christ for the sins of his church and people; the removing of the curse of the divine law, Christ having been made a curse for his people; and the necessity of that law being applied to the sinner's conscience by the invincible power of the Spirit.

It was his highest ambition to exalt Christ upon the pole of the gospel as the plague of death and the destruction of the grave; also the power of his resurrection, and the glory of his ascension, and the ever-prevalence of his intercession. Christ, in his offices, characters and relationship to his people he blessedly set forth. Finished salvation, all of grace from first to last, was the joy of his heart and the boast of his song, and he often exclaimed, "Immortal honours crown his brow for ever," as he expresses it in that precious hymn composed by him:

> "Immortal honours rest on Jesus' head,
> My God, my portion, and my living bread;
> In him I live, upon him cast my care;
> He saves from death, destruction, and despair."

The glorious Person and Godhead of the Holy Spirit he constantly and firmly maintained, insisting upon the power of God the Holy Ghost to quicken the dead sinner, to convince him of his sins and sinfulness, and bring him with a broken heart to Jesus' feet, and to begin and carry on and complete the work of grace in the souls of his people, and in the personal application of the precious truths of God to the soul with vital power. Thus he constantly vindicated the personal work of the Spirit in the souls of his people, and proved from the Scriptures that without this a profession of religion is but a dead form.

Nor was our brother deficient in preaching up practical godliness, for as the body without the soul is dead, so faith, if it does not produce good works, is dead also. He constantly enjoined the precepts and exhortations of the gospel upon the household of faith, upon evangelical principles. I hope I shall never forget a sermon that he preached for us at Rochdale, above thirty years ago, from these words: "Whoso offereth praise glorifieth me; and to him that ordereth his conversation aright will I show the salvation of God." In speaking of what it was to have our conversation ordered aright, I never heard practical godliness so preached up by any man, neither before nor since. So, while he preached up the great and glorious doctrines of the gospel, and insisted upon an experimental acquaintance with those doctrines by the unctuous teaching of God the Holy Ghost, he vindicated the practical effects these truths produce.

His work is done. He has finished his course with joy, and the ministry which he had received from the Lord Jesus, having testified the gospel of God by the grace of God which was given unto him. He has fought the good fight of faith, finished his course and kept the faith, and has now received the crown of righteousness given by Christ, the great Judge of all, unto all them that love his appearing, which crown, I know, he is joyfully casting at the Redeemer's feet, who hath loved him and washed him from all his sins in his own blood, and hath made him a king and a priest unto God and his Father, to whom be all the glory and dominion, for ever and ever.

To the bereaved church and congregation meeting for divine worship in St. George's Road, I would say, you have lost a faithful, affectionate pastor that cared for your peace and prosperity, that was willing to endure all things for your sakes that you might obtain salvation, which is in Christ Jesus, with eternal glory. Truly, he has very gladly spent and been spent for you. Your loss is great, such as none can replace but the great Head of the church. The Lord give you a spirit of prayer that he may send you another faithful pastor after his own heart, who shall feed you with knowledge and understanding, that, as good old Berridge sings,

> "As one Elijah dies,
> True prophet of the Lord,
> May some Elisha rise,
> To blaze the gospel word.
> And fast as sheep to Jesus go,
> May lambs recruit his fold below."

To the inhabitants of the town of Manchester I would say, you have lost a valuable citizen. He was a true patriot, a decided advocate for good government and for civil and religious liberty, and a determined enemy to tyranny and oppression. The welfare of the community at large lay near his heart. He was a real philanthropist; he loved his fellow-men, and took pleasure in doing good to all men, especially to the household of faith. In him the poor have lost a friend, who did all he could to assist them. He was kind and hospitable to all around him.

I doubt not that a great proportion of this large assembly joins with me in saying that we do deeply sympathise with the aged widow and bereaved family of our departed brother; and I pray that this afflicting dispensation may be sanctified to their real good, that his God may be their God and their Guide through life, and that they may, if consistent with the will of our heavenly Father, meet him before the throne of God and the Lamb.

To you, my friends, who are come here to show your respect to him whose mortal remains we have committed to the cold and silent grave, I would say, we know not how soon the grave may be opened for our reception, and our friends and relatives called together to follow these our mortal bodies to their long homes; for "it is appointed unto men once to die, but after this the judgment." And may the Lord enable us to examine ourselves, that we may see how matters stand between God and our own souls; and may he grant that it may be our happiness to be found amongst them who are born of God, and who are built for eternity upon Christ, the Rock of Ages; that we may be found clothed in the wedding garment, and washed from all our sins in the fountain of Emmanuel's precious blood, and sanctified by his Holy Spirit; that we may be made meet to be partakers of the inheritance of the saints in light.

Though death and the grave are solemn and doleful themes, yet the believer, by faith in Jesus, is enabled to triumph over the king of terrors, with all his frightful powers, as in the language of the apostle, "O death, where is thy sting? O grave, where is thy victory? The sting of death is sin, and the strength of sin is the law; but thanks be to God who giveth us the victory" over the world, sin, death and hell, "through our Lord Jesus Christ." This was the faith of our dear brother in the prospect of death, and now, as he said on his dying bed, he is "shouting Victory! victory! victory!" through the blood of the Lamb, and the word of his testimony, in an upper and a better world. May this be our happy lot, for his name and mercy's sake.

8. THE FUNERAL SERMON FOR
WILLIAM GADSBY

Preached at the Baptist Chapel, St. George's Road, Manchester, on February 14th, 1844

[Mr. Kershaw comments on the service as follows:

On the morning that the funeral sermon was preached there was a crowd of people in the street before ten o'clock, waiting for the chapel doors to be opened; and some time before the service commenced the place was crowded, aisles and vestries; and hundreds went away that could not get within the doors, there being from fifteen hundred to two thousand people in the place. At half-past ten o'clock the solemn service commenced by singing the 469th hymn:

> *"My soul, this curious house of clay,*
> *Thy present frail abode,*
> *Must quickly fall to worms a prey,*
> *And thou return to God."*

The 6th chapter of Isaiah was read before prayer. Before sermon, the 158th hymn was sung:

> *"Sweet the moments, rich in blessing,*
> *Which before the cross I spend,"*

this hymn having been made a blessing to Mr. Gadsby's soul above twenty years ago; and he often spoke of it in his ministry. After sermon, the 667th hymn, composed by Mr. Gadsby, was sung by the great congregation with much solemnity. This hymn contains a true portrait of the ministry of Mr. Gadsby; and the last verse contained the feelings of his whole heart and soul:

> *"O that my soul could love and praise him more,*
> *His beauties trace, his majesty adore,*
> *Live near his heart, upon his bosom lean,*
> *Obey his voice, and all his will esteem!"]*

The dispensation of the Lord in removing his aged and honoured servant by the hand of death, who has for so many years stood on Zion's walls in this place, is the means of calling this great congregation together. The Lord be graciously pleased to humble us and to solemnise our minds, and may both the hearts and minds of speaker and hearers be lifted up unto the great Head of the church, to ask that he would bless his servant in speaking, and you in hearing, that we may "find it good to wait upon the Lord."

The text that I have to call your attention to you will find on record in the 3rd chapter of St. Paul's Epistle to the Ephesians, and the 8th verse: "*Less than the least of all*." And, as if the language of St. Paul was not sufficient to express the humiliating feelings and views of our departed brother, he was wont to exclaim, in addition to these words, "Less than nothing, and vanity."

My beloved, I cannot do justice to the subject, and to the character of the deceased as a minister of the everlasting gospel, without reading and taking into consideration the whole verse: "*Unto me, who am less than the least of all saints, is this grace given, that I should preach among the Gentiles the unsearchable riches of Christ*" (Eph. 3. 8).

There are three things, as leading principles in these words, that I would, with the help of the Lord, call your serious attention unto. Believe me, my friends, when I say by the help of the Lord, that it is not a vain petition dropping from my lips, for I feel myself placed this moment in those circumstances that if ever I stood in need of the help of the Lord in the ministration of the word, it is this morning. Brethren, pray for me that the Lord may be with me and bless me, that justice in some measure may be done to the great subject we have under consideration.

But to return. There are three things unto which I would call your attention:

I.   The best, the greatest and the most extensively useful men have always had the most humble views of themselves.

II.   Take notice of the grace that was given to St. Paul.

III.   The great and glorious end to be accomplished by the gift of that grace, namely, "that he might preach among the Gentiles the unsearchable riches of Christ."

I. In the first place, that the best, the greatest and most extensively useful of all the Lord's servants have invariably had the most humiliating views and feelings concerning themselves. The truth of this statement I would prove from witnesses produced from the sacred records. And the first is Abraham, the father of the faithful and the friend of God, the progenitor of a numerous family, more in number than the stars of heaven, which cannot be numbered. Now see the humility, solemnity and the lowliness of this venerable patriarch's mind when appearing before the Lord to plead the cause of the ungodly of that day, who dwelt upon the plains of Sodom and Gomorrah. Hear his language, which was the inward feelings of his heart and soul before God: "Suffer me, who am but dust and ashes, to speak unto thee but this once." This is the feeling of every heaven-born and spirit-taught soul under the canopy of the heavens, poor, sinful dust and ashes, nothing, and less than nothing and vanity before the great Jehovah.

Again. Jacob, the father of the twelve patriarchs, unto whom the Lord gave the honourable appellation of "a prince who had power with God and with men, and prevailed"; Jacob, in the very peculiar trials and difficulties he met with in the day of his trouble, gave himself unto prayer, and in his solemn approach to the Majesty of heaven, that he might spread his cause before the Lord his God, he makes use of these memorable words, "I am not worthy of the least of all the mercies, and of all the truth, which thou hast showed unto thy servant." He was a great man, made so by the grace of God, and yet in his own feelings and views, a poor worthless worm. Hence that God, that knew the humility of Jacob's soul, addresses him, making use of a metaphor to express the feelings of his mind: "Fear not, worm Jacob, and ye men of Israel." He was a great man, and yet he took a very low estimate of himself; and unless you and I have the same feeling before the Lord, we are not of them that are truly humbled in the dust by the power of divine grace.

> "Great God, how infinite art thou!
> What worthless worms are we!"

There is a verse in one of Dr. Watts's hymns on this subject that is the inward feeling of God's family when in their right minds, and as there is more in it than in some whole sermons, I will read it:

> "A guilty, weak, and helpless worm,
>   On thy kind arms I fall:
>   Be thou my strength and righteousness,
>   My Jesus, and my all."

Beloved, if this is our character, and we fall into the arms of Jesus Christ, we shall not fall into hell, for underneath are his everlasting arms, and the eternal God is our refuge.

Again, beloved. Moses, the greatest of Jewish lawgivers, who in his day was the most humble and valuable of the Lord's servants; see the humility of his soul when the Lord speaks to him in the burning bush, and says he has seen the affliction of his people, and that Moses is to go as the honoured instrument to lead them out of bondage. Moses, feeling his own sinfulness and unworthiness, in his humility says, "Lord, who am I, that I should go unto Pharaoh, and that I should bring forth the children of Israel out of Egypt?" Send not me; send by whom thou wilt, but not by me; I am "of a slow tongue"; and thus he begs, in the humility of his mind, to be excused. But the Lord had intended him as leader of the Jews out of Egyptian bondage and through the wilderness, even to the very borders of Canaan.

Again, my friends. The most valuable and useful men have ever been the most humble men. See it in the instance of Gideon. Gideon was threshing his corn in the barn, and the angel of the Lord tells him he must go and deliver the Lord's people from the hands of the Midianites. "What! me, Lord?" says Gideon, in his surprise at the mission he is appointed to; "I am the least in all my father's house, and my family is poor Manasseh." But so it was; and thus the Lord makes use of the most unlikely of his creatures to accomplish his ends, that his glory may shine the more resplendently bright. And what shall I say more? If time would permit, I might speak of David, of Isaiah, and of Jeremiah.

We come down to a later period. St. Paul exclaims, in the language of our text, "Unto me, who am less than the least of all saints, is this grace given, that I should preach among the Gentiles the unsearchable riches of Christ." St. Paul, on this subject, draws two contrasts. In the first, he contrasts himself with his brethren in the ministry. He says, "I am the least of the apostles, and am not meet to be called an apostle"; "Less than the least of all the apostles of the Lord Jesus Christ." This is truly esteeming others better than ourselves. In our text he draws another contrast between himself and the saints of the most high God: "Unto me, who am less than the least of all saints, is this grace given," and as our friend was wont to add, "less than nothing, and vanity."

God Almighty grant that we may have the same humility of soul, the same loathing of ourselves and humbling of ourselves in the dust and upon the dunghill before the Lord, for the Lord raiseth the poor out of the dust, and the beggar from off the dunghill, that he may set them among princes, and make them inherit the throne of glory, while the rich, the proud and the high-minded are sent empty away. A question arose among the disciples – for they were frail creatures like ourselves, and liable to the sin of human pride – and they said, "Which of us is to be the greatest?" A child was called, and from this metaphor Christ teaches them the value of humility: "He that is the least among you, the same shall be the greatest." Humility is a beautiful garment to wear by all the household of faith, and it is very beautiful indeed when seen as the garment of a minister of Christ. Hence says the apostle, the Christian minister is "not to be a novice, lest, being lifted up with pride, he fall into the condemnation of the devil."

My friends, pride is bad anywhere, but to me it appears worst in the pulpit; and if we look at the present race of ministers, what pride is seen in them! We find there is very little humility indeed in the pulpit. When I look at the pride of men in the ministry, I am sick at heart. I am heartily sick of the pride which I continually find rising up in my own mind, and I pray to God to keep it down. The more humble a minister of Jesus is, the more entire his dependence upon the Lord, the more useful that man will be, and the more precious he will be. May we have the apostolic feeling in our ministry, "less than the least of all saints."

II. We proceed to the second part of our subject, *the grace given to St. Paul.* By the term "grace," in its general acceptation, we understand "free, unmerited mercy and favour," favour bestowed upon the worthless and the unworthy. God has loved his people with an everlasting and electing love; and this is of grace. "Even so, then, at this present time also, there is a remnant according to the election of grace; and if by grace, then it is no more of works, otherwise grace is no more grace; but if it be of works, then it is no more of grace, otherwise work is no more work." This grace was given us in Christ Jesus before the world was. Our salvation is of grace, "For by grace are ye saved, through faith, and that not of yourselves; it is the gift of God; not of works, lest any man should boast." It is "of faith that it might be by grace, to the end that the promise of life and salvation might be sure" to all the Lord's spiritual seed.

The great and glorious work of Christ in our redemption is of grace from first to last, and is freely given to his people. But I cannot enlarge upon this subject. Effectual calling is of grace; hence the apostle says, "But when it pleased God, who separated me from my mother's womb, and called me by his grace," for the Lord is found of them that sought him not, and made manifest to them that asked not for him.

We have grace given us to so support our minds in our troubles. When Paul had the thorn in the flesh, and besought

the Lord thrice that it might depart from him, the Lord said
unto him, "My grace is sufficient for thee, for my strength is
made perfect in weakness." It is by the grace of God that we
persevere in the divine life, and endure to the end. We are
exhorted to "come boldly to the throne of grace, that we may
obtain mercy, and find grace to help in time of need." My
friends, we need God's grace to comfort and support us; hence
the cry of the heaven-born soul is, "Lord, help me"; and the
Lord says, "I will help thee; I will uphold thee with the right
hand of my righteousness." There is an inseparable connection between the gift of grace and immortal glory, so that
every possessor of divine grace shall be carried safely through.

O my friends, has not my departed brother been for
nearly forty years maintaining this principle of the grace of
God in election, unfurling the banner of electing love? Has he
not been insisting upon the irresistible grace of the Spirit in
regeneration, proving that where God begins the work of
grace in the souls of his people, he will carry that work on until
the day of Christ Jesus, and that the consummation of that
grace shall redound to the honour and glory of a Triune
Jehovah?

And here, my friends, I may mention a circumstance. A
good old friend of mine, a Scotsman, went one night with me
from Rochdale to Heywood to hear Mr. Gadsby, who
preached that night in a place crowded to suffocation from
these words: "Who art thou, O great mountain? before
Zerubbabel thou shalt become a plain: and he shall bring forth
the headstone thereof with shoutings, crying, Grace, grace
unto it"; from which he showed that the salvation of the
church of God was begun, carried on and completed by the
grace of God; and that it was worked in the hearts of his
people by the blessed Spirit; and my friend, as we went home,
said, "I tell you what, parson, he has told us a good tale. I
should like to walk seven miles again tomorrow night to hear
such another." My friend was like the Gentiles who requested

that the same truths might be spoken to them the next Sabbath day.

"Unto me, who am less than the least of all saints, is this grace given, that I should preach among the Gentiles the unsearchable riches of Christ." Beloved, in the observations made in reference to grace, we have not come to grace as practically defined by the apostle in the text. When he says, "Unto me, who am less than the least of all saints, is this grace given," we are to understand that he has in view that grace given him by the great Head of the church to qualify him for the great and glorious work of the ministry. A man may be a gracious and a well taught man, an experimental man, a learned man as it respects the arts and sciences of the day, a useful man in the church, and yet not have the grace of God given him to preach the glorious gospel of God our Saviour. No man taketh this office upon himself but he that is called to that work, as was Aaron. Paul was an honoured instrument, called of God to preach the gospel to the Gentiles. He was not only called by grace, but he had grace given him by the great Head of the church to preach the Word of life. Christ, who has ascended up on high and led captivity captive, gives gifts unto men, ministerial gifts, to fit and qualify them for the work of the ministry, "some apostles, some prophets, and some pastors and teachers, for the perfecting of the saints, for the work of the ministry, for the edifying of the body of Christ." Jesus Christ is the Lord of the harvest, and it is he alone that can send forth labourers into his vineyard. Paul himself said that he was called of Christ.

Now, I read the preceding verse, "Whereof I was made a minister, according to the gift of the grace of God given unto me by the effectual working of his power." Beloved, there is an effectual working of the power of the Lord in the soul of that man God is bringing forth, and whom he is about to thrust forward into his vineyard. St. Paul alludes to the same principle when he says, "I am the least of the apostles, and am not meet to be called an apostle, because I persecuted the church of God; but, by the grace of God, I am what I am, and his grace, which was bestowed upon me, was not in vain, for I laboured more abundantly than they all." If he had stopped here, one might have thought he was exalting himself, but he says, "Yet, not I, but the grace of God which was with me." Thus he had special grace given him to enlarge his heart, to make him valiant, to make him stand fast in the truth, to support him in preaching to Gentile sinners the unsearchable riches of the Lord Jesus Christ. The disciples were good and gracious men, designed by the Lord for the work of the ministry, but they were not to go forth until they were endued with power from on high. "Tarry ye at Jerusalem until ye be endued with power from on high."

A great many men are for becoming ministers of the Word who have not the sanction of heaven. Such men become a trouble to themselves, and a trouble to the church. They are like Ahimaaz, who would be the bearer of tidings to David, whether Joab would or not; and away he went and he outran the true messenger; but when he came to the king and was asked, "Is the young man Absalom safe?" he answered, "When Joab sent the king's servant, and me thy servant, I saw a great tumult, but I knew not what it was." "O, stand by," says David; "let Cushi the true messenger come." My friend, it is a sore evil for any man who has not the sanction of the great Head of the church to go forth in the name of the Lord.

Now, I know many of you will agree with me that our departed brother Gadsby was a man called by God's grace, and that he was called to preach the Word of God to poor Gentile sinners; and the Lord laid it upon him with that solemn weight that he could not rest, either night or day. As I said over his grave, he had that sensibility of his unfitness for the great work of the ministry that he said, "Lord, let me die rather than go into the ministry"; for he would have chosen death rather than go into the ministry with the awful re-

sponsibility resting upon him of having taken upon him a
work to which he was not called. And I have heard him relate
one thing humorously, illustrative of the sensibility with
which he was affected about the time of his call to the ministry. He was by trade a stocking-maker, and he wove the clock
of the stocking to go up the shin instead of up the ankle; and
he mentioned it to his wife, who made the observation, "It is
time for thee either to give over preaching or weaving; for
thou spoilest all thou dost."

And so, my friends, it is with those who are called to this
great work: this is the working of the Lord's Spirit, which is as
a burning fire in their souls. As in the case of Jeremiah, such
men need thrusting forward. And there is that sweet savour
and power attending their preaching that the people feel they
are the right men; they will say, "I believe such a man to be a
true preacher of the Lord Jesus Christ, because what he says
comes home to me with power." And thus it is the working of
the Lord in the souls of the people that gives evidence that
they are the men that the Lord hath sent to preach the unsearchable riches of Christ. These men need drawing into the
ministry, for they enter upon it with fear and trembling.

Well, but some will say, is not human learning necessary?
Is it not right to go to some college to learn Latin, Greek,
Hebrew and get a knowledge of the sciences? My friends, I
have not one objection to human learning, provided it is left
where it should be – at the bottom of the pulpit stairs, at the
foot of the mount, where Abraham left the ass; for the gospel
needs no human adornment to set it forth. Paul was a learned
man, brought up at the feet of Gamaliel, and he understood
the arts and sciences of the day; but when preaching the
unsearchable riches of Christ, he laid his human learning by
and said, "And I, brethren, when I came unto you, came not
with excellency of speech and of man's wisdom, declaring unto
you the testimony of God; for I determined not to know any
thing among you, save Jesus Christ and him crucified." And

again he says, "My speech and my preaching was not with
enticing words of man's wisdom, but in demonstration of the
Spirit, and of power." Such was the preaching of St. Paul, and
such has been the ministry of our departed brother.

III. We hasten to the third and last part of the text,
which is "*the unsearchable riches of Christ.*" This is a great
subject, and neither our time nor the strength of my body will
allow me to go into it so fully as I ought on this memorable
occasion; but I will throw out a few observations, leaving the
illustration of them in some measure to yourselves.   "The
unsearchable riches of Christ." He that was rich, for our sakes
became poor, that we through his poverty might become rich.
He was born in a stable, laid in a manger; "the foxes had holes,
and the birds of the air had nests," but the incarnate Son of
God "had not where to lay his head." But he is the Most High
God, the possessor of the heavens and the earth, and all that
therein is. Hear what he says, "Riches and honour are with
me; yea, durable riches and righteousness." The gold and
silver are his, the cattle upon a thousand hills are his, the
fishes that swim about in the great and wide sea are his, and
are all marshalled by him, and made use of at his pleasure. If
a prophet in the wilderness wants food, he sends the ravens to
feed him; if a rebellious prophet is cast overboard, a fish is
made the instrument of his preservation, that he may fulfil the
high purposes for which he was appointed. And here we have
the eternal power of the Lord Jesus Christ, whose unsearchable riches the Apostle Paul preached to Gentile sinners.

But, my brethren, it is the riches of Christ as the
God-Man and Mediator to which the apostle particularly alludes; God in human nature, in his mediatorial character.
Christ is the law-fulfilling righteousness of his people; his
obedience to the law is called the best robe, the wedding
garment, the garment of praise for the spirit of heaviness. The
heaven-born soul is made to feel that he is altogether as an
unclean thing, and all his righteousnesses are but as filthy

rags. We are law-breakers; but Christ, in his active obedience, is our great Law-fulfiller. Christ is of God made unto us wisdom and righteousness, sanctification and redemption. He was made sin for us, that we might be made the righteousness of God in him. Now, in reference to the value of Christ's righteousness, which is of God imputed to his church and people, we find it alluded to as the most valuable, the most durable, the most resplendently bright, the most glorious of all robes. When the psalmist David speaks of it, he says, "It is a garment of wrought gold"; he calls it "a garment of needle-work." My heart is enlarged, my friends; but I want time. It is a rich robe, the righteousness of Jesus Christ; and the poorest worms on earth clothed in it shall be raised to the highest heights of glory: they shall shine brighter and more glorious than angels. "Upon thy right hand did stand the queen in gold of Ophir." Now, these unsearchable riches are the robe wrought out by Christ, and preached by St. Paul and every one of God's sent servants. "Blessed are they that hunger and thirst after righteousness," as St. Paul did when he counted all things but loss for Christ, and so earnestly desired to be found in Christ, "not having on our own righteousness, which is of the law, but that which is by the faith of Jesus, the righteousness which is of God by faith."

But again, beloved. There is a rich efficacy, a divine value in the atoning blood of the Lord Jesus Christ that it beggars language to describe. The riches and the preciousness of the blood of Emmanuel, the incarnate God, are beyond thought to conceive. The preciousness and richness of the blood of our Lord Jesus Christ appear from two considerations. First, as a redemption price. The election of grace fell in Adam with the rest of mankind, and we are sunk in sin, guilt and condemnation. Sin is an infinite evil, a transgression of the law of an infinite God; and its just demerit is an infinite or eternal punishment. Without the shedding of blood there can be no remission of sin; not the blood of bulls and goats; it must be a sacrifice of a nobler name and richer blood than these – no less a sacrifice than the blood of Emmanuel, the incarnate God. Hence St. Paul says, "Feed the church of God, which he hath purchased with his own blood." "Redeemed," says Peter, "not with corruptible things, such as silver and gold, but with the precious blood of Christ." Christ took our nature, yet without sin; all our sins were upon him by imputation, and in our nature he suffered, bled and died, was made a curse for us, and obtained eternal redemption for us by the blood of the cross. If we had all the silver and the gold in the world, and the cattle upon a thousand hills, and ten thousand rivers of oil, and the fruit of our own body, even our first-born, and would sacrifice all, it would be infinitely short as a sacrifice to God for the sin of our souls.

Beloved, the atoning blood of Jesus Christ is a definite atonement, and not an indefinite one as some affirm. Your late pastor preached the atonement of Christ as bounded by the line of God's election; he vindicated the absolute certainty which there is that all the redeemed of the Lord shall be landed safe in glory. "For the ransomed of the Lord shall return, and come to Zion with songs and everlasting joy upon their heads; they shall obtain joy and gladness, and sorrow and sighing shall flee away." Christ must and will see of the travail of his soul, and be satisfied. The redeemed of the Lord cannot be brought into condemnation; for their sins are all put away by the blood of the Lamb. The curse of the law is removed out of the way. Christ has been made a curse for us, and death and hell are vanquished foes. "Who shall lay anything to the charge of God's elect? It is God that justifieth. Who is he that condemneth? It is Christ that died, yea rather, that is risen again, who is even at the right hand of God, who also maketh intercession for us." Rich and precious must that blood be that inevitably secures the salvation and glorification of the church of the living God.

But again, beloved. The riches of the blood of Christ appear from another consideration; it is a cure to the wounded, troubled conscience that nothing else can heal. The poor sinner feels his sins to be a burden; and the more he strives to get rid of his burden, the greater he feels it to be. Wretched and miserable, he drags on heavily. The devil tells him there is nothing but hell for him. Some of his worldly friends are for the poor sinner to go into what they call "good company," to ease him of his burden; but it is all in vain. Not all the carnal pleasures or riches in the world, not all the noble names and titles that can be given, not all the applause that can be heaped upon him by his fellow mortals can lessen his burden. Dr. Watts understood this when he said,

> "Were I possessor of the earth,
>   And called the stars my own;
>   Without thy graces and thyself,
>   I were a wretch undone."

What is the cure for such a conscience? The Apostle John tells us when he says, "The blood of Jesus Christ, his Son, cleanseth us from all sin." When the Holy Spirit makes manifest the precious blood of Jesus in the soul of the poor sinner, the burden is removed, the hard heart is softened; law-terrors, doubts and fears subside; and the devil flees, for he cannot stand his ground when King Jesus appears in the sinner's conscience with his great atonement. Blessed be the Lord, on this subject I stand here as a witness for God to the truth of these things; for I felt the power of the atonement made manifest in my soul by the power of the Holy Ghost thirty years ago. Beloved, I do not know how it is with you, but I could not live if I did not at times feel that I had a living hope in the atoning blood of the Lamb. I am daily plagued with sin, and am sighing and mourning because of the evils of my heart and the sin of nature. "O wretched man that I am! Who shall deliver me from the body of this death." But I have this hope, that sin cannot damn me. It has been done away with by the shedding of the blood of Jesus Christ. Sin is removed by the sacrifice of Christ so that when it is sought for, it cannot be found: it is cast into the depths of the sea of Emmanuel's precious blood. Of this rich and precious blood, the redeemed of the Lord are singing in heaven, "Unto him that loved us, and washed us from our sins in his own blood." The riches of this precious blood your pastor preached to you, and now he is shouting, "Victory, victory!" through the precious blood of the Lamb and the word of his testimony.

But I observe again, beloved, in reference to "the un-searchable riches of Christ," there is a rich, inexhaustible fulness treasured up in him; "for it hath pleased the Father that in him should all fulness dwell," and out of his fulness are we to receive "grace for grace." Christ is the provision of his Father's house, the feast of fat things full of marrow, with wines on the lees, well refined; he is the fatted calf, the paschal lamb, the hidden manna, the wine of the kingdom, the water of life. The invitation is given, "Eat, O friends, and drink, O beloved"; "Come, buy wine and milk, without money and without price." Nothing can satisfy the Lord's hungry poor but Christ; he is to them the bread of eternal life.

"They eat his flesh and drink his blood,
And by and in him live."

In Christ there is rich, almighty strength to support poor, weak, sinful worms, and rich power to keep us, to preserve us, and to hold us up; for "he giveth power to the faint, and to them that have no might he increaseth strength." In Christ there is rich wisdom to guide and direct his people in all their difficulties; he is the "Wonderful Counsellor." Let us be often knocking at his door; for "if any man lack wisdom, let him ask of God," who is so rich that he gives wisdom to his people liberally, and he "upbraideth not." There is not a spiritual blessing that we stand in need of but it is treasured up in Christ. He is our rich friend, that "sticketh closer than a brother"; who is gone before us and has taken possession of the rich inheritance which is reserved in heaven for us. There is a rich kingdom prepared for all who love and fear the Lord; and there are mansions of bliss, white robes, palms of victory and crowns of glory. Our rich Elder Brother has taken possession of all these blessed things for his people, and will see that we are put into the actual possession of them. Hear his voice: "Let not your heart be troubled. Ye believe in God; believe also in me. In my Father's house are many mansions; if it were not so, I would have told you. I go to prepare a place for you. ... and I will come again and receive you to myself, that where I am, there ye may be also." This is what the true Christian wants; he will never be satisfied till he is where Jesus is. Then "I shall be satisfied when I awake in thy likeness."

My friends, by way of conclusion, you will reasonably expect that I shall say something relative to our departed brother. Were I to begin to praise and exalt him as a poor, vile, guilty creature, I should be insulting the memory of him, who so often exclaimed from this pulpit with St. Paul, "Yea, doubtless, and I count all things but loss for the excellency of the knowledge of Christ Jesus my Lord, for whom I have suffered the loss of all things, and do count them but dung that I may win Christ." How often has he lifted up his voice and said, "But God forbid that I should glory, save in Jesus Christ and him crucified"!

As a particular account of the early part of our departed brother's life will shortly be published, I shall not particularly refer to it at this time. It is well known that he has stood on Zion's walls in this place for nearly forty years. The Lord, in the dispensation of his providence, brought him here, having a great work for him to do in this large and populous town and neighbourhood. He had a great flood of opposition to encounter for many years after he came to Manchester. I do believe that Lancashire never had a more valuable man in it, made so by the grace of God, than the late William Gadsby was; and I never knew a man that has been more belied than he has been. The abominably false reports that the enemies of God and truth have circulated concerning him are amazingly numerous; but by well-doing he has been enabled to put to silence the ignorance of foolish men. As a good man, his steps were ordered by the Lord, and he delighted in his way. As I said over his grave, so I say again, I have never seen the words of the wise man more strikingly fulfilled than in him, "When a man's ways please the Lord, he maketh even his enemies to be at peace with him." The cry of the public, who have known him and have been watching him for years, has been, and still is, "Gadsby is an honest, upright, straightforward, honourable, good man."

Thus the Lord gave him many, very many friends, even amongst those that did not love the truths that he preached. It may be said of him, that the grace of God shone exceedingly bright in him. He stood valiantly for the truth of the Lord upon the earth; he did not turn, like the weathercock, from this side to the other side, according to circumstances, to please his fellow ministers. No, my friends, no; he feared no man's frowns, he courted no man's smiles, but with a brow like brass and a face like tempered steel, he stood in the truth of God to the last breath that he breathed. The honour and the glory of the Lord, the furtherance of the gospel, and the peace and prosperity of Zion lay near his heart. Such men are invaluable to all around them, however worthless and little they may be in their own estimation.

To the church of Christ meeting here I would say, you have lost a faithful, zealous, laborious, kind and affectionate pastor, who was truly an able minister of Jesus Christ, not of the letter, but of the spirit. My dear brethren and sisters in the Lord, I feel for you in your bereaved circumstances. Your loss is such as none can repair but the Head of the church. The Lord pour down his Holy Spirit into your souls, that you may cry mightily unto him that

"As one Elijah dies,
True prophet of the Lord,"

some Elisha may be sent amongst you to blaze the gospel abroad in this large town and neighbourhood. As an old friend of my departed brother, and I can truly say as a friend of yours, I would give you a word of advice. You will have to go on for some time with supplies. I warn you to call in no supply but such men as were in soul union with your late pastor; men that love and preach the same great and glorious truths, having the same end in view, namely, the abasement of the sinner and the exaltation of the dear Redeemer. If there should arise individuals among you that want something novel, be kind and courteous to them, but keep firm to the truth of God that you have had so long preached amongst you. Tell them that if they are not satisfied with the doctrines preached amongst you, they had best go quietly away; for, depend upon it, were you to swerve from that truth so long maintained amongst you, dissension and divisions would ensue amongst you. If there should come any man unto you and bring not this doctrine, receive him not into your house, neither bid him God speed. "Go to the Lord for direction," was the advice of your minister upon his dying bed. You, my brethren, the deacons of the church, go to the Lord for wisdom profitably to direct you in your present circumstances, that you may fill your office well. To the members of the church at large I would say, Go to the Lord, and ask him to guide and direct you, and enable you to fill up your places in the church becoming your characters. Be concerned, my friends, for the honour and glory of God, for peace and truth, and for the welfare of Zion; and the Lord be your helper.

In the death of our beloved brother, the town of Manchester has lost one of its most valuable citizens. I recollect well that when he broke his leg some time ago when walking in his own garden, one of your public journals took notice of the accident; and the paragraph, after noticing the fact, contained a sentiment which was both just and true: "The cessation from labour of such a man as Mr. Gadsby is a public calamity." If, then, the laying aside of the man of God for a few weeks was a public calamity, must not the removal of such a man by the hand of death be a much greater one? In him, Manchester has lost a citizen concerned for civil and religious liberty, who was an enemy to tyranny and oppression. In him, the poor have lost a kind and benevolent friend, whose heart and purse were ever open to relieve them. I believe I shall not go beyond the bounds of truth when I say that for the last three years Mr. Gadsby, out of his own private pocket and money sent him by friends at a distance, has not been giving less than £1 a week.* Somebody will miss this! Amongst the poor his loss will be greatly felt. To the poor I would say, The Lord liveth; and if your heavenly Father has taken away one true friend, he can raise us another; for he knows what his poor saints stand in need of.

And to the family of my esteemed brother I would say, you have lost one of the most kind and affectionate parents; one who has cared for your welfare; one who has offered up many prayers that the blessing of God might be on your heads, as a God of providence, but more especially that he might bless you with grace. You will hear his voice no more in supplication for you on earth. His tears are bottled up in heaven; and now that his body is laid low, and his soul has taken its departure, O that his God may be your God, and guide you down to the chambers of mortality, and receive you to glory, that you may meet him again in heaven.

But I come more especially to notice the last week of his life and sickness. It was his wish that his life and work might be finished together. It was his great wish for a long time that he might die in the pulpit, exalting Christ and him crucified

* Since preaching the sermon, I have been told by one of Mr. Gadsby's executors that, instead of saying £1 a week, if I had said £3 a week, I should have been nearer the truth. – J. K.

upon the pole of the gospel; and though in that wish he was disappointed, there was not a long period between the cessation of the one and the occurrence of the other. It is only three weeks since he preached in this chapel from the text, "When thou passest through the waters, I will be with thee; and through the rivers, they shall not overflow thee." This was on the Sunday morning; and summing up what he had gone through, he made particular mention that the last flood the Christian had to pass through was the Jordan of death. He was just going into the river himself, and was evidently aware of it.

On Tuesday morning the Lord's hand laid fast hold on him; and at night he repeated, as he lay in bed, the 61st chapter of Isaiah, "The Spirit of the Lord God is upon me, because the Lord hath anointed me to preach good tidings unto the meek." He spoke of the power of the Lord to support him, and of Christ being anointed as the great Prophet, Priest and King of his church and people, and of his being anointed to comfort the mourners in Zion. And on the Wednesday morning, still feeling that the outward man was tottering and sinking, that the hand of death had hold of him, he gave himself up. He saw the monster death, the king of terrors, making rapid strides; but to him the monster had no dread; to him the king of terrors did not appear as a king of terrors; and in the welcome anticipation of his dissolution he said, "I shall soon be able to shout, Victory, victory, victory! in the presence of my God." So that, my friends, he enjoyed a precious faith that sustained him to the last.

On the Thursday I came from Rochdale to see him and found him very sick in body; and I cannot forget the look he looked at me as he said, "John, my preaching's all over!" I asked him how his mind was. "O," he said, "Christ is glorious." He attempted to speak of Christ, but his breathing and cough were so bad that he could not get the words out; and I asked him to let me speak for him. I spoke of Christ, as God

gave me ability, in his covenant relation to his church and
people, and in his incarnation and perfect obedience to the
law, as the law-fulfilling righteousness of his people; of the
triumph of his cross, and the power of his resurrection; and of
his ascension to glory, and his now living in the high court of
heaven to intercede for his people. Through these things he
assisted me, giving his sanction, approbation and hearty
approval to the things that I said. And he said, "There is a
verse of a hymn on my mind, and I cannot get it off; it keeps
coming again and again continually"; and the good man began to repeat it, and got through all but the last line, notwithstanding his cough:

> "'Tis to credit contradictions,
>   Talk with him one never sees;
> Cry and groan beneath afflictions,
>   Yet to dread the thoughts of ease:
> 'Tis to feel the fight against us,
>   Yet the victory hope to gain;
> To believe that Christ has cleansed us,
>   Though the leprosy remain."

This is a deep verse, my friends; and my brother had every
word of it in his heart and in his soul. Before we parted, I read
the 23rd Psalm and Isaiah chapter 12, and as I prayed with him
he gave his hearty "Amen" to the solemn words in such a
manner as we never heard him do before; and at the end he
gave his hearty "Amen" to mine, that what we prayed for
might be given.

On the Friday he was worse in his body. He said, "Religion is nothing without power"; and he said to my friend
Ashworth that there was nothing on his mind so much as the
feeling that he might not have been sufficiently kind to the
poor. Now the *Manchester Times* of last Saturday but one said
he went from house to house, and he was continually feeding
the poor; and yet Satan came upon him, to harass his mind
that he had not done enough for the poor. Friend Ashworth
said, "Mr. Gadsby, the devil could not have assailed you upon

a worse ground than this; for since you could not go to relieve the poor, I have been going for you."

But we come to the last day, Saturday; and on that day he desired that the 12th chapter of Romans might be read to him. This chapter is all upon practical godliness. Now, let me digress for a moment. Our brother has been a doctrinal, experimental and practical preacher; and yet you know he has been called, through the length and breadth of the land, "The Antinomian of Manchester," a denier of good works, an enemy to piety, and so on. But, my friends, though he has been thus belied, he was all practice himself; and a more practical Christian has rarely been known. And the chapter having been read, he said, "Let us pray"; and he prayed with that humility and power that surprised all the friends in the room. He called upon the Lord to keep the church humble at Jesus' feet; to bless them, and to bless his family; and his whole soul seemed to go up to Christ in the prayer. Not much more than two hours before the Lord took him, he said, "I shall soon be shouting, Victory, victory, victory! in the kingdom of my Father"; and the last words heard from him were, "I shall soon be singing, Glory, glory, glory! in an upper and a better world."*

Thus lived and died this great man, a monument of the love of the Lord Jesus Christ, an ornament to the Word he preached; and now he is gone we may truly say of him, "Mark the perfect man, and behold the upright; for the end of that man is peace." Amen and amen.

* I find I was in error here. The last words he uttered were, "Free grace, free grace, free grace!" – J. K.

9. THE ONLY TRUE GROUND OF REJOICING

Preached at Zoar Chapel, Great Alie Street, London, on April 10th, 1845.

Text: *"The poor among men shall rejoice in the Holy One of Israel"* *(Isaiah 29. 19).*

There are two things, as leading principles in our text, that I want, by the help of the Lord, to call your attention to. The first is, to say a little of *"the poor among men."* And secondly, to show that they *"shall rejoice in the Holy One of Israel."*

I. In the first place, then, let us notice *"the poor among men"* that are here spoken of by the prophet. Now, in a doctrinal point of view, they are the very characters that the Apostle Peter dedicates his epistles to. "Peter, an apostle of Jesus Christ, to the strangers scattered throughout Pontus, Galatia, Cappadocia, Asia, and Bithynia." And he gives them the honoured and honourable appellation of "Elect according to the foreknowledge of God the Father, through sanctification of the Spirit, unto obedience and sprinkling of the blood of Jesus Christ."

The doctrine of God's election is clearly revealed in the sacred Scriptures. Everlasting, electing love is the spring and fountain of every blessing of grace and salvation. As, for instance, if you and I feelingly and experimentally know our spiritual poverty and destitution, our knowledge of it has for its origin God's covenant love and covenant mercy. But upon this I shall not dwell now.

"The poor among men" intended by the words of the text are "the redeemed of the Lord"; those who are redeemed by the precious blood of the Lord Jesus Christ from sin, the curse of the law and the pit of destruction. God's election and Christ's redemption are coupled and bound up together. All that Jehovah the Father loved, he gave into the hand of Christ their covenant Head. Christ in the covenant became their bond, their Surety and their Mediator; and, in the fulness of time, according to covenant engagements, he came forward, appeared in our nature, made of a woman, made under the law (the right of redemption falling upon him) to redeem his people from under "the curse of the law," being made a curse for them.

But we observe, in the next place, my friends, that the objects of the Father's love, and the purchase of Christ's blood, cannot be known, only as God the Holy Ghost makes them manifest. The Lord's people, in their Adam-fall state, are no better than the rest of the world; they all have had their conversation among their ungodly neighbours in time past in the lusts of their flesh, fulfilling the desires of the flesh and of the mind, and have by nature the same wrathful dispositions as others.

Now here I pause. And I say to you and myself, let us look back to how we were living when the Lord arrested us in our conscience. It has done me good many a time to look back, and I have often viewed with astonishment and wonder the riches of God's grace that made me to differ from what I once was, and from my sinful companions that surrounded me. It is "by the grace of God" we are what we are as Christians and believers; we have nothing but what we have received from the Lord, and all the glory from first to last redounds to him alone. The saint of God that knows these things feels a something rising up from the very bottom of his heart, which says, "Not unto us, not unto us, O Lord, but unto thy name give glory, for thy mercy and for thy truth's sake." My friends, keep your minds fixed upon two points; and the two points are these: one is, that God's religion in the soul of a poor sinner always lays that sinner low; and the other, that God's religion in the sinner's soul always lifts the Lord Jesus Christ very high.

A good old gracious friend of mine I had in the north for many years, who was a great blessing to me when I first entered the ministry and who performed many good things for me as an instrument in God's hand, used to say, "There are two points which you can never push too far in preaching; and these are, to lay the sinner low in the dust of abasement, and exalt the riches of God's grace in the salvation of the soul."

But to return. We were observing that none can tell who the Lord's people are till God the Spirit makes them manifest. The Lord knows who they are: "Having this seal, the Lord knoweth them that are his." "Yes," say some, "He knows them when they begin to turn to him, when they accept the offers and proffers of salvation, and take hold of his grace; he knows them then." My friends, that is not God's way of working. He knows his sheep before he gives them eternal life; he says, "My sheep hear my voice, and I know them, and they follow me: and I give unto them eternal life, and they shall never perish, neither shall any man pluck them out of my hand." In God's religion, life is the first thing given. The poor sinner is dead in trespasses and sins. The Lord Jesus Christ is a "quickening spirit"; and he has "power over all flesh, to give eternal life to as many as the Father gave him." And, in regeneration, the Holy Spirit makes no mistake. As a Spirit of knowledge, he knows who the Lord's covenant people are; and when the set time to favour Zion comes, he arrests them in the conscience. Saul was one of these vessels of mercy; and Zacchaeus also was a monument of grace; and therefore, at the appointed moment, the Lord the Spirit quickened them into spiritual life. There are not any whose names are written in the Lamb's book of life but what the blessed Spirit either has regenerated, or will in due time regenerate and begin the good work of grace in their precious souls, and carry it on in the face of every opposition from within and from without, from sin, men and devils. It is a good doctrine, my friends. Where God begins the work, he will surely carry it on and finish it till at last he lands the soul safe in immortal glory. He does not give the poor sinner a stock of grace to live on and cultivate. No, no! It is God's grace that cultivates the poor sinner, and not the poor sinner that cultivates the grace of God.

But now, my friends, we will come more into the experimental part of the text. The "poor among men" are those that feel their spiritual poverty and destitution. A man may be a nobleman and possess immense wealth; yea, he may be a king, wear a crown on his head and wield a sceptre in his hand, and yet be one of "the poor among men." For instance, David, the king of Israel, was one of "the poor among men," in a spiritual point of view. And every one of you, my friends, here tonight who feels his spiritual poverty and destitution, the Holy Ghost has found room in your very heart and soul for the language of the man after God's own heart. What were the words of David that we have room for and which so fit us? "But I am poor and needy; yet the Lord thinketh upon me." "But I am poor and sorrowful: let thy salvation, O God, set me up on high." "I am a poor, mourning, sorrowful, sighing, groaning, weak, vile helpless and worthless worm." This is a description of the feelings of David, and of every one of the Lord's quickened family, "the poor among men," who "shall rejoice in the Holy One of Israel." A man may be as poor as poverty can make him in a literal point of view, and yet be very proud and high-minded in himself. "There are that make themselves (imaginary) rich, and yet have nothing; and there are that make themselves poor, and yet have great riches." It is a great blessing, my friends, feelingly and experimentally to know our poverty and destitution before God. "Blessed are the poor in spirit, for theirs is the kingdom of heaven."

Now these are the characters that God has a special regard to. "Thus saith the Lord, The heaven is my throne, and the earth is my footstool: where is the house that ye build unto me? and where is the place of my rest? For all those things hath mine hand made, and all those things have been, saith the Lord: but to this man will I look, even to him that is poor and of a contrite spirit, and trembleth at my word." The first term that God here makes use of suits me well – "to him that is poor." I very generally feel my poverty and destitution, and cannot join in with those that say "they are rich, increased in goods, and have need of nothing"; for I feel by daily experience that I am "wretched, miserable, poor, blind and naked." It is a mercy to know this, my friends. The Pharisee did not know it; but the poor publican did, and groaned before God on account of it.

But then, in reference to the next term, I mostly feel my lack of it – "a contrite spirit." Now instead of having, generally, a humble and contrite spirit, a broken-down, feeling heart before the Lord, I am mourning and crying over a hard and barren heart and a stubborn mind, beseeching the Lord to take away this stony heart and give me a heart of flesh, a feeling heart. I am sighing and mourning because of a corrupt heart, unclean thoughts and vain and foolish imaginations, which make me cry out, "Create in me a clean heart, O God, and renew a right spirit within me." Well, my friends, be it so. If you have the feelings I have described, you are the very characters who stand in need of what God has promised to give – a new heart, a right spirit and a tender conscience. But the Lord will be enquired of by the house of Israel that he may do these things for them. They have feelings of deep necessity; and they cry to the Lord that he would hear their prayer and regard their cry. Now then, God says, "To this man will I look, even to him that is poor, and of a contrite spirit, and trembleth at my word." The Lord hears a humble spirit before a spirit of presumption; and though such may have many fears and tremblings, yet they shall be brought to rejoice with trembling.

Do you not see, then, that God has a special regard to these "poor among men," these spiritually poor who feel their inward poverty and destitution before the Lord? The psalmist speaks on the subject thus: "He will regard the cry of the destitute, and will not despise their prayer." The destitute, then, are such as have nothing of their own, those who feel themselves only a mass of sin, weakness and helplessness before the Lord.

Now these are the characters, my friends. The Lord strips them of all the imaginary goodness they once thought they had; he empties them of all this, brings down their high looks and breaks their rocky hearts, and thus he makes the poor soul feel his weakness, that he cannot save himself, nor do that which is the alone work of the Lord the Spirit. And thus these really "poor among men" feel the importance of the Lord's own words: "Without me ye can do nothing." Now Paul was one of these "poor among men"; he felt that he could do nothing by his own power or ability, but he could do all things by the power of Christ strengthening him.

II.   But secondly. "The poor among men," the destitute, the weak, the helpless, the lost and the undone, "*shall rejoice in the Holy One of Israel*." Indeed, my friends, they have nothing else to rejoice in. "The poor among men," God's spiritually poor people, cannot rejoice in the world or the things of it. There is nothing in it that will do them good, nor indeed can they be satisfied with anything short of the rich treasure which is treasured up in the Lord of life and glory. Thus it is that the truly poverty-stricken, bankrupt, undone sinner and Jesus Christ, in his glorious salvation, rich treasure and inexhaustible fulness, meet so blessedly together, the One being so adapted to the other. A full sinner and a full Saviour will not do together at all; but an empty sinner and a full Saviour – a filthy, vile and polluted sinner and the efficacious blood of Christ to cleanse it away – a naked and undone sinner and the robe of Christ's justifying righteousness – a weak and helpless worm and the power of the mighty God of Jacob to keep, support and hold him up – these things blessedly harmonize together. And this is God's way of working.

"The poor among men shall rejoice in the Holy One of Israel"; for they cannot rejoice either in themselves, or in the world. "Finally, my brethren," says Paul, "rejoice in the Lord"; and God takes very good care that Christ alone shall be the ground and basis of all their joy and consolation. Instead of "the poor among men" rejoicing and triumphing in themselves, the more they are led to see what dwells and lurks within, the more they are brought to groan and cry out to the Lord under the burden of it. Looking to ourselves will bring us nothing but sighing and sorrowing. "We that are in this tabernacle do groan, being burdened." "For in me, that is, in my flesh, dwelleth no good thing." No, all the goodness is in "the Holy One of Israel."

Paul understood these things well, and he explains in the seventh of Romans in a heartfelt way what every one of "the poor among men," spoken of in our text, knows something about; he says, "O wretched man that I am, who shall deliver me from the body of this death!" This is the inward feeling of every one of the Lord's saints concerning themselves. There is no rejoicing in our wretchedness, nor any triumphing in our sinfulness and vileness. Whatever some men may say, who brand us with rejoicing in our corruptions and wretched feelings, they do not do us justice, my friends; for instead of rejoicing in my weakness and infirmities, my very soul is mourning and sorrowing because of these things before God; so that my cry is, "Dear Lord, hold and keep me up; preserve me from evil; be thou my guide and keeper all through the wilderness, and land me at last safely in glory where I shall praise thee for evermore."

"The poor among men shall rejoice in the Holy One of Israel." It is Christ alone that is the Christian's rejoicing. Paul speaks of it thus: "We are the circumcision, which worship God in the spirit, and rejoice in Christ Jesus, and have no confidence in the flesh." This is the way God circumcises the hearts of his people with the circumcision of Christ, made without hands, which cuts them off from all hope of saving themselves; and by the circumcising knife of his law, he stops their mouth from all boastings and brings them in guilty and condemned. The Holy Ghost leads them away from self to a precious Jesus. He leads to a discovery of Christ in all his covenant characters, and shows how he took their case into his hands before all worlds. He opens up to them the glories of Christ in his incarnation; he shows them that "it is a faithful saying, and worthy of all acceptation, that Christ Jesus came into the world to save sinners." So that this is the ground of their rejoicing, that Jesus Christ is an able, willing, glorious and an all-sufficient Saviour.

"The poor among men" rejoice in a finished salvation, all of grace; not a salvation partly accomplished by Christ and the rest made up by the sinner. A gospel of this kind will not save "the poor among men." I tried for months at saving myself in this way, and when I missed it here and missed it there, I tried it again, for I was determined to hit it. I could see no way of salvation only by being good; therefore I resolved to be good. But with all my trying and tugging, I felt myself to be getting weaker and weaker and further and further off from God, till I was afraid at last that I should surely sink under the terrors of God in a broken law in the waves of damnation, if there were no other way of salvation than my own. I wanted now something more than my good doings. O, my friends, it is dreadful work thus to sink in "the horrible pit and the miry clay." But however painful, it is profitable. The more sick we are made of ourselves, the more we are brought to feel our own weakness and inability, the more will be our joy and rejoicing in Christ Jesus, "the Holy One of Israel."

"The poor among men," then, rejoice that salvation is finished – that sin is for ever put away by the sacrifice of Jesus – that law and justice are satisfied – that everlasting right-eousness is wrought out and brought in – that the world is overcome – that death and hell are conquered, for

> "Hell and our sins resist our course,
> But hell and sin are vanquished foes;
> Our Jesus nailed them to the cross,
> And sang the triumph when he rose."

Thus, as the believer is enabled to look away from self by faith to a precious Christ – to see Christ in the triumphs of his cross – Christ in the power of his resurrection – Christ in the power of his ascension, for the God of salvation is "gone up with a shout" – as the Holy Spirit leads "the poor among men" by faith to the place where Christ, the Forerunner, has for us entered, there is a spring of joy and gladness rising up in the soul, which has a precious Christ and a finished salvation at the bottom of it. And O what sweetness and consolation there is to the heart when Christ is thus received, believed on and triumphed in!

The Lord Jesus Christ, in our text, is called "*The Holy One of Israel.*" And this he is experimentally felt to be by all God's spiritual Israel. But I shall not detain you tonight in reference to "Israel" by defining the term particularly. Let it suffice that Paul says, "They are not all Israel, which are of Israel: neither, because they are the seed of Abraham, are they all children"; but the children of the promise are counted for the seed. A man might be able to trace his genealogy from the patriarchs, and yet not be an Israelite in the best sense of the word. We are Gentiles according to the flesh; but though this is the case, many of us here, I trust, are of the spiritual Israel. But whether Jew or Gentile, if we are of the true circumcision, we are made to know that there is no holiness in ourselves, but that it is all in a precious Jesus. Christ is our "all in all."

"The poor among men shall rejoice in the Holy One of Israel"; for he is their holiness; they cannot produce it in themselves. What holiness can you find in your heart? The words of Mr. Hart have come into my mind with over- whelming power many times, for I find that I have the daily feelings of them in my soul. He says,

> "That we're unholy needs no proof,
>   We sorely feel the fall;
> But Christ has holiness enough
>   To sanctify us all."

And let him but make that holiness manifest in thy soul, poor sinner, and thou wilt rejoice "in Christ Jesus, who of God is made unto us wisdom, and righteousness, and sanctification, and redemption." Christ is "the Holy One" of his spiritual Israel. We have no holiness in ourselves. Paul had none, yet the dear child of God is ready to say, "O that I was as Paul! He was indeed a vessel of mercy! O that I felt as Paul felt!" And do you not feel as Paul felt? "When I would do good," he says, "evil is present with me." Do you not find that he describes your feelings in the seventh of Romans? If you do, you know that there is no purity or holiness in your hearts by nature. Now, my friends, I make two very broad assertions, but I will stand fast to them – there is not one particle or grain of true holiness in the whole world but what comes from Christ, "the Holy One of Israel"; and there is not one grain of holiness amongst the "spirits of just men made perfect" now before the throne but what has emanated from a precious Christ, "the Holy One of Israel." As all natural light is from the sun, so all spiritual holiness is from Christ, "the Holy One of Israel."

Now the Lord Jesus Christ is "the Holy One of Israel," whether we speak of him in his complex character, or as God. He is holy in all his attributes and in all his operations; so much so that he is said to be, "Glorious in holiness, fearful in praises, doing wonders," both in "the armies of heaven, and among the inhabitants of the earth." They that appear before him are said to veil their faces, exclaiming with holy admiration, "Holy, holy, holy is the Lord of Hosts."

And if we look at the human nature of our Lord Jesus Christ, he is "the Holy One of Israel"; for though he was "made of a woman, made under the law," partaking of the nature of the woman, yet he was not of a sinful nature. Here is a part of the mystery: "Great is the mystery of godliness." How he could be made of a woman, partake of the nature of the woman, and that woman a fallen creature like the rest of mankind, and yet be holy himself is a mystery. But so it is. The angel said to her, "That Holy Thing which shall be born of thee" – not that impure thing, but "that Holy Thing" shall be called "the Son of God." He was "holy, harmless, undefiled, separate from sinners, and made higher than the heavens." He was the immaculate Jesus; the "Lamb without blemish and without spot, whom God verily foreordained." So that in his complex character, as God-man, he is the perfection of beauty, purity and holiness; so much so that the divine Father, in viewing his Person and all that appertained to him, exclaimed, "This is my beloved Son, in whom I am well pleased."

He is "the Holy One of Israel," also, not only in the constitution of his Person, but in all the thoughts of his heart, in all the expressions of his lips and in all the actions of his life. Nothing but holiness and purity ever centred in him or flowed from him; so that he is "the Holy One of Israel" in the strictest sense of the word. He is now enthroned in glory, inhabiting the praises of his Israel above. He is "the Holy One of Israel" in the realms of bliss. And as I before said, all the holiness and purity of the redeemed comes from him; they owe it all to him. In him they exult and glory, and cast their crowns at his blessed feet, while they sing "the song of Moses and the Lamb."

"The poor among men," then, shall rejoice in this precious Christ, "the Holy One of Israel." We can find no holiness in ourselves; but Jesus Christ has a holiness which is made over to us. Now, I know I am on ground which many of our professedly pious religionists do not like. The very sound of "imputed holiness" they abhor and detest; they are for having a holiness in themselves.

Indeed, my friends, I was in this hole for many years. There was one text which I was always hitting at; it was this: "Blessed be the God and Father of our Lord Jesus Christ, who hath blessed us with all spiritual blessings in heavenly places in Christ; according as he hath chosen us in him before the foundation of the world, that we should be holy and without blame before him in love." I maintained that I was chosen of

God before all worlds; that I was chosen to be holy in myself; that I was to grow in grace till I became holy and unblameable before God. I aimed at this year after year but could never attain to it. Instead of attaining to holiness and unblameableness, I saw myself to be more and more unholy; to be blameable in this and blameable in that; and if my outward walk and conversation was such that my brethren could not blame, nor the world lay hold of, my conscience was always accusing and blaming me. I was groaning and mourning about as a poor, guilty wretch; and I believe if I live to be fourscore years old, it will be the same.

So that there is no holiness in us as sinners, in which we can stand unblameable before God, but what is in Christ. Blessed be God, we have a holiness and unblameableness in the Lord Jesus Christ in which we stand before him holy as Christ is holy and pure as Christ is pure. What does the church say? There are two words – they are very broad but very firm. Speaking of herself as she is in herself, she says, "Black" – speaking of herself as she viewed herself in Christ by the eye of living faith, she says, "Comely," through "the comeliness which thou hast put upon me." Again; *black,* "as the tents of Kedar" – *white,* "as the curtains of Solomon." The Lord, addressing the church as she is in Christ, says, "Thou art all fair, my love; there is no spot in thee."

> "And lest the shadow of a spot
>   Should on my soul be found,
>   He took the robe the Saviour wrought,
>   And cast it all around."

So that Christ is "the Holy One of Israel" and the holiness of his people Israel, and it is only as they stand in him that they are holy and unblameable before a just and righteous God in love. If any man were to tell me that he was holy and unblameable before God in any other way than in Christ, I should know that he was a liar, and the Bible would prove it; for it says, "If we say we have no sin, we deceive ourselves, and

the truth is not in us." Man in his best estate is vanity; what
then must he be in his worst? What does the church say? "We
are all as an unclean thing, and all our righteousnesses are as
filthy rags; and we all do fade as a leaf; and our iniquities like
the wind have carried us away." But as the church is viewed
in Christ, it is said, "He hath not beheld iniquity in Jacob,
neither hath he seen perverseness in Israel: the Lord his God
is with him, and the shout of a King is among them."

The Lord enable us, then, to trust alone in a precious
Christ, and not to attempt to cleanse ourselves from our defilement. We might as well attempt to wash a black skin white
as to effect it; for, "Can the Ethiopian change his skin, or the
leopard his spots? then may ye also do good that are accustomed to do evil." But in the Lord Jesus Christ there is
righteousness to justify us; in the Lord Jesus Christ there is
efficacious blood to cleanse us; in the Lord Jesus Christ there
is holiness to sanctify us; and in him there is everything that
we can stand in need of. Thus there is great ground for "the
poor among men" to rejoice in "the Holy One of Israel," and
in him alone.

"Well," say some, "but is there not a holy and divine
nature communicated from God to his people?" Yes, there is;
and that is a great blessing indeed. Christ has taken our
nature into union with his divine nature, and in that nature
he has bled and died for us, sin being condemned in his flesh.
In that nature he has been made a curse for us, and wrought
out and brought in an everlasting righteousness; and this is
imputed to us. He has gone to heaven, and taken our nature
with him. He now appears in the presence of his Father:

> "Arrayed in mortal flesh, he like an angel stands,
>   And holds the promises and pardons in his hands."

And as sure as he lives to represent us and plead our cause
before the throne, so in the set time to favour us, in the hour
of regeneration, he implants within us a holy principle, a new
nature, a meek and quiet spirit – the new man of the heart, the

new man of grace – and which is of the very nature of the Lord
in respect of holiness.

But what is the result or effect of this? Does the Lord
communicate to us this holy and "divine nature" to renovate
or change our old Adam nature into holiness, purity and
perfection? Some will have it so. They say that a new nature
is so communicated that it changes our old nature, and the
whole lump becomes holy and pure. And this is what they call
"progressive sanctification," getting better and better every
day, more pure and holy as they advance in years, till at last
they become free from sin, when God takes them to glory like
a shock of corn fully ripe is gathered into the garner. But is it
so with you, my friends? Are you getting better and holier as
you grow older? I am at a point about it in my own experience. The old man of sin is still the old man of sin, "corrupt
according to his deceitful lusts"; and he will still be the old
man of sin while we are in these bodies: "for the flesh lusteth
against the spirit, and the spirit against the flesh; and these are
contrary the one to the other; so that ye cannot do the things
that ye would." What shall we ever see in the Shulamite but
"the company of two armies"? It is only as "grace reigns
through righteousness unto eternal life," and as the Lord
enables us to wield the weapons of our spiritual warfare, which
"are not carnal, but mighty through God to the pulling down
of strong holds, casting down imaginations, and every high
thing that exalteth itself against the knowledge of God, and
bringing into captivity every thought to the obedience of
Christ," that we shall raise the song of triumph and tread
upon the necks of our enemies.

When the Lord appears in the conscience, bringing light
and gladness, it is a day season to our souls; and then the ugly
beasts of prey skulk into their holes and dens, because they
cannot stand the light, power and glory of the Lord. But
when we come into a night of darkness in our experience, then
these beasts come forth from their lurking places and prey

upon our souls. O, my friends, what are we in the night season? We feel shocked at ourselves; we feel that we are nothing but vile, guilty and miserable wretches. But, blessed be the Lord, our holiness is in "the Holy One of Israel."

"And the poor among men *shall* rejoice in the Holy One of Israel." Now mark, my friends, in our text we have one of God's *shalls*. It does not say, "the poor among men" shall have an offer and proffer of salvation, and then if they accept it, and their faith lays hold of it, they "shall rejoice in the Holy One of Israel." No, no: there would be no rejoicing on such grounds as these. If there were anything to be done by men, I am sure I could not do it, for I am so helpless, weak and feeble in spiritual things that I can neither exert faith nor lay hold of any promise whatever; and when I am in the dark, I can only grope about and feel as blind and as stupid as a fool.

How are we to rejoice, then, in "the Holy One of Israel"? Why, when the Holy Spirit puts faith into our hearts and the Word of God lays hold of us, then our faith lays hold of the Word of God. And this is the best way, my friends. The poor child of God is brought to feel that he cannot embrace salvation when he will, nor enjoy it when he pleases. Our springs of comfort are all in the Lord; and it is only when he works in us by his blessed Spirit that we feel joy and gladness.

He says, "The poor among men *shall* rejoice in the Holy One of Israel"; and what God says *shall be* must be. Neither sin, men nor devils can turn one of God's *shalls* or *wills* upside down. His *shalls* and *wills* are as firm as his throne; and as surely as he says, "The poor among men *shall* rejoice in the Holy One of Israel," so certainly will it be. The Lord will come and pay the poor sinner a visit; and when he comes into the heart, and sheds abroad his love there by the Holy Spirit (O, my friends, have you ever felt it?), there is "joy unspeakable and full of glory." I have felt it, and I want to feel more of it; it is so sweet and blessed, and makes the heart so joyful.

When the Lord is thus graciously pleased to come, and by the efficacy of his blood to purge our conscience and speak peace and pardon to it by saying to us, "Son, or daughter, thy sins which are many are all forgiven thee," then joy will spring up in the soul more than in the heart of the man whose corn and wine are increased. When the Spirit comes and reveals this to us, as he doth not to the world, our joy and comfort abound in the Lord; he leads us from ourselves to Christ, and makes him our "all in all." It is our happiness, then, to sink into nothing and to lie low at his blessed feet. Now, my friends, is it so with you?

It is a great source of comfort and joy that "the Holy One of Israel" is a Friend that "loveth at all times, and that sticketh closer than a brother." The Lord does not change as you and I do. There are no ups and downs, colds and hots with him. No; Jesus Christ, "the Holy One of Israel" – and really it does my soul good to think of it, even before I speak it – is "the same yesterday, and today, and for ever." Let us feel as we may, "the Holy One of Israel," who hath loved us from the beginning, will love us to the end. Blessed be his name, he will take care of us, watch over us for good, hold us up in life, and at last land us safely in glory, where we shall shout his praise for evermore!

10. SALVATION BY GRACE

Substance of a Sermon preached at Zoar Chapel, Great Alie Street, London, on Lord's Day morning, April 12th, 1846.

Text: *"For by grace are ye saved, through faith; and that not of yourselves; it is the gift of God. Not of works, lest any man should boast"* *(Ephesians 2. 8, 9).*

My beloved friends, as we had this precious portion of God's holy Word under consideration last Lord's day, we will come at once to the second part of our subject, that the *enjoyment* of our interest in the salvation of Christ is by faith.

What a blessing, beloved, for us that the work of salvation is finished. The poor sinner is made to feel his lost, ruined and undone state. It is necessary in this part of our subject to draw a line of distinction between the real, genuine faith of a believer and the faith that a man may have and yet not be quickened by God the Holy Spirit. Now, there is what is called a nominal, natural faith. James, speaking on this subject, says, "Thou believest that there is one God. Thou doest well!" Better be so than to be an infidel, to deny the Supreme Being. But recollect, the devils believe this, and they tremble. The devils believe that Jesus is the Saviour of his people, for the devils cried out, "Art thou come to torment us before the time?" And in another place, "Jesus I know, and Paul I know; but who are ye?" So you see there is a faith that both men and devils may have, and yet be destitute of living faith.

The Lord, speaking in the parable of the sower, said there were some who for a while believed, but in time of temptation fell away. Paul had to do with a great many of this sort, who for a time believed, but in the time of temptation and trial they left him. So, you see, there is a faith that we have a command over as regards assenting and consenting to the word of truth; but the real faith of God's elect we can no more command than we can command our souls to leave our bodies. Now, my friends, it becomes you and me to have a godly jealousy to know whether we are in the faith for, as it respects genuine faith, it is the gift of God the Holy Spirit; it is a limb of the new creature. Paul says, "For we are not of those that draw back unto perdition, but of those that believe to the saving of the soul."

It is called the faith of God's elect; and why is it called the faith of God's elect? Because it is wrought in the children of God and none else. You see this proved. "Now faith cometh by hearing, and hearing by the Word of God." The apostles preached the Word, and the Lord gave it success; and then it is written, "As many as were *ordained to eternal life* believed."

"By grace are ye saved, and that not of yourselves; it is the gift of God." The faith of the elect is a plant that never grew in nature's garden. He who has this faith believes all that God says in his holy Word, not only because it is in the Word of God, but because he feels and knows these things in his heart. What is it without the feeling? It is, as John Berridge says, not worth a groat. The child of God does not want to go to those great commentators, such as Dr. Gill, Dr. Hawker, Matthew Henry, and other great men, from which many of our parsons get their sermons. No; he has it in his heart. I must stick to feeling. Some parsons say, "Bother your feelings!" Well, I cannot think so. If I had been out and come home very hungry, and saw a good table spread, and plenty of good things talked about, that would not satisfy my hunger. I must eat the things myself to be satisfied.

Christ is the Author of our faith; and not only is he the Author, but he carries on the work of grace in our hearts. Some professors talk about their faith, that they can believe when they like. I know I cannot. The child of God knows by daily experience that he feels dark and shut up, and cannot lay hold on a single promise. It just comes to my mind about a gracious woman that came seven miles to join our church. She said that she was tossed to and fro in her mind for a long time to know whether she was one of the elect. She could not see how it could be; till one morning, when she awoke, these words came to her with power: "The new and living way! The new and living way!" "O," she said, "I saw that Jesus was the way," and from that she got comfort; and often from such texts as these does the Lord give us comfort. "I am the way, the truth, and the life. No man cometh to the Father but by me."

Now may the Lord assist me to show to some poor, cast-down sinners that they have faith; and O that he may be with us. You do really and truly in your hearts confess before God that you feel guilty, lost, ruined and undone. Well, poor souls, there must be life to feel your deadness; there must be light to see your darkness. The great object of your faith is the Lord Jesus Christ; you love him. I know a man who said he could never think he was a believer, he never thought he had faith, until one night, he said, "Our parson preached from these words: 'Unto you that believe he is precious'; and as he was speaking, I did feel him precious to my soul, and I said, 'I have faith.'" There is a verse of a hymn on the subject on which we are now dwelling; it is addressed as a prayer to the Holy Ghost:

"Assure my conscience of her part
In the Redeemer's blood;
And bear thy witness with my heart,
That I am born of God."

This is what the child of God wants to know, whether he is interested in the love of Jesus. You know that Jesus is the Saviour of his people, and that none of them will ever be lost. You have no doubts about that; but this is not enough for you, you want to feel that he is yours. It is as Hart says,

"True religion's more than notion;
Something must be known and felt."

"And that not of yourselves." Now we must go to the fountain head. God saw all the elect from everlasting. So far will the Arminians go with us. Let them have it their way. They say "that God saw all those that would accept his grace, and be good; so he loved them." Why, if so, it would contradict our text: "Not of works, lest any man should boast." "Where is boasting, then? It is excluded. By what law? of works? Nay; but by the law of faith." It would contradict the truth of God. I should have room to boast if, as they say, God loved me because he foresaw I should be a good man. He loved us because he would love, and for no other reason; for so far from the creature loving, he is at enmity with God and strives against him. So "it is not of him that willeth, nor of him that runneth, but of God that showeth mercy." And again: "And the children being not yet born, neither having done good or evil, that the purpose of God according to election might stand, not of works, but of him that calleth; it was said unto her, The elder shall serve the younger; as it is written, Jacob have I loved, but Esau have I hated."

If I were like what some professors talk about, I would not go groping all the day long, and be obliged to cry, and sigh, and groan for a few crumbs; all darkness, and not able to lay hold on a single promise. "Truth, Lord, yet the dogs eat of the crumbs that fall from the Master's table."

"Not of works, lest any man should boast." Where were you and I, beloved, when the Lord first called us? I look back and remember as fresh as if it were but yesterday, 200 miles from here. I was at enmity with God. I used to go roaming about on the Lord's day, instead of going to chapel. I used to hate my father's religion. I did not hate him as my father; but when I came home at night I could not rest. I was uneasy in my conscience. I felt the wrath of God against me, and when I look back and see my old companions in iniquity, for I sometimes do (for it hath pleased God to keep me in the same place), this text will often start up in my mind: "Who maketh thee to differ from another?" There was one of my companions who was more steady than I, for I used to drag and urge him on; but the Lord in his mercy has been pleased to take me and leave him. Where is boasting, then?

There was another of my old companions that got on well and became a manufacturer, and the devil used to tease me very much about him, and told me that if I had gone on as he had, I should have got on well in the world. But after I had been with you six weeks, when I got home, my wife said to me, "Do you know Abel is broke all to pieces, and can only pay three shillings in the pound?" "Well," said I, "I'm a better man. I'm a better man. I can pay twenty shillings to the pound, and a pound left." But after a time, some of my friends said to me, "Do you know Abel has attempted to hang himself?" "Where is boasting, then? It is excluded."

Paul said, "God forbid that I should glory, save in the cross of our Lord Jesus Christ"; and unto him alone must we give all the glory. "Not unto us, O Lord, not unto us, but unto thy name give glory, for thy mercy and for thy truth's sake."

11. THE RIGHTEOUS AND THEIR PRAYERS

Preached at Bedworth, October 27th, 1846

Text: *"For the eyes of the Lord are over the righteous, and his ears are open unto their prayers; but the face of the Lord is against them that do evil"* (1 Peter 3. 12).

The Apostle Peter begins this Epistle by mentioning that great and glorious doctrine of the everlasting gospel – the particular, everlasting love of Jehovah the Father. He commences with a divine and experimental question, with the truth as it is in the Lord Jesus Christ, and then proceeds to its particular effects, bringing forward sundry exhortations which are blessedly adapted to meet the feelings of the Lord's living family who are living in the enjoyment of God's precious truth.

Doctrine in its own place is blessed and precious; it is heart food, heart comfort and consolation. But we cannot live upon God's blessed truth unless we taste it, handle it, and feel its solemn importance and blessed reality. With the enjoyment of God's precious truth in our hearts we shall be constrained to live to his honour and glory, and the precepts and exhortations of the Word will become as meat and drink to our souls.

The chapter whence our text is taken principally contains exhortations. But, not to be tedious in our introductory observations, we will come at once to the subject in hand.

"For the eyes of the Lord are over the righteous, and his ears are open unto their prayers; but the face of the Lord is against them that do evil."

I.   I would take notice of *the character of the righteous.*

II.   *The prayer of the righteous*, which the Lord hears.

III.   *The declaration*, that "the face of the Lord is against them that do evil."

I.   We are to take notice of the *righteous*. But where can we find a just and righteous man? Such a man cannot be found as we stand in relation to the first Adam. The assertion is broad and pointed, but it is true. The Lord himself looked down from heaven to see if he could find any that did good and that sinned not, and he found none – none righteous among the fallen sons and daughters of apostate Adam – no, not one. All flesh has corrupted its way. Man's very nature is contaminated with sin. He is born in sin and shapen in iniquity. His heart is carnal, and is enmity against God. The thoughts and imaginations of man's heart are evil, only evil, and that continually. It is therefore vain for us to think of finding a righteous man on these grounds.

Yet there *are* righteous men, and the eyes of the Lord are upon them. And these souls are constituted righteous in God's sight as they stand in union with the Lord Jesus Christ, and as interested in his redemption. Christ is the Second Adam; and there is no way whereby the guilty sinner can be constituted righteous and be accepted in God's sight but as he stands interested in the glorious Person and the perfect obedience and blood-shedding of the dear Redeemer.

God's law is a just and holy law. Its requirements are just; and it demands righteousness, uprightness and perfection in nature, in heart, in thought, in word and in action. And where that uprightness and perfection are not found, all that the law can do is to curse and condemn.

But this perfect obedience can never be found in us. You that are born of God, and know that in yourselves dwelleth no good thing, feel that in God's sight you are altogether as an unclean thing, and that all your righteousnesses are as filthy rags. You must therefore have a better righteousness than your own or sink to rise no more.

But in the Lord Jesus Christ there is that perfection which the law demands. If we look at his nature, he was "holy, harmless, undefiled, and separate from sinners." His heart was holy, his thoughts were pure, and perfect grace was poured into his lips; beauty and perfection shone in all he did and said, insomuch that the eyes of divine justice in the holy law were upon the covenant Head – our Elder Brother – from the manger to the cross. His thoughts were watched. His actions were marked. His words were listened to. And God solemnly exclaims concerning him that he is "well pleased for his righteousness' sake. He hath magnified the law and made it honourable." Thus the law has been honourably and gloriously fulfilled by the dear Redeemer – observe, not on his own account, but as the covenant Head of his mystical body, the Bridegroom of his chosen bride. And this he did in his active obedience to the divine law for his church and people; and it is by the act of Jehovah imputed and made over to poor sinners.

Now, the Word of God abounds with demonstrative proofs of these things, but time would fail me to refer to more than two or three.

Paul, speaking of the righteousness that is by faith, says, "Of him are ye in Christ Jesus." That is, loved in him, saved in him, complete in him and accepted in him. "Of him are ye in Christ Jesus." And this Jesus Christ is made of the Father the wisdom of the elect, to guide and direct them, and their complete righteousness, sanctification and redemption. He is "of God made unto us wisdom, righteousness, sanctification, and redemption." I was going to say that this text is a cluster of the sweetest gospel grace that we have in the Scriptures. Our righteousness, you see, is not to be found in ourselves – it is in the Lord Jesus Christ. And these things are of God.

"Surely shall one say, in the Lord have I righteousness and strength." Now, why is this spoken in the singular number? Because it is the language of Christ's spouse. Jesus has not two brides, and he hates putting away. It is the bride that speaks, and says, "Surely in the Lord have I righteousness and strength," righteousness to justify me and constitute me accepted in the sight of the Lord.

This righteousness, enjoyed by faith, makes the church to sing, "I will greatly rejoice in the Lord, my soul shall be joyful in my God; for he hath clothed me with the garments of salvation, he hath covered me with the robe of righteousness, as a bridegroom decketh himself with ornaments, and as a bride adorneth herself with her jewels."

> "And lest the shadow of a spot
>   Should on my soul be found,
>   He took the robe the Saviour wrought,
>   And cast it all around."

Do you, my friends, desire a righteousness like this? The Saviour said, "Blessed are they that hunger and thirst after righteousness, for they shall be filled." There was a time when Saul of Tarsus went about like the rest to establish a righteousness of his own, by his prayers and alms deeds, zealous for the law and the tradition of the fathers. He was wrapped up in it, and rested in it. But when Jesus met him on his way to Damascus, and when in the power of the Holy Ghost the commandment came, "sin revived, and he died." What a wretch he was in the sight of God's holy law, looking at that law as in a looking-glass, and viewing himself to see what a vile, guilty wretch he was! The Lord stripped him there and emptied him of self and self-sufficiency. Then he could say, "But what things were gain to me, those I counted loss for Christ." I do not know that there is a passage in the Bible that I have more upon my spirit than the third chapter of Philippians, verses seven and eight. Then the words of Paul in the ninth verse, how many of you have felt them? "And be found in him (in Jesus), not having mine own righteousness which is of the law; but that which is through the faith of Christ, the righteousness which is of God by faith." This is sure to be the soul-breathing of every poor sinner that is under divine teaching. "The just shall live by faith." They shall look from themselves to the dear Redeemer, and so rejoice in him as their law-fulfilling righteousness. "Blessed is the man unto whom the Lord will not impute sin," but righteousness.

The doctrine of imputed righteousness is contemned and slighted by some persons because they say it does away with inward holiness. But it secures inward holiness. It is

impossible for a poor sinner to enjoy righteousness in the Lord
Jesus Christ, as the law-fulfilling righteousness, and rejoice in
him as such, without his being made a partaker of divine grace
and having a principle of holiness in his soul.

Some may say, "I have gone on very well so far, but now
you leave me behind; when you contend for holiness in the
soul, I am afraid I have it not."

When a sinner is born again, he is made a partaker of the
divine nature. Christ took our nature in the womb of the
virgin, and in our nature he suffered, bled and died. He
entered heaven with our nature, and John saw him as "a Lamb
as it had been slain." He wears our nature still; our nature is
gone to glory in union with the Lord's divine nature; and in
regeneration every spiritual child is made a partaker of the
holy nature of the Lord Jesus Christ. And where that divine
principle is implanted in the soul of a poor sinner, he shall
certainly go to heaven. "He who sanctifieth, and they who are
sanctified are all of one; for which cause he is not ashamed to
call them brethren" – bone of his bone, and flesh of his flesh.

"But," says the child of God, "I want you to prove it."
Well, we will try to do so. Every poor sinner who is born of
God is made a partaker of divine grace in regeneration, and he
will feel somewhat as follows: where there is the grace of God
in the soul, there will be a hatred to and an abhorrence of sin.
And where there is a hatred to sin, there will be a forsaking of
our sin and a coming out from ungodly connections. This is
the grace of God, and is a holy principle. The grace of God
"teaches us to deny ungodliness and worldly lusts; and that we
should live soberly, righteously, and godly in this present
world." So that where this grace of our Lord is given and the
divine nature implanted, there will be a fleeing from sin as
from a pestilence.

But to come more closely to the matter still. If you and I
are real, living souls spiritually, and partake of the divine
nature of the Lord Jesus Christ, we shall hate to feel that sin

which dwells and works in us, which our nearest and dearest
friends know nothing of, but is known only to God and
ourselves. Yes, where there is the grace of God, a divine
principle is implanted, and that precious soul hates his own
vain thoughts because of the sin that dwells within him and
works in his mind. Then follows a mourning before the Lord,
and this is from the grace of God that is in the soul. He hates
and abhors himself, and becomes his own burden and trouble,
because of sin that lives and works within him.

Souls thus circumstanced know not where to go; but
wherever they go these feelings and the Lord's grace go with
them. God's grace is in their hearts, and he will take them to
glory.

"The eyes of the Lord are over the righteous, and his ears
are open to their prayers; but the face of the Lord is against
them that do evil." Now, when this divine nature is implanted
in the soul of a sinner, it will be evidenced in another way.
There will be holy desires, and pantings, and breathings after
the Lord Jesus Christ. There will be a desire to be conformed
to the image of Christ – a concern to have the mind, likeness
and spirit of Christ; and they will anxiously wish to live to the
honour and glory of that precious Jesus who is the ground and
foundation of their hope. This gives the following particular
evidence of a righteous man: "He that doeth righteousness is
righteous." "No man gathers grapes from thorns, or figs from
thistles."

I make nothing of those who have got doctrine in their
head, and never feel soul-humility at the feet of Jesus. They do
not feel their need of the blood of Jesus to cleanse their souls,
nor of his righteousness to justify them. They do not love to
glorify him with their bodies and their spirits, which are his.
True religion produces its own effects, and those are to honour
and glorify the Lord.

II. Leaving the first part of our subject, namely, the
character of the righteous, I will call your attention to their

prayer. "The eyes of the Lord are over the righteous, and his ears are open unto their prayers."

Let me make a few remarks upon *prayer* itself. In reference to prayer there is an important distinction to be made. It is one thing to *say prayers* and another thing to *pray*. We may buy prayers, say prayers and make prayers, yet never pray at all. I put the question thus, for I wish you all to think how a man may learn prayers by rote and repeat them night and morning, yet unless the words of those prayers be felt in the heart and soul of him that prays, he does not truly pray. We may have a prayer-book, and read prayers in church or chapel, or before our family, or by the bedside of a sick friend; but however good and weighty the words in themselves may be, if they are only read and heard, and not felt in the souls of the persons engaged therein, it is not prayer. The Pharisees made long prayers, but God says they drew near to him with their mouths, and honoured him with their lips, but their hearts were far from him. It is mockery to repeat words to God in which we have no feeling. It is to be feared that in these days we live among many who are only sayers of prayers, and never pray.

But our text speaks of *true* prayer: "His ears are open unto their prayers." To come, then, to this true prayer. Prayer is the breathing of the heaven-born soul after God. It is the immediate effect of the fulfilment of that solemn promise, that very solemn and needful promise: "I will pour upon the house of David, and upon the inhabitants of Jerusalem, the Spirit of grace and of supplications." Now, the Lord pours his Holy Spirit into the soul of us poor sinners; and that Spirit convinces us of our sin, makes us see and feel our wretchedness and misery, and leads us to see where those blessings are of which we stand in need, so that we pour out our hearts and souls before the Lord in earnest fervent prayers. Thus true prayer is the spiritual breathing of a poor sinner before God.

Paul was a Pharisee of the Pharisees, and made long prayers; but he never prayed at all spiritually while a Pharisee, and God never acknowledged him as a praying soul. But after the Lord met him on the road to Damascus, and the Holy Spirit, the grace of God, had taken possession of his soul, he truly and spiritually prayed to the Lord. And the Lord spoke unto his servant Ananias and said, "Go thy way, and thou wilt find one Saul of Tarsus, for behold he prayeth; and speak such words to him as I shall tell thee." But Ananias was afraid, and answered, "Lord, I have heard what evil he hath done to thy saints at Jerusalem; and here he hath authority from the chief priests to bind all that call upon thy name: why send me into the paw of this Benjamite, this ravening wolf?" But the Lord said unto him, "Go thy way, he is one of my chosen; and I will tell thee something more, he is a praying soul." Ananias was ready then to say, "Bless thy name, I will go if there is a cry in his heart for mercy."

To this day, when the grace of God arrests a poor soul, that soul begins to cry. And God's religion, that will stand the test of life or death and the judgment of the great day, begins in the language of the poor publican, "God be merciful to me a sinner." God's religion in the heart of the dear family of faith is, "God be merciful to me it sinner." On a dying bed and on the banks of Jordan it is the same. So that in true prayer there is a confession of our sin and guilt, there is a coming before God guilty and condemned, and there is a calling upon him for mercy, for help and for deliverance. And as the Lord moves by his Spirit, the souls of the saints go after him. Thus you see "the eyes of the Lord are over the righteous, and his ears are open unto their prayers."

Thousands of true prayers go up to God when there is not a word spoken. What! pray to God without words? Yes; and if you know not this, you never truly prayed. We will just look at one text, and I have thanked God many a time it is in the Bible. It is in the eighth chapter of Romans: "For we know not what to pray for as we ought." We are such dark, ignorant wretches, such bewildered creatures, when we come before the Lord that we know not what to say nor how to begin. We cannot put our feelings into words if our salvation depended upon it. But the Holy Ghost as the Spirit of grace and supplication, "helpeth our infirmities, and maketh intercession for us with groanings that cannot be uttered. And he that searcheth the hearts knoweth what is the mind of the Spirit, because he maketh intercession for the saints according to the will of God." Therefore real prayer to God is in the heartfelt sigh, and groan, and moan, arising from a sense of our sinfulness, vileness, weakness and helplessness. I would come lower still, for the psalmist says, "All my desires (the desire of my soul, when there are no words) all my desires are before thee, and my groaning is not hid from thee. Thine eyes are over me (over the desires of my heart), and thine ears are attentive to my sighs and groans."

Many a time, as the dear child of God is moving about his house, or going over his farm, or engaged in his business, he ponders these things over in his soul. I like pondering Christians better than great talkers. When he is pondering in his soul before the Lord, and feeling his own sinfulness, weakness, unworthiness, worthlessness and vileness, and says in the very feeling of his mind, "Ah! Lord, thou knowest what a vile wretch I am; thou knowest what a weak helpless worm I am; thou knowest my heart; thine eyes are upon it, and thou knowest I cannot do what I wish to do" – there is more prayer in that "Ah, Lord!" than there is in a million words; and that very "Ah, Lord!" enters into the ears of the Lord God of Sabaoth, and is accepted as true prayer. The psalmist says upon this very subject, "Let the sighing of the prisoner come before thee. According to the greatness of thy power, preserve thou those that are appointed to die." Come, poor soul, the Lord heareth all thy sighs, and all thy groans and breathings after himself. "He regardeth the prayer of the destitute, and will not despise their prayer." O what good things and what encouraging things for the Lord's family that are panting after him!

That there may be prayer where no words are we have proof in the case of Hannah, the wife of Elkanah. She was a woman "of a sorrowful spirit"; and where did she go to in her sorrow? To the best place she could go to, to the temple of the Lord; and she prayed unto the Lord with sore weeping, that he would remember her and deliver her. She went into the temple, and the Lord met with her and blessed her; but as she was engaged in prayer, it is said that her lips moved and she prayed in her heart. There was a motion of the lips, it is true, but there was no sound of words. Now, I like those people that pray in their hearts. Heart prayer is prayer to the Lord from the soul. Eli sat by a pillar or post in the temple; and, looking at her, said, "Is she drunk?" Suspicion rose high in the mind of the priest of the Most High God that the woman was intoxicated. A holy indignation rose in his mind, that a female should come in the house of God in that state. "Put away thy wine, thou daughter of Belial, why comest thou here to mock?" Such a mode of attack was very grievous from the Lord's priest, who should have spoken a word of comfort to her soul. And Hannah said, "No, my lord, count not thine handmaid a daughter of Belial, for I am a woman of a sorrowful spirit, and have poured out my soul to the Lord." How it changed the mind of Eli when she lifted up her head and looked towards him, and spoke those few words! That knit the heart of Eli to her, so that the union which took place then never was dissolved, and never will be to all eternity. What was it that she said to him? "Count not thine handmaid a daughter of Belial, for I am a woman of a sorrowful spirit, and have been pouring out my soul before the Lord God of Israel." And when Eli heard that this was the case he said, "The Lord God of Israel grant thee thy petitions." And so it was. The eyes of the Lord were over her and his ears were open unto her prayer, and there was a blessed answer in the gift of Samuel. "The eyes of the Lord are over the righteous, and his ears are open unto their prayers."

Now, though I have been speaking very particularly about mental prayer, do not mistake me. I do not say a word against a child of God coming before the Lord, as the prophet says, and taking with him words, and turning unto the Lord and saying unto him, "Take away all mine iniquity." It is blessed when God pours the Holy Spirit in our souls, when we have liberty and enlargement of soul before the Lord, and can tell him our troubles and plead his promises, and put him in remembrance of the words he has spoken. Sometimes it has been the case with us when we have had such nearness unto the Lord, and we have told him everything we have felt. And as we have been petitioning for mercy, the Holy Ghost has brought the promise to our mind. Then we have felt sweet nearness and familiarity with the Lord at a throne of grace, drawing near by faith. It is a solemn thing to have God sensibly with us, and feel a familiarity with him. This is to have communion with the Father and with the Lord Jesus Christ, under the immediate influence of the Holy Ghost. Such seasons are very few, however. May God give us more of them, more times of nearness to himself and familiarity with our Lord in prayer and meditation. Then shall we prove the truth of our text, "The eyes of the Lord are over the righteous and his ears are open unto their prayer."

The eyes of the Lord are over all his people in all their troubles and trials. Poor Jonah made a mistake when in the belly of the fish, for then he said, "I am cast out of thy sight." But he was not unseen by his God. David says, "If I take the wings of the morning, and dwell in the uttermost parts of the sea, even there shall thy hand lead me and thy right hand shall hold me." There is no fleeing from the presence of the Lord, no hiding from the all-seeing eye of God. The Lord saw Jonah in the fish's belly, and moved the prophet's mind to say, "I will look again towards thy holy temple." There is a looking again in the minds of God's people when in trouble, and a longing after the Lord in heart and affection. But his eyes are over them, and his ears are open unto their prayers; and he marks their prayers when they are in trouble.

For instance, when Israel was in Egyptian bondage, his eye was over them; and when the time of deliverance came he appeared to Moses in the bush, and said, "I have seen the affliction of my people." He had watched their affliction and heard their cry, and now he came down to deliver them. He came to deliver them when they were before the Red Sea with rocks and mountains on either hand, and Pharaoh's army at their heels. Moses, it is said, cried to the Lord, and yet we have no account of words being employed in his cry. I believe he used no words that his friends could hear, but in his heart and soul he cried mightily for the Lord to make known his power and deliver them. The Lord's eyes were over them in their extremity, and he commanded Moses to smite the waters. He did so, and the waters parted and made a way for them. "The sea saw it and fled," and the people passed over on dry ground. Israel was a typical people, and the dealings of God with them set forth his dealings with his spiritual family in all ages.

"His ears are open unto their prayer." Take another instance. When Elijah, obliged to flee for speaking the truth in the name of the Lord, was in the wilderness, the Lord did not forget him; and when he was without food, the Lord sent him some help and provision. Why, the eyes of the Lord were upon his servant, and in answer to prayer the Lord appointed ravens to feed him; and they brought him bread and flesh in the morning, and bread and flesh in the evening, and he drank of the brook. "Now I have seen this," the prophet would say, "I shall never doubt the Lord again." But says the Lord, "I will try thy faith and patience." Soon the brook dried up, and the ravens ceased to bring him food. Then he cried again to the Lord for help; the Lord said, "Go thy way to Zarephath, a city of Zidon, and dwell there; behold I have commanded a widow woman there to sustain thee, for thou art mine after all; mine eyes are upon thee." The prophet went to Zarephath, and when he was about to enter the city, he met a poor woman. Now, speaking after the manner of men, this woman should have had plenty of victuals in her pantry for the man; but if this had been the case, the power, majesty and glory of the Lord would have been eclipsed. Well, as the man approaches the city, the woman comes out. Wearied with travelling, and parched with thirst, Elijah says, "Fetch me some water that I may drink." And as she is hasting to fetch it, he calls after her, and says, "Bring me, I pray thee, a morsel of bread in thine hand." The woman stands and looks at the prophet, and says, "Man, as thy soul liveth, I have but a handful of meal in a barrel, and a little oil in a cruse; these are for my son and me to live, and I was coming out to gather two sticks to dress up the last, and then I and my poor son must die." No, no; that was carnal reason. The woman had been crying to the Lord, and help was come. What! help come with a man oppressed with hunger? Yes. It came with the prophet, for he says, "Go thy way, do as thou hast said; but make me thereof a little cake first; for thus saith the Lord God of Israel, the barrel of meal shall not waste, neither shall the cruse of oil fail, until the day that the Lord sendeth rain upon the earth. The Lord will take care of thee and me; I have it by faith and have confidence in God." Bless his precious name! his eyes are over the righteous.

Again. Consider that eminent servant of the Most High God, who was hated and persecuted for righteousness' sake, concerning whom his enemies said, "We shall not find occasion against this Daniel, except we find it concerning the law of his God." Let us pause here a moment. May our conduct and conversation in the church of God, in the family and in worldly transactions be so that the enemies of God and truth may find no occasion against us unless it be in the law of our God. Well, Daniel's enemies conspired against him on this very principle, and went with canting hypocritical faces to the king. They wanted the king to make a decree and sign it so that it should not be altered, that if any man asked a petition of any god or man for thirty days, save of the king, he should be cast into a den of lions. This was made a law, made and signed according to the law of the Medes and Persians, that altered not. It was just suited to the pride and ambition of the king. The day came in which it was put in force. Daniel knew that the design of this law was to entangle him; but did he desist from prayer in the face of danger? No; but we are told he entered his chamber, his window being open towards Jerusalem. There he kneeled and prayed every morning, and then again at noon, and then again in the evening.

Daniel was discovered by his enemies, and accused before the king. The king, loving Daniel, set his heart to deliver him, and laboured for it until the going down of the sun, but could not. So Daniel had to be cast into the den of lions. But the eyes of his God were upon him, and his ears were open unto his cry, and the Lord sent his angel and stopped the lions' mouths. And doubtless, Daniel was far more happy in the den of lions than the king was on his princely couch. Early in the morning, however, the king came to the den of lions, and cried, "O Daniel, servant of the Most High God, is thy God able to deliver? has he delivered? if thou canst, speak, let me hear thy voice." Hearing the distress of his mind from the tone of his voice, Daniel answers, "True, O king, my God hath sent his angel and shut the lions' mouths, that they have not hurt me. His eyes are upon me, and as a wall of fire round about me. So that I am a monument of his mercy, and have proved his power."

But to come to the New Testament for illustration of our subject. We will notice an instance, and then conclude. We read in the Acts of the Apostles that Peter was cast into the common prison; and in the morning, when the jailor went to fetch the prisoner out, he was gone, for the angel of the Lord had opened the prison doors and set him free. And when the officers went and reported the circumstance, they wondered and doubted whereunto it would grow; they could not tell what would be the end of these things.

When Peter was taken the second time and put in the prison, however, he was put in bonds and locked fast between two soldiers. All the doors too, inner and outer, were locked and barred, and made as safe as they could be, so that he might not be delivered this time. Now they have him, they think, quite secure. All these things being settled, Peter's friends met at the Nazarenes' rendezvous to pray on behalf of Peter. Now "the eyes of the Lord are over the righteous, and his ears are open to their prayers." Their cry was, "O Lord, help thy servant: thine arm is not shortened, neither is anything too hard for the Lord. O Lord, come down; rend the heavens, and make a way for thy servant to escape." And in answer to their petitions, the great Jehovah said to his angel, "Go and fetch my servant Peter out of yonder jail." The angel descends into the jail, into the very place where Peter is. And the angel, with solemn majesty, says unto him, "Arise, and follow me." And he arose, and left his companions, and followed him. But while going forward, Peter thinks it is all a dream. When he is brought out into the city, however, the angel's work is done, and he ascends to immortal glory. The angel gone, Peter stood and looked around. He thought he had been dreaming, but it was no dream. He was really delivered. And while he thought of his marvellous deliverance, he remembered where his friends would be, and there he went. A damsel named Rhoda came to the door, and knowing Peter's voice, said, "It is Peter;" but they said unto her, "It is not Peter; thou art mad; he is fast in prison." But Rhoda says, "It is Peter; do I not know his voice?" She opened the door, however; and Peter came in and rehearsed the mighty acts of the Lord in sending his angel and delivering his servant from prison.

"The eyes of the Lord are over the righteous, and his ears are open unto their prayers."

I must not trespass longer on your time. May God Almighty bless the word spoken, that it may do you good. Amen.

12. A PROTEST

Preached at the Baptist Chapel, St George's Road, Manchester, on January 23rd, 1848

Text: *"And searched the Scriptures daily, whether those things were so" (Acts 17. 11).*

[Before the death of William Gadsby, the notions had appeared in the church at Manchester that a child of God cannot backslide, that the Lord does not chastise his people for sin, and that sin in thought is as great an offence to God as sin in action. These errors led to a separation and the setting up of another church in Manchester. John Kershaw felt constrained to preach this sermon as a protest, and it was immediately published as a pamphlet at the request of the church.

J. C. Philpot, perceiving its importance, reviewed the sermon in four long articles in the 1848 Gospel Standard.

There seems to be some mistake on page 168. Mr. Kershaw confuses two distinct things – the Spirit of God and the new man of grace. J. C. Philpot makes this point in his review of the sermon.]

St. Paul, writing to the church at Ephesus, exhorts the brethren to pray for all saints; and he adds, "And for me, that utterance may be given unto me, that I may open my mouth boldly, to make known the mystery of the gospel."

Beloved, if the great Apostle of the Gentiles had to entreat an interest in the prayers of the brethren, how much more reason has such a poor, sinful dust and ashes as myself to desire an interest in your prayers at this time. Brethren, pray for me that my eye may be kept single to the honour and glory of the Lord and the peace and prosperity of Zion; that I may preach the truth in love and in the fear of the Lord, under the immediate influence of the Holy Spirit; that I may speak as the oracle of God, and with the ability which God giveth me, that he may be glorified, and good may be done in the name and by the power of our Lord Jesus Christ.

The summer before your late and esteemed pastor died, he and I, in the providence of God, were cast into the company of a clergyman of the Established Church, vicar of a neighbouring parish. After the compliments which usually pass on such occasions, he being informed who my friend was, looked very earnestly at him, and said, "Well, Mr. Gadsby, I have often heard of you, but never recollect seeing you before; you are a much older man than I expected." "Ah!" said my friend, "I have attained to more than threescore years and ten, and as good old Dr. Hawker was wont to say after he had attained that age, I am living upon borrowed days." The vicar, still looking earnestly at my friend, continued, "Mr. Gadsby, I suppose you stand directly opposed to all such men as myself." Mr. Gadsby replied, "O! no, doctor; you are greatly mistaken. I do not stand opposed to you or any man in the land. There is not a man upon earth whom I do not feel wishful to benefit so far as lies in my power. I do not stand opposed to men, but to erroneous principles and practices." My dear friends, I feel thankful to the Lord that I can even now say the same as your esteemed pastor said.

The Lord has put it into my heart "to do good to all men, especially to the household of faith." It is neither men nor church that I stand opposed to as such but to those principles and doctrines, both in theory and practice, which stand opposed to the Word of God, and to the real happiness, peace and prosperity of Zion.

On the present occasion you are aware that I stand pledged to enter a solemn and scriptural protest against the following errors:

I.   That a child of God cannot backslide.
II. That the Lord does not chastise his children for sin.
III. That sin in the thought of the heart is as great an offence to God as sin in the outward action.

Beloved, these principles are either true or false; either in accordance with the records of heaven or opposed to them.

Let us in examination follow the noble example of the Bereans spoken of in our text, who "searched the Scriptures daily, whether those things were so." The Lord enable us to try the principles under consideration by the same rule, bringing them to the standard of God's Word, Christian experience, and "the doctrines which are according to godliness."

I.   The first is that a child of God — that is, a good man who is born again of God, and who has been blessed with the fear of the Lord in his heart — cannot backslide. Now, this is roundly, boldly and unflinchingly maintained by certain persons who profess to follow the doctrines and precepts of God's holy Word. In the examination of these principles, we shall have to inquire on what they conceive these opinions to be founded, and how far they are consistent with the truth of God. To prove that a child of God cannot backslide, it is argued that a regenerated man possesses two natures, an old man of sin and a new man of grace; that the old man of sin never made any progress in the divine life nor ever can; consequently that he can never go back from that in which he has never made any advances. It is also contended that the new man of grace never sinned nor ever can sin, so that he likewise can never go back or imbibe the least stain or particle of sin. Now as this is said to be the constitution of a Christian, viz., that the old man of sin never made any advances in the divine life, so that he can never go back, and as the new man of grace cannot sin, the question is, How can the child of God backslide?

Beloved, the statement we have just given of the constitution of a child of God is a very superficial notion, falling far short of the true scriptural definition of what constitutes a regenerated man. There are four things here to be considered:
1.   The body.
2.   The soul.
3.   The old man of sin.
4.   The new man of grace.

In the first creation God formed the body of man out of the dust of the earth, and after it was formed it was an inanimate mass, cold and lifeless. "The Lord God breathed into his nostrils the breath of life, and man became a living soul." Here we have man, a creature of God, with a body and a living soul — an immortal spirit, good, upright and perfect, as first turned out of the hands of the great Creator.

In man's primeval state we find that he had body and soul, but no old man of sin nor new man of grace. But after the Fall, through the disobedience of our first parents, man became subject to the old man of sin, "which is corrupt according to the deceitful lusts," under its domineering power, and was led away captive by Satan, "the prince of the power of the air, the spirit that now worketh in the children of disobedience." Thus we have a body, a soul and an old man of sin, but in this state no new man of grace. A man becomes a new creature only when he is born again of God, and thus made the subject of a divine nature, or a "new man which, after God, is created in righteousness and true holiness." This new man of grace is holy and pure as its divine Author, and neither is nor can be contaminated with sin.

This being the constitution of a regenerate man, the question arises: In backsliding, what part of this nature is it that backslides? I grant at once to my opponents that it is not the old man of sin nor the new man of grace. The question then still occurs, What is it? I answer, *It is the soul of the Christian.*

When the soul and body of a good man are plunged into sin, it is under the influence of the old man of sin and Satan. "Every man is tempted, when he is drawn aside of his own lust, and enticed" (James 1. 14). But those who boldly maintain that the soul of a good man cannot go back, tell us at the same time that to charge the soul of a quickened or regenerated sinner with sinning "is nothing short of blasphemy." Beloved, we have to try this statement and, like the Bereans, we will "search the Scriptures to see whether those things are so."

Now, the soul of a good man either *can* or *cannot* sin. Let us try, therefore, both sides of the question, and show from the Word of God and Christian experience that the soul of the regenerated is sometimes under the influence of the new man of grace implanted by the Spirit, and at other times under the influence of Satan and the old man of sin.

When the soul is under the influence of the Spirit and grace of God, it is sure to go forward in the divine life and in the means of grace. But when the soul of a child of God is under the influence of sin and Satan, he is sure to go back. Here is the seat and source of the Christian warfare, where "the flesh lusteth against the spirit, and the spirit against the flesh; and these are contrary the one to the other, so that ye cannot do the things that ye would." And this causes a struggling within; as it is written, "What will ye see in the Shulamite? As it were the company of two armies."

It is said that "in the mouth of two or three witnesses every word shall be established." It will be admitted that David was a good man, for the Lord calls him a man "after his own heart." We will, therefore, let David speak on this matter. His soul being under the influence of the new man of grace, he longed to live to the honour and glory of God, and nothing but the Lord could satisfy his soul. Hear what he says: "As the hart panteth after the water brooks, so panteth my soul after thee, O God. My soul thirsteth for God, for the living God: when shall I come and appear before God?" (Psalm 42. 1, 2). "O God, thou art my God; early will I seek thee. My soul thirsteth for thee, my flesh longeth for thee in a dry and thirsty land where no water is (Psalm 63. 1.) "My soul followeth hard after God." Are there not seasons, beloved, when you, like David, feel your very heart and soul going out after God in fervent breathings, hungerings and thirstings after him whom your soul loveth? You want to know more of him as your Saviour and Redeemer; to feel your interest in his love, by having it shed abroad in your heart by the Holy Ghost that is given unto us, and in his precious, atoning blood; that you may be found in the Redeemer's robe of righteousness; that you may be found bound up with him in the bundle of life, and be his in that day when he makes up his jewels. Are not your souls at times going out after God, praying that you may be conformed to the image of his Son, that the mind that was in Christ Jesus may be in you, that you may live to his honour and glory the few days you may have to sojourn in this time state, and that the Lord will land you safe in heaven, to be for ever in his presence, where there is "fulness of joy and pleasures for evermore"?

My dear friends, our souls at such times are going forward, making advances in the divine life under the influence and power of the Spirit, the new man of grace in the soul. But are these always the feelings of our soul? Alas! no. David, the man after God's own heart, expresses himself in very different language when his poor soul was under the temptations of Satan and the workings of the flesh, the old man of sin. Hear what he says: "My soul cleaveth to the dust: quicken thou me according to thy Word" (Psalm 119. 25). At this time both the old and new man were at work in his soul. Under the power of the old man his soul clave to the dust; under the influence of the new man of grace his soul longed to feel more of the quickening power and grace of God. The indwelling and working of sin in his poor soul often made him sigh and groan, yea, and "roar" before the Lord.

Beloved, you who fear God and know the plague of your own hearts, is it not so with you? Are you not plagued with vain thoughts and worldly-mindedness? Do not your souls cleave to the dust, feeling yourselves so weak and helpless that you cannot deliver yourselves and, like the psalmist, you feel a daily need of the quickening influence of God's grace to speed you in his ways?

Again, David says, "He restoreth my soul; he leadeth me in paths of righteousness, for his name's sake" (Psalm 23. 3). David's soul like ours, when left to himself, the evils of his own heart and the power of the old man of sin, wandered and strayed from the Lord and the thoughts and imaginations of his heart were evil, foolish and vain. Hence he says, "I hate vain thoughts"; and again he says, "Thou tellest my wanderings." "For I have gone astray like a lost sheep; seek thy servant." I cannot give you a clearer, more concise and experimental explanation than does Watts in the following lines:

"My soul hath gone too far astray,
My feet too often slipped;
Yet since I've not forgot thy ways,
Restore thy wandering sheep."

I solemnly declare, in the name and fear of the Lord, that there is not a heaven-born and Spirit-taught soul in this congregation but what experimentally knows these things in a greater or less degree; and those who do not are out of the secret, and know not the spiritual warfare there is in the soul of every man of God. His soul is often wandering from the Lord, so that the pen of inspired truth warrants us in positively affirming that there is such a thing as backsliding.

Again. David says, "My soul refuseth to be comforted." Under what influence was his soul at this time? Under that of the new man of grace? O! no; if that had been the case, he would have reasoned as on another occasion: "Why art thou cast down, O my soul? and why art thou disquieted within me? Hope thou in God, for I shall yet praise him, who is the health of my countenance, and my God." This is the language of the new man of grace, to encourage the soul in its troubles and castings-down. But when he says, "My soul refuseth to be comforted," it is under the influence of a fretful spirit, the old man of sin; and thus we see, as I said before, that under the influence of grace, the soul of a man of God advances in the divine life, and in the ways of the Lord; but under the influence of the old man of sin, he draws back.

We have another witness, my friends, to bring forward from the Word of God. Like the Bereans, let us be diligent in searching the Scriptures whether these things are so. Job was a man of God. The Lord, speaking of him to Satan, said, "Hast thou considered my servant Job, that there is none like him in all the earth, a perfect and upright man, one that feareth God and escheweth evil?" He had severe trials in the loss of his property and his family. In the midst of these trying dispensations, his mind was kept calm and his soul stayed upon the Lord, so that he could in his heart and soul say, "The Lord gave, and the Lord hath taken away; blessed be the name of the Lord." "In all this Job sinned not, nor charged God foolishly." And when given up into the hands of Satan, with sore affliction upon his body, and his wife, who should have been a comfort and a help-mate for him in these calamities, said unto him, "Curse God and die," the Lord was still with him to comfort and support his soul, so that he said unto her, "Thou speakest as one of the foolish women speaketh. What? shall we receive good at the hand of God, and shall we not receive evil?" "In all this did not Job sin with his lips." Under the influence of the new man of grace, Job could bless and praise the Lord in all his afflictions, and say, "Though he slay me, yet will I trust in him"; he could "kiss the rod and him that hath appointed it," and say with Eli, "It is the Lord: let him do what seemeth him good."

How very different, however, were Job's feelings when, under the influence of the old man of sin, he cursed the day of his birth! He says many strange things: "My soul chooseth strangling, and death rather than life; even that it would please God to destroy me; that he would let loose his hand, and cut me off." Poor, afflicted Job was not one of those who tell us it is nothing short of blasphemy to say that the soul of a good man can sin. He had such wretched, sinful feelings in his soul at times as caused him to say, "My soul is weary of my life"; "Behold I am vile"; "Wherefore I abhor myself and repent in dust and ashes."

Thus we see that when Job was under the influence of the new man of grace, he could bless and praise the Lord in the midst of trouble; but when under the influence of the old man of sin, he murmured and repined.

In the next place, let us call in the testimony of the church of the living God, the spouse of Christ, who, when under the influence of the Spirit of the Lord, exclaims, as we have it from the mouth of the prophet, "I will greatly rejoice in the Lord; my soul shall be joyful in my God; for he hath clothed me with the garment of salvation, he hath covered me with the robe of righteousness" (Isaiah 61. 10).

How different from this are the feelings and language of the church of God when under the influence of the old man of sin, carnal reasonings, unbelieving fears and temptations! Zion said, "The Lord hath forsaken me, and my Lord hath forgotten me." She was now in her feelings as a woman forsaken and grieved in spirit, and ready to say, "Will the Lord cast off for ever? and will he be favourable no more? Is his mercy clean gone for ever? doth his promise fail for evermore? Hath God forgotten to be gracious? hath he in anger shut up his tender mercies?" Alas! my friends, this is our infirmity!

How evident it is from the testimony of God, and from Christian experience, that the souls of the children of God go forward in the divine life when under the blessed influence of the new man of grace, but that, under the influence of sin and Satan, they go back, or backslide from the Lord! St. Paul says, "But we are not of them who draw back unto perdition, but of them that believe to the saving of the soul," (Heb. 10. 39), intimating that the soul of a Christian may draw back, that he may fall outwardly into sin, that he may turn from the Lord, as Solomon, David, Peter and many others have done, whose backslidings have been healed and whose immortal spirits are now in glory. Such, though they fell, were not of them that draw back to perdition, but believed to the saving of their souls.

They were not like the disciples that went back and walked no more with the Lord. These, like many professed disciples in our day, follow the Lord for the sake of the loaves and fishes. "It is happened unto them according to the true proverb, The dog is turned to his own vomit again, and the sow that was washed to her wallowing in the mire." But remember, they were dogs and sows before, and they were the same after. Sheep may fall into the ditch and get besmeared with dirt, but they are sheep still, and the mire is not their natural element. So with a spiritual sheep of Christ. It may fall into sin and stain its outer garments, but sin is not its element; it shall hate the garments spotted with the flesh, as David did, when he said, "My wounds stink and are corrupt because of my foolishness." "The just man falleth seven times, and riseth up again"; but "though he fall he shall not be utterly cast down, for the Lord upholdeth him with his hand." Christ gives his sheep "eternal life, and they shall never perish." They "hear his voice" and "follow him"; they believe in him, and shall not come into condemnation. Paul was confident that where God begins the good work of grace in the soul of a poor sinner, "he will perform it until the day of Jesus Christ."

It is our mercy that there is an inseparable connection between the gift of God's grace to a poor sinner and eternal glory. "He will give grace and glory," so that the soul that is made a partaker of divine grace is as certain of heaven as his Lord and Master, who is gone to prepare a place for him. Whatever ups and downs, tossings and tempests, we may have in the wilderness, if we are the Lord's we shall be safe at last. "The ransomed of the Lord shall return, and come to Zion with songs, and everlasting joy upon their heads; they shall obtain joy and gladness, and sorrow and sighing shall flee away."

Beloved, following the example of the Bereans, who searched the Scriptures daily to see whether these things were so; that is, whether the truly regenerated child of God can fall into sin and outwardly backslide from the Lord, let us next turn our attention to the third chapter of the Prophecy of

Jeremiah. "O no," say the advocates against backsliding, "it is
no use turning to prophesies of that sort." Why not? "Because," say they, "such are not spoken to the regenerated
church and people of God, but to the Jews as a nation, or to
the ten revolted tribes, who are exhorted to return to those
laws and statutes which they had left."

But hear the word of the Lord: "Go and proclaim these
words towards the north, and say, Return, thou backsliding
Israel, saith the Lord, and I will not cause mine anger to fall
upon you, for I am merciful, saith the Lord, and I will not keep
anger for ever." Whatever intentions the Lord might have in
this proclamation in reference to the Jews as a nation, it is
more especially designed by the Holy Spirit for God's elect and
regenerate children in every age of the world, who are encouraged to acknowledge their iniquities, their multiplied
transgressions and backslidings against the Lord, and the
promise of mercy shall be fulfilled, "The Lord is merciful to
their unrighteousnesses"; and the poor backslider has to sing
with the church of old, "Though thou wast angry with me,
thine anger is turned away, and thou comfortedst me." O the
amazing love and mercy of the Lord displayed to poor back-
sliders in the following gospel invitation: "Turn, O backsliding
children, for I am married unto you"; not only to the Jews in
a national point of view, but to the remnant amongst them
according to the election of grace, whom he hath betrothed
unto himself in righteousness, lovingkindness, mercy and
faithfulness.   And what an exceeding great and precious
gospel promise we have connected with this invitation: "And
I will take you one of a city and two of a family, and I will bring
you to Zion, and I will give you pastors according to mine own
heart, which shall feed you with knowledge and understanding."

How often are we in this gospel dispensation putting the
Lord in remembrance of these promises, and pleading with
him, not upon old covenant ground, but in Jesus' name, for

the fulfilment of them! Beloved, if these things only have to do with the Jews as a nation, and have nothing to do with the Spirit and Word of the Lord Jesus Christ and his spiritual backsliding children, we are praying for what he has not promised to grant.

That the word spoken by the prophet Jeremiah was attended with the power of the Spirit to the souls of his own spiritual people is evident from the 22nd verse of the third chapter: "Return, ye backsliding children, and I will heal your backslidings. And they said, Behold, we come unto thee, for thou art the Lord our God." And how did they come unto him? We cannot describe it better than in the language of the poor, returning prodigal: "I will arise and go to my father, and will say unto him, Father, I have sinned against heaven and before thee, and am no more worthy to be called thy son; make me as one of thy hired servants." "Behold, we come unto thee," and this is the manner of their coming. "For thou art the Lord our God," not only the Lord our God as the God of nature and of nations, but the Lord our God as the God of grace and salvation. This is evident from the next verse: "Truly in vain is salvation hoped for from the hills and from the multitude of mountains; truly in the Lord our God is the salvation of Israel," who says to his backsliding, returning children, "Your sins and iniquities I will remember no more."

This is Bible language, my friends, and the security we have that poor souls, who have backslidden from the Lord God of their salvation, may and must return with weeping and supplication, being assured they shall meet with a gracious reception like the poor prodigal.

Beloved, following the noble example of the Bereans, who searched the Scriptures whether these things were so, we will come to the 14th chapter of Jeremiah, beginning at the 7th verse, and take special notice of Jeremiah's prayer. The great advocates against backsliding say that Jeremiah did not pour out the prayer under the influence of the Holy Spirit of God.

They are well aware if they admit that, all their foundation is gone for maintaining the system. As I read this prayer, such of you as are praying souls, listen, judge, examine; for we either pray under the immediate operation of the Spirit of God, or in our own spirit, and I will leave you to judge whether the language of the prophet be from the fleshly feelings of his soul or the bedewing influence of the Holy Spirit: "O Lord, though our iniquities testify against us, do thou it for thy names's sake, for our backslidings are many; we have sinned against thee. O the hope of Israel, the Saviour thereof in the time of trouble, why shouldest thou be as a stranger in the land, and as a wayfaring man that turneth aside to tarry for a night? Why shouldest thou be as a man astonied, as a mighty man that cannot save? Yet thou, O Lord, art in the midst of us, and we are called by thy name; leave us not."

Now I dare say some of you will be surprised, and in your feelings stagger, being ready to say, "Is it possible for any man professing godliness to say the prophet did not thus pray under the immediate influence of the Holy Spirit?" I assure you that this is really the state of the case. But let us look again at the first verse of the quotation: "O Lord, though our iniquities testify against us, do thou it for thy name's sake, for our backslidings are many; we have sinned against thee." Was Jeremiah a good and gracious man? Most assuredly, and a prophet of the Lord too. Mark well, my friends, in his prayer he does not say, "your backslidings are many," but "our backslidings are many"; he embodies himself in the confession of sin and humiliation before the Lord. For though he might never have joined the people in outward backslidings, he knew what it was to be a backslider in heart and affections from the Lord, so that he felt the truth of what he was saying, and in his heart, under the influence of the Spirit of God, he intended to include himself when saying, "For *our* backslidings are many," and he entreated the Lord to have mercy upon them though they had sinned against him.

Beloved, judge for yourselves whether there is any foundation from this part of the Word of God for denying that the child of God may revolt, go from his privileges and from his God, falling thereby into sin, and bringing a scandal on the cause of Christ.

The eleventh verse of this chapter is referred to in attempting to prove that the prophet Jeremiah was not moved by the Holy Spirit when he offered up this prayer where the Lord says, "Pray not for this people for their good"; but so far from this quotation proving what is asserted, I conceive it rather goes to prove the contrary, viz., that the prayer we have read, which evidently speaks the feelings and language of a heaven-born and Spirit-taught soul, was for himself and the Lord's spiritual people with whom he had to do. There never was such heartfelt confession of sin and pleading with the Lord as we have in Jeremiah's prayer, without its being of the inditing of the Holy Ghost. If the Lord works a desire in the soul of a poor sinner for any spiritual blessing, that blessing is treasured up for him in Christ Jesus, in whom it hath pleased the Father that all fulness should dwell. He will not say "to the seed of Jacob, Seek ye me in vain."

When the Lord said, "Pray not for this people for their good," it was in the time of the famine. He was not to pray for rain that the famine might cease, nor for deliverance from their enemies that they might not go into captivity; for these things were determined on by the Lord, and he would not revoke his purpose. He does not at all forbid his praying for their repentance and reformation, nor for eternal life and salvation for the remnant of his people yet amongst them, for this would be contrary to his Word and the whole spirit of the gospel. He was only forbidden to pray for external good things.

We will now leave the chapter we have been commenting upon, and turn our attention to the 14th chapter of Hosea, which we are told is addressed to the Jews as a nation. This appears to be the stronghold of our opponents, and if it be removed, the foundation they build upon is gone. Israel as a nation was in many things typical of God's spiritual Israel. When they were in easy circumstances they forgot the Lord, forsook his ordinances, and backslid from him. But when brought into fresh troubles and given into the hands of their enemies, they repented of their sins, returned unto the Lord, and besought him that he would deliver them. In this the spiritual Israelite sees a portrait of himself. What the Lord says by the mouth of the prophet Hosea meets his case, and is designed by the Lord for his comfort: "O Israel, return unto the Lord thy God, for thou hast fallen by thine iniquity. Take with you words and turn to the Lord; say unto him, Take away all iniquity, and receive us graciously; so will we render the calves of our lips. Ashur shall not save us; we will not ride upon horses, neither will we say any more to the work of our hands, Ye are our gods, for in thee the fatherless findeth mercy. I will heal their backsliding" (mark this, my friends; there must have been backslidings or there would have been none to heal;) "I will love them freely, for mine anger is turned away from them." The Lord here says he will heal our backslidings and love us still.

The word of the Lord by the prophet Hosea has been made a blessing to thousands of his family who never were of the Jewish nation, being Israelites spiritually and not naturally, who have backslidden from the Lord, but through grace have been enabled to return unto him saying, "Take away the burden of sin that lies upon my conscience; cleanse me, O Lord, from all iniquity; receive me graciously and love me freely." And have they not met with a gracious reception? O yes; their backslidings have been healed and the Lord has loved them freely, so that they have offered the sacrifice of praise to God continually, giving thanks unto his name.

We have now gone through the doctrinal part of the first branch of our subject, and have proved, from the Word of God and Christian experience, that a real child of God does sometimes draw back, but not to perdition. That a good, gracious man, under the power of indwelling sin, the allurements of the world, and the temptations of Satan, sometimes falls into outward sin, and thus backslides in heart as well as conduct from the Lord.

Beloved, you well remember what I said at the commencement of this discourse, viz. that it was not persons or Christian communities I stood opposed to, as such, but to principles and practices which are not according to the Word of God. As every tree is known by its fruit, I will show you what sort of fruit this non-backsliding principle has produced; and I will not go to London, where it has caused much strife and confusion, but will content myself by looking a little nearer home, in Manchester for instance, and we will try the fruits which this doctrine has produced. Some years ago a sermon was preached and published, the object of which was to prove that a good man cannot backslide. Your venerable pastor saw that sermon, read it carefully over, and was much grieved in his heart to see such error fall either from the pulpit or the press. He was afterwards entreated to let the author of that sermon* occupy his pulpit during his absence in London, but he resolutely refused, saying, "No such man shall ever fill my pulpit." Some time afterwards, your late pastor and the author of that sermon met together in London. Whilst there, your esteemed minister proved, from the Word of God and Christian experience, that the principle laid down in that sermon was false, and with such demonstration that its author acknowledged his error, and said, "I am sorry I ever published it." On the strength of that acknowledgment and upon the ground of that pernicious doctrine being relinquished, your pastor gave way and allowed the author to preach for him. After he had done so, to the surprise and grief of many, he revived the old error, and published the same erroneous

* James Wells (1803-1872), minister of the Surrey Tabernacle, London.

doctrine as boldly and unflinchingly as ever. Mr. Gadsby, as an honest God-fearing man, could not sanction such glaring inconsistency of conduct, and said that no such man should ever again occupy his pulpit.

Now, my dear friends, your minister was either right or wrong in this determination. I solemnly contend that he was right. "If there come any unto you and bring not this doctrine, receive him not into your houses; neither bid him God-speed, for he that biddeth him God-speed is partaker of his evil deeds." Paul "gave no place to error, no not for an hour, that the truth of the Gospel might continue." What was the result of your minister and deacons refusing him the pulpit, and the majority of God's people who came here to worship justifying them in so doing? The very Sabbath but one after your pastor had left for his annual visit to London, several members of the church and congregation who had been laying their heads together in the dark (men love darkness rather then light when their deeds are evil), unknown to your officers and the church, arranged their plans and invited another minister to another chapel in the town which they had hired for the occasion. They were so carried away with the errors propagated, and with the talents and ablity of its author, that they determined to make a split, and soon carried this determination into effect.

Now, I say the division that took place in this church the summer before your late pastor died was caused by the doctrine alluded to, its author and advocate. Pause, my friends, while you think of this division. Strife and contention is the fruit of error, and especially of that I am contending against: "A tree is known by its fruit."

But they say, "Our object is not contention, but peace." If this be so, let us in the first place have truth and sound gospel, and peace will follow. Let the error be confessed and rooted out. Let this unscriptural conduct, in causing division and the many hard and unbecoming speeches used against your late pastor, be acknowledged with godly sorrow, and my heart is open to receive them and take them by the hand; *but never till then.*

I met your revered pastor in London just after this crisis. I had been down to Brighton, and on returning I called upon a friend in London with whom your minister was stopping. "Friend Kershaw," said he, "are you aware there is a complete division in the church at Manchester?" I told him I was not. "It is but too true," he replied, "and poor Mr. Gadsby knew nothing of it till he reached Leicester. You will find him at such a place, in great trouble." I went, and never shall I forget the sighs and groans I heard him utter as he took up the lamentation: "I have nourished and brought up children, and they have rebelled against me." Did not your pastor say at the last annual school meeting, which he attended only twenty-six days before his death, alluding to these principles and practices in the people that had left you, "I do not know what they mean, unless it be to break the old fellow's heart"? Ah, my dear friends, these things brought down his grey hairs with sorrow to the grave. I hear a voice from heaven, and it is the voice of the Lord; "Touch not mine anointed, and do my prophets no harm." Your late pastor was an injured man, greatly touched in his feelings, hurt in his very soul, and much abused in his character; though no man I ever knew was more exemplary in his conduct and conversation, both in his family, in the church of God, and in the world.

Now let us try this conduct by the Word of God as the Bereans did, searching the Scriptures. If our principles be pure, such will be our practice and will stand the test of God's Word. Paul, writing to the Thessalonians, says, "And we beseech you, brethren, to know them which labour among you, and are over you in the Lord and admonish you, and to esteem them very highly in love for their work's sake. And be at peace among yourselves." And, "Obey them that rule over you." Mark well, beloved, the next clause: "And submit yourselves, for they watch for your souls as they that must give account, that they may do it with joy and not with grief, for that is unprofitable for you" (Heb. 13. 17). The Lord will chastise his own children who are guilty of such conduct. Some of them have already had the rod in measure, and it is surely meet they should: "With such measure as ye mete, it shall be measured to you again; yea, pressed down, running over."

I would, if possible, go to the foundation of the matter, and stand valiant for the truth in all its parts and branches, fearing no consequences, for these are the words of truth and soberness, faithful sayings, and therefore worthy of all acceptation. I would again, therefore, affirm that this non-backsliding system, and no other, along with its advocate and propounder, caused that unhappy division here; and I am confident, from undeniable proof, that the advocate for this doctrine, if he cannot get his ambitious desires and inclinations gratified, will not hesitate going to any place to effect a division.

Mr. Gadsby and myself were in the habit of preaching occasionally in Bradford for more than twenty years. The effect of our labours was seen in the formation of a church there some few years since, and a chapel has been built. The author of the system I am contending against went there some time ago, and such was the spirit he manifested that they had no inclination to have him again. However, without waiting for an invitation, he wrote to let them know that he intended coming again at such a time, and for two nights; and also that he purposed going to Leeds. He requested the Bradford friends to write to him immediately and send the name of someone in Leeds to whom he could send word as to his intentions, inasmuch as the times and places where he was going to preach must be announced upon the cover of the *Gospel Ambassador*. The officers of the church at Bradford consulted together what was best to be done in this business.

They knew that he had been the means of greatly embittering their old friend Mr. Gadsby's last days, and the cause of much strife and contention amongst their Manchester friends. In the end, therefore, they concluded to write and inform him that they declined accepting his offered services. Upon receiving this, he immediately returned a long letter, bitterly censuring and condemning their conduct in refusing his ministry. In it he expressed his determination to go down to Bradford and see about forming another church. He accordingly came. A room was got for him, and he did all in his power to divide the people, promising that if they would hire a room he would send them supplies from London.

I do not at this time wish to notice the foul and unjust attack he made upon me in his letter to my Bradford friends, but if you will look at the second edition of your late pastor's Memoir, you will find the letter, printed from its author's own handwriting. Yorkshiremen have the reputation of being rather long-headed. One of them called upon me, and stated all the circumstances. He said, "They wanted sadly to drag me into it, but I sat down and counted the cost. I thought to myself, 'If the supplies are to come from London, where is the money to come from to pay for their journey, lodging, wages, etc.?' and besides," said he, "some of those the most forward in this business are, in their moral character, such as I can have nothing to do with."

In all congregations there are individuals to be found whose conduct has been such as to cause the church of God to execute the discipline of the Lord's house upon them. These too frequently are exceedingly disaffected towards their minister and the officers in the church and, like the drowning man, ever ready to catch at a straw. It is well known amongst us in the north that such characters are they who have drunk most deeply of the errors I am exposing, and are great followers and admirers of the individual who advocates those pernicious principles.

In following the example of the Bereans, we find it recorded in the Scriptures that we are to "mark them which cause divisions and offences contrary to the doctrine which ye have learned, and avoid them, for they are such as serve not our Lord Jesus Christ, but their own belly, and by good words and fair speeches, deceive the hearts of the simple." This is the fruit, my friends; but is it good fruit produced by the influence and Spirit of the Lord? I think not: "For God is not the author of such confusion" in the churches of his saints, "but of peace."

II. We hasten to the second part of our subject; namely, *That the Lord does not chastise his children for sin.* Now I have said in the former part of this discourse that there is no principle promulgated, be it ever so contrary to the scope of God's Word, but its advocates find some ground upon which they profess to base it. Thus they who advocate the doctrine of non-chastisement for sin tell us that the Lord has no rod to chastise them with; all the sins and iniquities of his people having been laid upon Christ, who has put all our sins away by the sacrifice of himself, made an end of them, so that when they are sought for they cannot be found; and that as Christ has endured the curse of the law due to our sins, having been made a curse for us and having drunk up even the very dregs of penal wrath, we, therefore, stand complete and accepted in him, all our scarlet and crimson sins washed away in his blood, and our souls clothed in his perfect robe of righteousness.

Then it may be asked, "Are you going to agree with the advocates of non-chastisement?" By no means. I shall introduce my views upon this subject by drawing your attention to what is said in the Word of God respecting it; and I cannot do this better than by naming what took place many years ago. At that time I went to supply a destitute people in Yorkshire. I got there on the Saturday night, and several of the friends came to see me at the deacon's house, with whom

I was then staying. I soon found that they had been debating amongst themselves, and had become a little cross one with another. A minister had been supplying for them, who preached from Numbers 23. 21: "He hath not beheld iniquity in Jacob, neither hath he seen perverseness in Israel; the Lord his God is with him, and the shout of a king is among them." From their conversation, I found the minister had preached well, setting forth the union between Christ and his people, proving from the Word of God that as the church stood in Christ, God could not see any sin in her, but that she was all fair, and without spot or blemish. Some of the friends contended that the Lord did see sin in his people, and that he chastised them for it too. Thus the argument was renewed in my presence.

At length my opinion was appealed to. I said, "Both parties are right, though there is an apparent contradiction. As the church stands in Christ before a holy, just and righteous God in his law, she stands as free from sin as Christ, and as white as snow, without spot, wrinkle or stain of sin; the church being complete and accepted in the Beloved. But mark well, there is another relationship that we stand in to our covenant God and Father. We are his adopted children, and he hath sent forth the Spirit of his Son into our hearts, saying, Abba, Father. As our heavenly Father, he hath given his children many precepts which it is both our duty and privilege to obey, from a principle of love to him for the great things he hath done for our souls. He watches over us in love and with an observing eye, and is well-pleased with our obedience to his commands, precepts and exhortations, and he is displeased with our disobedience, and assuredly will chastise us for it."

Beloved, like the Bereans, let us "search the Scriptures to see whether these things be so." The Lord is well-pleased with the obedience of his children, which springs from a principle of love to him, and is done with a single eye to his honour and glory; and this is called the obedience of faith, for "without faith it is impossible to please God." Before Enoch was translated, he had this testimony that he pleased God. The Lord works in his people by his Spirit "that which is well pleasing in his sight." Through Jesus Christ we are exhorted to "walk worthy of the Lord unto all pleasing, being fruitful in every good word and work," and, "to do good and to communicate to forget not, for with such sacrifices God is well pleased." "For God is not unrighteous to forget your work of faith and labour of love, which ye have showed toward his name, in that ye have ministered to the saints, and do minister." But, beloved, "when we have," as the Master tells us, "done all," we see so much sin and weakness in what we do that we are heartily willing to count ourselves "unprofitable servants," and say we have done only that which it was our duty to do; nay, not so much. And we have to sing this God-honouring, Christ-exalting, and soul-comforting song:

"The best obedience of my hands
Dares not appear before thy throne;
But faith can answer thy demands,
By pleading what my Lord has done."

Let us take a view of the other side of the question. Is the Lord well-pleased with the disobedience of his children, and does he not chastise for it? Let us, as in the former part of our subject, bring forward our witnesses from the Scriptures, "that," as St. Paul says, "every word may be established."

David was a man of God, born and taught of him, but in an unguarded hour, through the power and under the temptations of Satan, he fell awfully and grievously into sin, when he committed adultery with Bathsheba, the wife of Uriah the Hittite and, to cover his sin, gave orders unto Joab to set him in the front of the battle, that he might be slain with the sword of the children of Ammon. The awful and foul fall of David is left upon record, not to encourage us to sin that grace may abound, but rather as a beacon on a hill to deter us from lusting after evil things as he did. The eyes of the Lord,

as a Father, however, were upon his child David in this matter. Though he loved him as one of his people in Christ Jesus
his covenant Head, he did not love his sin; as it is written, "But
the thing that David did displeased the Lord." As a Father, he
was displeased with the unbecoming conduct of his son. He
therefore sent Nathan the prophet to him. But you shall have
David's own words. Turn your attention to the 89th Psalm:
"His seed also will I make to endure for ever, and his throne as
the days of heaven. If his children forsake my law and walk
not in my judgments, if they break my statutes and keep not
my commandments, then will I visit their transgressions with
the rod, and their iniquity with stripes." He will do it in
fatherly love and mercy. And (for ever blessed be his holy
name!) it is a mercy that he does not cast his backsliding
children off. But he says, "Nevertheless, my lovingkindness
will I not utterly take from him, nor suffer my faithfulness to
fail; my covenant will I not break, nor alter the thing that is
gone out of my lips. Once have I sworn by my holiness that
I will not lie unto David."

"Ah!" say the advocates of non-chastisement, "mark well,
it is said, 'My lovingkindness will I not utterly take from him,'
that is from Christ." True, but as the Father hath loved
Christ, even so hath he loved his people in Christ, and
notwithstanding our many inward and outward backslidings,
his mercy will he not take away, neither will he suffer his
faithfulness to fail, nor break his covenant, nor alter the Word
that is gone out of his mouth. My friends, let men say what
they will, this is the Word of the Lord.

The Lord, in chastening his people, frequently makes use
of their own froward and rebellious conduct, so that they are
beaten, in fact, with their own rod. And be assured no stripes
smart so much as those when we are beaten by our own sinful
ways. Now that such is the case appears evident from what
the Lord says in Jeremiah 2. 19: "Thine own wickedness shall
correct thee, and thy backslidings shall reprove thee. Know,

therefore, and see that it is an evil thing and bitter that thou hast forsaken the Lord thy God, and that my fear is not in thee." That is, the fear of the Lord is not in exercise in the souls of his people when they fall into sin, for "it is to hate evil," and "is a fountain of life, to depart from the snares of death."

Brethren, if we sow to the flesh we must of the flesh reap corruption, as we shall see if we go back to the case of David, and hear Nathan, by way of parable, introduce the melancholy errand on which the Lord had sent him. When he speaks of the rich man who had spared his own flocks and taken the poor man's ewe lamb, David exclaims, "As the Lord liveth, the man that has done this thing shall surely die, and he shall restore the lamb fourfold, because he did this thing, and because he had no pity." Nathan, as the Lord's servant, corrected him with his own rod when he said unto him, "Thou art the man. Thus saith the Lord God of Israel, I anointed thee king over Israel, and delivered thee out of the hand of Saul. Wherefore hast thou despised the commandment of the Lord to do evil in his sight? Thou hast killed Uriah the Hittite with the sword, and hast taken his wife to be thy wife. Now, therefore, the sword shall never depart from thine house." The reproof given by Nathan entered with power into David's conscience. He cried out, in the bitterness of his soul, "I acknowledge my transgression, and my sin is ever before me. Against thee, thee only, have I sinned, and done this evil in thy sight, that thou mightest be clear when thou judgest." Nathan saw that his heart was broken with godly sorrow for sin, and to comfort the mourner he said unto him, "The Lord hath put away thy sin; thou shalt not die." David, feeling its guilt and burden, wanted to feel it removed from his conscience, and cried out, "Deliver me from bloodguiltiness, O God, thou God of my salvation." Though the Lord forgave David, David never forgave himself. He knew that what he had done was dishonouring to his Lord and Master, grieving

to the brethren, and that he had given great occasion to the
enemies to blaspheme.

The Lord made good the word spoken by his servant
Nathan. Evil was continually rising up in his own family.
Amnon casts a lustful eye upon his sister Tamar. Absalom,
enraged at the conduct of Amnon, is determined to be re-
venged, and slays him. Absalom rises in rebellion against his
own father and, guided by Ahithophel, David's most intimate
friend and counsellor, steals away the hearts of the people, so
that David had to flee for his life. O the sorrows, sighs and
groans that his poor soul had to pass through from the time of
his fall to the day of his death. But though the Lord visited his
transgressions with his fatherly rod, he did not take away his
lovingkindness from him, nor suffer his faithfulness to fail, but
was his God and guide even unto death. In his last moments
he was enabled to say, by precious faith, "Although my house
be not so with God, yet he hath made with me an everlasting
covenant, ordered in all things and sure, for this is all my
salvation and all my desire, although he make it not to grow."

Now, my dear friends, does not the case of David prove to
a demonstration the falsity of the doctrine that the Lord does
not chastise his people for sin? The Lord says, "As many as I
love I rebuke and chasten." "Behold, happy is the man whom
God correcteth; therefore despise not thou the chastening of
the Lord."

> "Bastards may escape the rod,
> Sunk in earthly, vain delight,
> But the true-born child of God
> Must not, would not, if he might."

To prove that the Lord does chastise his people for sin, we
will call our second witness, namely, Ephraim, for as with him,
so with every child of God, either in a greater or lesser degree
(Jer. 31. 18, 19): "I have surely heard Ephraim bemoaning
himself thus, Thou hast chastised me, and I was chastised."
When yoked up in the old weather-beaten path of tribulation,

he had been "as a bullock unaccustomed to the yoke," kicking and plunging, murmuring and repining, till he was sick of his rebellion, and then he cries out, "Turn thou me and I shall be turned, for thou art the Lord my God." Ephraim could not turn his own captivity, so he cries to the Lord to turn him. "Surely after that I was turned, I repented, and after that I was instructed, I smote upon my thigh; I was ashamed, yea, even confounded, because I did bear the reproach of my youth." This is the account Ephraim gives of himself, and of the dealings of the Lord with him. In the next place the Lord speaks concerning his froward child, and says, "Is Ephraim my dear son? is he a pleasant child? for since I spake against him I do earnestly remember him still: therefore my bowels are troubled for him; I will surely have mercy upon him, saith the Lord." Hence true it is that

> "Oft he chastised, but ne'er forsook
> The people that he chose!"

Beloved, let us next call in the testimony of the great Apostle of the Gentiles, as recorded in Heb. 12. 5-11. He says, "And ye have forgotten the exhortation which speaketh unto you as unto children, My son, despise not thou the chastening of the Lord, nor faint when thou art rebuked of him, for whom the Lord loveth he chasteneth, and scourgeth every son whom he receiveth. If ye endure chastening, God dealeth with you as with sons, for what son is he whom the father chasteneth not ? But if ye be without chastisement, whereof all are partakers, then are ye bastards, and not sons. Furthermore we have had fathers of our flesh which corrected us, and we gave them reverence: shall we not much rather be in subjection unto the Father of spirits, and live? For they verily for a few days chastened us after their own pleasure, but he for our profit, that we might be partakers of his holiness. Now, no chastening for the present seemeth to be joyous, but grievous; nevertheless afterward it yieldeth the peaceable fruit of righteousness unto them which are exercised thereby."

How clear it is from Paul's testimony that our heavenly Father, who hath made known unto us his mind and will concerning us, has given us "line upon line, and precept upon precept," to walk by; that he watches over us in love when we transgress his commandments; and in mercy to our souls, and for our profit, chastises us for our sins and disobedience, that we may reverence and fear him, "and be in subjection unto the Father of spirits, and live"! Thus he causes us to pass under his fatherly rod, that he may bring us into the bond of the covenant. Then it is that we can say with the prophet Micah, "Rejoice not against me, O mine enemy: when I fall, I shall arise; when I sit in darkness, the Lord shall be a light unto me. I will bear the indignation of the Lord" (not penal indignation as of an angry judge, but fatherly chastisement) "because I have sinned against him, until he plead my cause, and execute judgment for me: he will bring me forth to the light, and I shall behold his righteousness."

Thus we see that the doctrine of non-chastisement is not according to the Scriptures and the experience of the children of God. As such we reject it, and warn every man that he receive not such testimony.

So much for doctrine. We now come to the practical part of our subject: "The tree is known by its fruit." Our Lord and Master tells us that "every good tree bringeth forth good fruit, but a corrupt tree bringeth forth evil fruit." We have already proved that the doctrine of non-backsliding is a corrupt tree, and has brought forth evil fruit. Those who hold that the Lord does not chastise for sin profess to believe that they are free and clear from all sin, as they stand united to Christ, and the sword of divine justice will pass them by; that there is no fatherly rod of correction to come upon them, even if they fall into sin, or indulge themselves in the lusts of the flesh and gratify their sinful inclinations. O my dear friends, this is an awful doctrine. It is an open door for a life of licentiousness. The tree is bad, and the fruit evil. I hope none who stand

connected with this church maintain such pernicious principles. Your late pastor set his face like a flint against them. I
have for forty years been watching the conduct and conversation of persons who tell us that they are all safe and secure
in Christ, and have no doubts nor fears of their interest in
him. There being no chastisement for sin, they have indulged
themselves in it, so that I have had to take and preach from
the lamentation of Paul, recorded in Phil. 3. 17-19: "Brethren,
be followers together of me, and mark them which walk so as
ye have us for an ensample. For many walk, of whom I have
told you often, and now tell you even weeping, that they are
the enemies of the cross of Christ; whose end is destruction,
whose God is their belly, and whose glory is in their shame,
who mind earthly things."

My dear friends, the dutiful child, that loves and reveres
his parent, is afraid of offending him, or bringing upon himself
a father's frown and the rod of correction. So with those that
love and fear the Lord. It is their delight to honour and obey
their heavenly Father. Their prayer is, "O Lord forbid that I
should sin against thee, lest thou in a little fatherly wrath hide
thy face from me, and bring me under thy chastising hand."
My heart's desire to the great Head of the church for you is
that he would keep you from all evil, with your eye single to
his honour and glory in all that you do and say, walking
together in the fear of the Lord, that in the comfort of the
Holy Ghost you may be multiplied; "that you show forth the
praises of him who hath called you out of darkness into his
marvellous light"; "that you may be as a city set on a hill that
cannot be hid." The Lord grant it, for his name and mercy's
sake.

III. We now come to the third subject for examination,
viz.: That sin in the thought of the heart is as great an offence
to God as sin in the outward action. God forbid that I
should, in any word that may fall from my lips, say what is
calculated to palliate sin, or make it appear otherwise than an

offence against God, whether in our hearts, thoughts, words or actions. But it is sin in the heart when compared with outward actions that we have now to take into consideration.

Where is the man who fears God, and knows the plague of his own heart and the spirituality of the law, who does not know also that God takes cognizance of evil thoughts as well as evil actions, being an observer of the thoughts and intents of the heart, and a weigher of the actions of the children of men? This is clear from what our Lord says in his sermon on the mount: "Ye have heard that it was said by them of old time, Thou shalt not commit adultery; but I say unto you, that whosoever looketh on a woman to lust after her hath committed adultery with her already in his heart." All heaven-born and Spirit-taught souls know the spirituality of the law, and their own carnality, to the grief and sorrow of their hearts, causing many bitter sighs and groans in the inmost soul that none know anything of but God and themselves. I scruple not to say that David had committed adultery in his heart many times before he fell into it outwardly. But while he is struggling and fighting against it within, and wearying because of it, it was not so offensive to the Lord as when he fell into the outward act. No, no; the prophet is not sent to fasten conviction upon his conscience, and correct him for the inward thought; but when the deed is done, the name of the Lord and his cause dishonoured, the minds of the brethren wounded, and the mouths of enemies opened, saying, "Ah! ah! so would we have it," there is aggravation of the guilt. This must surely be more displeasing in the eye of the Lord than when it was only in the heart. The Lord keep and preserve us from outward sin, and from the belief that if we cannot keep out wicked thoughts we might as well indulge in outward actions, from the idea that it would not be more displeasing to the Lord. O my dear friends, this is a dangerous doctrine, leading to licentiousness both in heart and conduct. Dear Lord, preserve us from such errors.

I cannot forget what a sick man said to me on this subject when on a dying bed. He told me that he once had an argument with a deacon of the church of which he stood a member, who believed and contended that sin in the thought of the heart was as offensive to the Lord as sin in outward actions. "I told him," said he, "that I could not believe such a doctrine. For instance, I might go into a shop that was filled with various articles for the purpose of buying something I might stand in need of. While there I might feel a wicked thought come across my mind, tempting me to take that and the other article, and appropriate them to my own use. Now I hate such wicked thoughts, and in my mind fight against them, and come out of the shop without putting them into practice, bringing with me nothing but what I have honestly and honourably paid for. I feel ashamed of myself before the Lord for having had such wicked thoughts, but thankful I have been enabled to resist them, thus coming out clear of theft in the outward act. But," continued the dying man, "suppose I had taken something I had not paid for, and no one had known but God and my own conscience, I know that my case would have been a great deal worse, and I am confident that I should have felt a much greater burden on my conscience than if I had only been tempted to steal." Now, my friends, this is bringing the question to a practical bearing. If the man had stolen something, he would have had a conscience burning within him a thousand times hotter than if he had only thought of the theft in his mind, and had struggled against it and overcome it. The advocate for the doctrine we are contending against replied to my dying friend, in a subtle, sneering manner, quite peculiar to persons who hold these pernicious principles, "I admit it would have been worse for your outward character and reputation had you stolen something, and been detected, and punished by the law of the land." The dying man replied, "If there had been no disgrace, there would have been a stab in my heart and a wound in my conscience before the Lord when on my knees that would have driven me from his presence until restitution had been made." "If I regard iniquity in my heart, the Lord will not hear me."

Do not these things prove, my friends, the fallacy and unsoundness of such doctrine? To those who fear the Lord, the indwelling of sin we are daily struggling with and fighting against is quite enough, without having the outward acts to wound and grieve us. "For a wounded spirit who can bear?" Dear Lord, may the "weapons of our warfare not be carnal, but mighty through God to the pulling down of the strongholds" of sin and of Satan, bringing into captivity every foolish, sinful, vain "thought to the obedience of Christ."

Now, my dear friends, we have gone through the things first laid down: namely, that a child of God cannot backslide, that the Lord does not chastise his children for sin, and that sin in the thought of the heart is as offensive to God as sin in the outward action.

I am asked, "Who believes these things? We are told in the public press there are very few who are tainted with them." I am very glad to hear it, for the time was when these things were much talked of, and believed too, by many.

It is well known that I travel and preach a great deal, and converse with many that know and fear the Lord. I must, therefore, necessarily hear much of what is going on. The other day a friend said to me, "I went to Manchester one Sunday, and fell into conversation with persons who maintain that a child of God cannot backslide, and I said, 'Mr. Gadsby did not preach such doctrines; neither does Kershaw of Rochdale, nor M'Kenzie of Preston, believe and preach them.' 'Gadsby, Kershaw, M'Kenzie! what are they?' was the answer; 'they are nobody when compared with these excellent things and their advocates.'" This is not a solitary case. I could bring forward many. I shall be very glad when such unhallowed principles are got rid of. They have been a source of strife and contention wherever they have been promulgated.

But what I pray for is that God will so humble those who favour such principles that they may renounce them, and exhibit a conduct and conversation becoming the precepts and exhortations of the gospel. I shall then be ready to receive them into my heart and affections, and take them by the hand. I am charged with aiming to strike deadly blows at a certain interest in this town. God forbid that I should either in word or deed strike a blow at the cause of God and truth wherever it be, for there is nothing upon earth that lies so near my heart. But glad shall I be if the Lord enables me so to strike with the hammer of his Word that I may give a fatal blow to these unhallowed doctrines (Jer. 23. 29).

It would rejoice my heart to see other Baptist churches planted in this large and populous town, with spiritual pastors placed over them, preaching the gospel of Christ in love; these pastors walking together in the unity of the Spirit and the bond of peace, like your old minister and the late William Nunn, though of different denominations, so that when I come to Manchester I could preach in all their pulpits. But before this can be, we must have things upon a proper and scriptural basis. I speak from no bad feeling against individuals, but from a regard to the truth and Word of God.

These, friends, are my sentiments and views concerning the errors I have been opposing. I thank the Lord for having put such principles and feelings as I have declared into my heart, and in them I hope to live and die, and to stand by them in the name and fear of the Lord God of Israel. Amen and amen.

13. SPIRITUAL BLESSINGS IN CHRIST

Preached at Zoar Chapel, Great Alie Street, London, on April 18th, 1848.

Text: *"Blessed be the God and Father of our Lord Jesus Christ, who hath blessed us with all spiritual blessings in heavenly places in Christ" (Ephesians 1. 3).*

Beloved, many of you will recollect that we had these words under consideration last Thursday evening. We endeavoured to prove, in the *first* place, from the Word of God and Christian experience, that we shall never find anything in ourselves but sin and weakness, unworthiness and unprofitableness; and *secondly*, that as all the fulness of grace and salvation is treasured up in the Lord Jesus Christ, there must be corresponding weakness, emptiness and unprofitableness felt in us. But when it pleases the Lord, in the riches of his grace, to bless the soul with an enjoyment of himself and his precious truth, and with the comforts and consolations of his salvation, the result is, as in our text, that poor soul in return will bless, praise and magnify the God of his salvation.

"Blessed be the God and Father of our Lord Jesus Christ, who hath blessed us with all spiritual blessings in heavenly places in Christ." God hath blessed his people from the beginning with every needful new covenant blessing, treasured up in Christ Jesus their covenant Head. There is not a single blessing of grace and salvation which is not secured and deposited in him. Ah, my friends, it is well for us they are treasured up in Christ Jesus, because in him they are safe and secure. The Holy Spirit, in his appointed time, convinces the heart of the poor sinner of the want of these spiritual blessings; he gives him deeply to feel his need, and puts a cry in his heart after them. The Lord says, "I will yet for this be enquired of by the house of Israel, to do it for them." The poor sinner will never come to Christ, bow down before him and seek the Lord's blessing, until he is brought into poverty, destitution and indigent circumstances. He will never flee to Christ for refuge until every other resource fails him, and he is at his wits' end and knows not what to do. But, blessed be his name, Christ is a refuge for the helpless and the destitute.

We have these things blessedly set forth and traced out in the history of Joseph. He was a type of Christ. "Let the blessing come upon the head of Joseph, and upon the top of the head of him who was separated from his brethren." The spiritual Joseph is to be seen in it. When was it, my friends, that Joseph's brethren went to him, and made application for food? Not till they were in famine, when want and starvation stared them in the face. But why did they go to Joseph? Because all the supplies in Egypt were treasured up by him, and there was no getting them but through an application to Joseph. And when the sons of Jacob came to Joseph, they entered into his presence just like the poor sinner does into the presence of Jesus – they fell down before him. But Joseph knew his brethren; he remembered his dreams, and thought of the time when in the simplicity of his heart he told them how he dreamt they were all binding sheaves in the field, and how his sheaf arose and stood uppermost, while all the sheaves of his brethren fell down before him; and in consequence of revealing this dream to them, how they had envied him and conspired together to take away his life. But now he sees the fulfilment of it. In the time of their destitution and famine they come to him and fall down at his feet, entreating him to supply them with provision. And just so it is with the convinced sinner. He comes in his poor and needy circumstances and falls down before the Lord Jesus Christ, our spiritual Joseph. Now Joseph knew his brethren and felt for them; they were nigh his heart; and though he appeared to speak roughly at first, yet he could not long refrain from acknowledging them. He quickly turns aside to weep, for his bowels of compassion were moved towards them.

But, however strong the feeling of love and affection might have been that Joseph had towards his brethren, it was not one ten thousandth part so strong as Christ, our spiritual Joseph, has towards his people. Bless his precious name, he has made provision for them and treasured it up in himself. He brings the poor soul to his blessed feet, to fall down and supplicate for mercy. It is the hungry that are filled with good things, while the rich are sent empty away. And when the sinner is brought to feel his spiritual destitution, wretchedness, guilt and misery; when he finds that the world cannot afford him any help, and that he cannot help himself; when all creature refuge fails him; when all the streams of earthly comfort dry up, and they are proved to be broken cisterns that can hold no water, then it is that he comes and falls prostrate before the Lord at his blessed feet. The Lord draws him to himself, and says, "All that the Father giveth me shall come to me; and him that cometh" – in a destitute, lost, ruined and undone condition – "I will in no wise cast out."

But I must pause a moment or two to notice the characters here expressed. There are some it appears who will be "cast out." Who are they then that will be "cast out"? Those who come with a price in their hand; those who are rich and highminded; those who fancy they have some worth or worthiness, and use it as a plea with the Lord why they should have the blessing – all these he will cast out and send empty away. But those who come to him guilty, weak, helpless, ignorant, naked and filthy, without money and without price (bless his name for ever!) he will never cast them out. He knows your destitution, want and every spiritual blessing you stand in need of; and the supply is all treasured up in himself, that you may receive grace for grace. It is for such as you I desire tonight so to speak that the Word may be made a blessing to your never-dying souls.

"Blessed be the God and Father of our Lord Jesus Christ, who hath blessed us with all spiritual blessings in heavenly places in Christ."

I.   We have already spoken of the spiritual blessing of a *finished and complete salvation* by the Lord Jesus Christ, and that the enjoyment of it is inseparably connected with faith and repentance. Salvation is wholly and entirely of the Lord. His people are saved in him with an everlasting salvation. Faith and repentance are spiritual blessings communicated by the Lord to the heirs of promise, his elect people, and are wrought by the Holy Ghost in their hearts as fruits and effects of the salvation of the dear Redeemer.

II.   But to proceed a little further into this blessed subject, we observe, in the *second* place, in the Lord Jesus Christ we have the spiritual blessing of a *justifying righteousness.* We can never stand justified before a holy God in his righteous law on the ground of works, or of any worth or worthiness done by us. I do not know of a greater impossibility or absurdity than to suppose that justification before God can be obtained by anything the sinner can do, or by anything he may have done, or ever expects to do, either in whole or in part. The law demands purity and perfection, and the poor sinner is all impurity and imperfection; all therefore that the law can do is to curse and condemn the transgressor.

But let us hear what Paul says upon this subject: "Now we know that what things soever the law saith, it saith to them who are under the law; that every mouth may be stopped, and all the world may become guilty before God." God will stop the mouth of every elect vessel of mercy in this world. But those who are left in sin, and have not their mouth stopped here, will have it stopped at the judgment of the great day. God's elect are brought in guilty and condemned in their souls before God in a righteous law. They are made to feel what Paul says in the next verse: "Therefore by the deeds of the law there shall no flesh be justified in his sight; for by the law is the knowledge of sin." My friends, do we feel this? Has the Lord taught us this truth in our own souls? If so, we want the blessing of a free grace justification, which is only to be had in the Lord Jesus Christ. We shall find it nowhere else, I am sure. Hence the apostle says, "All have sinned, and come short of the glory of God."

Now friends, look where the blessing is: "Being justified freely by his grace through the redemption that is in Christ Jesus." Our justification by grace and acceptance with God is only to be found where it is treasured up – in Christ. You cannot find it in yourselves. It hath pleased the Father that in the Lord Jesus Christ all fulness should dwell for every poor, sensible soul who is brought by God the Spirit to confess his guilt and misery, feel his need, and have earnest desires, hungerings and thirstings after Christ's justifying right- eousness. The Lord brings his people to know that in his solemn presence they are altogether as an unclean thing, and that all their doings and righteousness are as filthy rags. They find that when they would do good evil is present with them; that the good they would they do not, while the evil they would not that they do. So that the poor soul who is brought more and more to feel his own evils, and to see that he has nothing in self to glory in, but that he is as an unclean thing before the Lord, will be led by the Holy Spirit to discover that his justification and acceptance is treasured up in a precious Christ; and he will burst out in the language of the church of old, "Surely shall one say, in the Lord have I righteousness and strength"; and again, "In the Lord shall all the seed of Israel be justified and shall glory." Our justification, our ac- ceptance and our glory before a holy God is in the Lord Jesus Christ. Boasting is excluded on every side. Hence the apostle says, "To declare at this time his righteousness: that he might be just, and the justifier of him which believeth in Jesus. Where is boasting then? It is excluded. By what law? of works? Nay, but by the law of faith."

This is the way, my friends, whereby we are considered just and accepted in Jesus Christ. "Be it known unto you, therefore, men and brethren, that through this Man is preached unto you the forgiveness of sins; and by him all that believe are justified from all things, from which ye could not be justified by the law of Moses." The righteousness of Christ is imputed to the poor sinner. "Blessed is the man unto whom the Lord imputeth not iniquity." The poor sinner's unrighteousness is washed away in the atoning blood of the Lamb; he is constituted righteous in the Lord Jesus Christ. Therefore, my friends, as we stand on the Rock of Ages, sin is done away; we are clad in the Redeemer's righteousness, and stand complete and accepted in the sight of Jehovah. But it is in Christ, my friends. And blessed be God that it is there.

But the children of God want not merely to know the doctrine of justification and acceptance in Christ; they want to have a blessed revelation of their interest in it powerfully made known to their heart and conscience by the Holy Spirit. Now the enjoyment of this is by faith; hence the apostle says, "Being justified by faith, we have peace with God through our Lord Jesus Christ." "The just shall live by faith." But faith is the gift of God. May the Lord enable thee, poor soul, to look from thyself to a precious Christ, to see that his perfect obedience is thine. The Lord enable thee to look to the atonement of Christ on the cross, whereby thy sins are done away. The Lord enable thee, poor sinner, to look to Jesus, and see the curse removed, sin atoned for, righteousness brought in, heaven opened, death abolished, and life and immortality brought to light. Wherever the blessed Spirit has begun the work of grace in the heart of a poor sinner, he will land that precious soul in immortal bliss and blessedness at last. O may he therefore now enable thee, poor soul, to look to and see the ability of Christ, to join in the language of the poet, and sing,

"A feeble saint shall win the day,
Though death and hell obstruct the way."

But it is in Christ, my friends; it is in Christ. "Blessed be the God and Father of our Lord Jesus Christ, who hath blessed us with all spiritual blessings in heavenly places in Christ."

III. But again; we observe, *thirdly,* there is the spiritual blessing of *redemption* – redemption from sin, iniquity and the curse of the law. But it is only to be found in Christ. Jesus Christ, the incarnate God, is the great Redeemer of his church and people. "Our Redeemer," says the prophet, "is strong"; he is strong to redeem, strong to deliver, and mighty to save. O that I could speak of him as I have him in my heart, bless his precious name! All might, power and ability is in Christ, and all to redeem us from sin, the curse of the law and the pit of destruction. But what is the ransom? What is the price, my friends? Silver and gold and corruptible things? O no. If a man had all the silver and gold in the earth, and the cattle upon a thousand hills, and could give them all for the sin of his soul, it would be contemned; yea, ten thousand rivers of oil would be a sacrifice insufficient.

But we have redemption in Christ. He is not only the great Redeemer; but marvellous to tell, he is also the ransom price. "Walk in love, as Christ also hath loved us, and hath given himself for us an offering and a sacrifice to God for a sweet-smelling savour." Mark the reading: he gives himself, his life, his blood, as an offering and a sacrifice to God for a sweet-smelling savour. When on the cross he suffered "the Just for the unjust"; when he bled, groaned and died for our sins, it was to redeem us from all iniquity, and to deliver us from the curse of the divine law by being made a curse for us. When he shed his precious blood for the remission of our sins, it was our ransom price. Bless his precious and immortal name, by sacrificing and offering himself up once for all, he has "obtained eternal redemption for us." Though it is lofty language, yet it is firm and sure – "*eternal redemption*"! "We have redemption." Where? "Through his blood," through his atoning sacrifice, "even the forgiveness of sins, according to the riches of his grace." He has redeemed his church and people, even millions of men by his blood; so that, my friends, he is of God "made unto us redemption."

Now this just suits the captive soul held in bondage and chains; he stands in need of just such a redemption price. When God arrests the poor soul by convincing him of sin, he is held fast in the chains and fetters of legal bondage, he is a captive soul in prison, shut up unto the faith of the gospel. I would not give a groat for a man's religion if he has never been in the prison and the low dungeon. Christ can never be precious to him as his salvation, nor his sacrifice prized, unless he has been there. "Bring my soul out of prison," says David, "that I may praise thy name." "Let the sighing of the prisoner come up before thee; according to the greatness of thy power preserve thou those that are appointed to die."

Now, when the poor soul is in prison, in chains and in condemnation, he wants deliverance from his captivity, but he feels that none upon earth can help or deliver him. O no; the blessed Saviour alone can deliver and save him. His atoning blood is the ransom price. He says, "The Spirit of the Lord God is upon me, because the Lord hath anointed me to preach good tidings unto the meek; he hath sent me to bind up the broken-hearted, to proclaim liberty to the captives, and the opening of the prison to them that are bound; to proclaim the acceptable year of the Lord." When this deliverance is proclaimed in the conscience of the poor sinner, the effect is as the Bible describes – it is "liberty to the captives." Our religion to stand the test must be according to the Scriptures; and the language of the inspired Word is, "Deliver him" (the poor, captive, bowed-down soul) "from going down to the pit; I have found a ransom for him" – the blood of the incarnate God. "As for thee," says Jehovah the Father to the dear Redeemer, "by the blood of thy covenant, I have sent forth thy prisoners out of the pit wherein there is no water." Mark it, my friends, God delivers the poor sinner by the blood of the covenant, the blood of the dear Redeemer. The Holy Spirit applies the atoning blood of Immanuel to the conscience of the convinced sinner, and he discovers to him that the debt of sin is paid, law and justice satisfied, hell defeated, death vanquished and glory obtained. And when the poor sinner sees and feels this in his conscience, he has the spiritual blessing of deliverance from guilt and condemnation, and is brought into the glorious liberty of the gospel. "Stand fast therefore in the liberty wherewith Christ hath made us free, and be not entangled again with the yoke of bondage." And again, "If the Son shall make you free, ye shall be free indeed."

Our freedom from the curse is a spiritual blessing in our covenant Head. Paul felt it, and said, "Blessed be the God and Father of our Lord Jesus Christ, who hath blessed us with all spiritual blessings in heavenly places in Christ." The spirit of liberty, gospel freedom, sweet peace in the conscience, pardon and redemption is all in Christ, my friends. And if we are blessed with these spiritual blessings in the Lord Jesus Christ, we are safe and secure to all eternity. The soul that is interested in Christ, the great Redeemer, is as sure of heaven as if he were there already. It is not as some freewillers wickedly tell their hearers: "There are thousands in hell for whom Christ shed his blood." O no, this can never be the case; for the Father has declared of the Son, "He shall see of the travail of his soul, and shall be satisfied." He could never be satisfied if the purchase of his blood, the ransom of his life, were to be lifting up their eyes in hell. "The ransomed of the Lord shall return, and come to Zion with songs and everlasting joy upon their heads; they shall obtain joy and gladness, and sorrow and sighing shall flee away." It is in Christ, my friends. The Lord keep you and me looking by precious faith to the Person of the great Redeemer, to his bloodshedding and justifying righteousness, for peace and salvation. It is the test of the household of faith.

Now, let us speak a word or two on Christian experience, in reference to the feelings that a Christian man finds working in his mind. Sin is the bane and plague of a child of God. It is in his heart and in his thoughts, and he cannot get rid of it.

It goes with him wherever he goes, and abides with him wherever he stays; and the misery which he feels on account of these things often makes him cry out with Job, "O Lord, I am vile." "What a wretch I am!" I tell you, my friends, if I were called by others what I frequently call myself, it would make me very angry; I should not like to be called such ugly names. But I cannot find any language vile enough to call myself in my own mind. The poor soul finds language beggared in describing what he sees of the depravity, guilt and wretchedness of his evil heart and fallen nature. But the mercy is, poor sinner, though thou art black in thyself, thou art fair and comely and without spot in a precious Christ. Thou art quite safe and secure in his blessed hands. He hath put away all thy sins and iniquities, and hath blotted them out as a thick cloud, and says, "When they are sought for, they shall not be found." He hath removed for ever the curse of the law from thee; therefore it is written, "Christ hath redeemed us from the curse of the law, being made a curse for us." We can, therefore, now sing with the poet,

> "Believing, we rejoice,
>   To see the curse remove;
> We bless the Lamb with cheerful voice,
>   And sing his bleeding love."

Yes, poor soul, thou wilt find it all right at last; thou art as sure of heaven as though thou wert there already. It is the will of thy Father that when thou art absent from the body, thou shalt be present with the Lord. The dear Redeemer will have the purchase of his soul with him; and he says, "Father I will that they also, whom thou hast given me, be with me where I am, that they may behold my glory." This is often a degree of strength, comfort and consolation to living souls. The poor sinner knows and feels what he is in himself as a worthless worm; but he rejoices in Christ Jesus, while he can put no trust or confidence in himself.

The spiritual blessings of redemption, peace, pardon, gospel liberty and rest for the soul come through the dear

Redeemer alone. I do not know whether you London folks find rest, peace and comfort anywhere else, but I know I do not. I find no rest, no confidence, no joy for my heart but in the glorious Person, the finished work, the justifying right-eousness and complete salvation of my incarnate God; and that has hitherto, and I believe it will continue to sustain me through every storm, tempest and trial that I may have to meet with to the end of my days. But it is all in a precious Christ. "Blessed be the God and Father of our Lord Jesus Christ, who hath blessed us with all spiritual blessings in heavenly places in Christ."

IV. But we observe, *fourthly*, that another spiritual blessing which is treasured up in Christ is his *atoning blood*. O what a blessed remedy this is for the worst of all maladies, the worst of all diseases! No disease ever did or can exist equal to the malady of sin, and for that very reason it is called a plague. There are many disorders which come upon the body, but they fall short of a plague. A plague is the worst kind of disease that can break out among mortals. When a plague bursts out in a populous district, it has been known to make awful work. We have heard, and some of us have read, of the plague that once broke out in this great metropolis, and how it swept away thousands upon thousands.

At the dedication of the temple, when Solomon, who was a type of the Lord Jesus Christ, stood praying for the Lord's blessing to rest on his church and people, among other things in his petition he particularly makes use of this plea before the Lord, that he would hear and regard from heaven every man that should know "the plague of his own heart" – the torment of his carnal heart, his refractory, rebellious, fretful heart, where swarms of evil thoughts and vain imaginations abound, which often makes the child of God so sick and weary of himself that he knows not what to do.

I knew a simple man in the country who was so plagued with the workings of his evil heart that to get a little ease from his torments, he thought he would try to walk it away. He set off walking and walking, and then he took to running as fast as he could till he was out of breath. But there it was in his heart, working, fretting and foaming. He could not get rid of it, nor run away from it; he felt the plague of his heart, and could only cry, "O wretched man that I am!" But after a time the Lord applied his precious, atoning blood to his conscience, and that gave him ease. And nothing but the blood of the Lamb can take away the smart or stop the plague of sin in the heart.

Blessed be God, in our text we have a great Deliverer set forth; and that Deliverer is a precious Christ. He is the great High Priest over the house of God, and the remedy is his atoning blood, the balm of Gilead. Poor soul, dost thou want thy conscience to be cleansed, thy heart to be purified, and thy sin and guilt to be washed away? Where canst thou look for these things but to a precious Christ? The blessing is in Christ, my friends, and nowhere else. My soul lives upon the truths I preach, and God forbid that I should speak anything to you but what I have experienced the blessedness of in my own soul.

Now the Lord says by the prophet, "In that day there shall be a fountain opened to the house of David and to the inhabitants of Jerusalem for sin and uncleanness." This is the precious blood of Jesus, Immanuel, the incarnate God. And what is this fountain opened for? "For sin and for uncleanness." So that if you have no knowledge of sin and uncleanness, the fountain is not opened for you; it is opened for the guilty, the vile and the filthy in their feelings. Come then, poor black and leprous sinners, to the fountain. I love the song:

> "Black, I to the fountain fly,
> Wash me, Saviour, or I die."

Come to the fountain; it is opened for those who feel the plague of their heart, who are burdened with sin and uncleanness, and whose cry is with the leper of old, "Unclean,

unclean." This fountain is opened to cleanse thee from sin and to purify thee from uncleanness. "Ah," says the poor child of God, "I want to get at it, and cannot." You may want to get at it by your own wisdom and strength; but, blessed be the Lord, it is not left to thy getting. If thou couldst get it when thou wouldst, then thou couldst do the work of the Holy Ghost.

But God has determined that thou shalt not do his work; hence the dear Redeemer tells his disciples that "when he, the Spirit of truth is come, he will guide you into all truth: for he shall not speak of himself; but whatsoever he shall hear, that shall he speak; and he will shew you things to come. He shall glorify me; for he shall receive of mine, and shall shew it unto you." The blessed Spirit takes the atoning blood of the Lamb and applies it to the conscience of the poor sinner; he removes the burden of sin and softens the heart; and the dear child of God feels the blessedness of that text, which I cannot speak without feeling its blessed and solemn import: "The blood of Jesus Christ his Son cleanseth us from all sin." This is its blessed effect. And the redeemed soul for a while sings in this vale of tears the same song as the glorified spirits above: "Unto him that hath loved us, and washed us from our sins in his own blood, and made us kings and priests unto God and his Father; to him be glory and dominion for ever and ever." "For if the blood of bulls and goats, and the ashes of an heifer sprinkling the unclean, sanctifieth to the purifying of the flesh; how much more shall the blood of Christ, who through the eternal Spirit offered himself without spot to God, purge your conscience from dead works to serve the living God." It is in Christ, my friends. The Holy Spirit takes the atoning blood of the Lamb, applies it afresh to the conscience with power, and bears witness to the spirit of the living family that they are the redeemed of the Lord. May we glory only in a precious Christ! "Blessed be the God and Father of our Lord Jesus Christ, who hath blessed us with all spiritual blessings in heavenly places in Christ."

Now my friends, your time is gone, and the strength of my body begins to fail me through much preaching. By way of conclusion, therefore, let me ask, what do you know of these things for yourself? Let me pause then for a moment and give you time to think.   Do you see your lost, ruined and undone state and condition as a sinner before the Lord? Do you feel the need of that salvation which is in Christ? Are you led by the teachings of the blessed Spirit of God never to expect acceptance or justification before him on the ground of you own doings? Is it the earnest desire and prayer of your soul to be saved completely by the redemption that is in Christ Jesus? Are you looking by faith to the great Redeemer for the washing away of all your sins through his precious blood? Is the Lord Jesus Christ the Rock on which your soul rests for life and salvation? Are you confiding and trusting in him as your great High Priest before the throne? If so, the Spirit has begun the work of grace in your soul; and he that has begun it will surely carry it on; and when the great conflagration of all things shall take place, you shall shout the triumphs of the Lamb, exalt his precious name, and glorify his great salvation for ever and ever.

But am I speaking to any individuals present who are strangers to these great and glorious truths in the experimental feelings of their heart and soul before the Lord? If I am, it is my province to declare to such of you as are careless about these solemn and eternal things that you are living without God and without hope in the world; that "God is angry with the wicked every day"; and that if you live and die in this state, enemies to God and his Word, you will die under the wrath of God and the curse of his holy law. "It is a fearful thing to fall into the hands of the living God." God out of Christ is "a consuming fire." If you live and die in impenitency and hardness of heart, you will fall into a fire that never can be quenched.

But how different the state and prospect of the poor child of God, who is resting by faith upon the dear Redeemer!

Pondering over these things in my mind this afternoon, I was desirous that I might be made a blessing to the Lord's children this evening. I felt a little comfort in my own soul while meditating on the words of the text; and I wanted to preach to the people of God the things which I have looked upon and handled and felt in my own experience of the Word of life.

And now, may we drop into the hands and everlasting arms of the dear Redeemer as poor guilty sinners. Then we shall be safe in every storm and tempest, while passing through this vale of tears, and at last live and reign with him in glory above for ever and ever. Amen.

14. THE BURDENED SOUL SUSTAINED.

Preached at East Street Chapel, Walworth, on April 25th, 1848.

Text: *"Cast thy burden upon the Lord, and he shall sustain thee; he will never suffer the righteous to be moved" (Psalm 55. 22).*

Beloved, without taking up any time by way of introductory observations, we will come immediately to the words of our text. And with the help of the Lord, we will, first, notice the *exhortation and the promise* connected with it. We are exhorted to "cast our burden upon the Lord"; and the promise stands for our encouragement, "he shall sustain us." In the second place, we have a *solemn declaration* made, "He will never suffer the righteous to be moved."

I. In the first place, let us notice *the exhortation*, "Cast thy burden upon the Lord." This is an exhortation that will not suit everyone. For instance,

1. If we look for a moment at the *careless, unthinking* world, who are rolling sin and iniquity under their tongue like a sweet morsel; who are lying down in sin and filth, and wallowing therein like the sow – these are not burdened. O no; Gallio-like, they neither care for sin, their never-dying souls, nor the awful realities of an opening eternity. We look at these with grief and pity; but we cannot say to them, "Stand by, I am holier than thou!" Many of us can look back, and say with humility, solemnity and thankfulness to God, "And such were some of us;" and we are obliged to tell the Lord, such we should have remained, living and dying, and have lifted up our eyes in hell, had it not been for the riches of God's grace in stopping us in our mad career of sin and folly. "Is not this a brand plucked from the fire?" is a question that may well be asked concerning each of us who know the Lord. My friends, a consideration of these things will humble us, solemnize our minds, and create in us, under the blessed influences of the Holy Spirit, thankfulness to God.

2.   But again. There are others whom the exhortation of our text will not fit, "Cast thy burden upon the Lord." Who are they? Those who have "*a form of godliness, but deny the power thereof.*" They come and go to the means of grace; they are members of Christian societies, living in every point of view what is called a pious life, and pleased and delighted with themselves. Thus they wrap it up, secure with a name to live while dead, having the mere profession, without the life and power of God in the soul. Such may with propriety be considered in the devil's cradle, in which immortal souls are lulled in the sleep of perdition, and, if grace prevent not, will sink them to the regions of the damned; for it is not everyone that saith, "Lord, Lord, shall enter into the kingdom of heaven."

3.   But, again. There are others whom the exhortation of our text does not fit, "Cast thy burden upon the Lord." Who are they? Such as have got *a sound creed* – the doctrines of grace in the head; who, like Balaam, can distinguish truth from error; but they have never had the fallow ground of their hearts ploughed up, they have never been brought with godly sorrow, weeping and supplication to the feet of Jesus. Whatever a man knows of the letter of truth in a way of profession, if he is never brought by the power of divine grace to the footstool of mercy, as a poor, guilty, broken-hearted sinner, he is but as "sounding brass and a tinkling cymbal." Such a profession as this will not avail him anything in the great and solemn day of God.

But, leaving the negative side of the question, let us come more closely to our text, "Cast thy burden upon the Lord, and he shall sustain thee; he will never suffer the righteous to be moved." When it pleases God, in the riches of his grace, to convince a poor soul, dead in trespasses and sins, of his lost and ruined state by nature, he quickens and makes him alive. God's religion and the soul of the poor sinner go together. When the Lord first begins the work of grace, he in general lays some particular outward sin on the conscience of the poor sinner of which he has been most guilty. As, for instance, Saul of Tarsus in his mad persecution of the church and people of God; and Zaccheus the publican, of his unjust and oppressive dealing. But when God sends an arrow of conviction into the soul, he not only discovers to him his present sins, but he reveals to his astonished view past sins; and as Job expresses it, makes him "to possess the sins and iniquities of his youth." Present and past sins rise up to view; they stare the poor sinner in his face, and appear in their scarlet and crimson hue, a thick, black cloud; and in the midst of their thickness and blackness an angry God is felt in a broken law. The poor sinner is now bowed down greatly; he feels the burden of sin in his conscience; for the Lord has laid it with a solemn weight upon his heart, and it presses him down to the dust of death. He is oppressed with it, and cries out with David, "Mine iniquities are gone over mine head; as an heavy burden they are too heavy for me" (Psalm 38. 4). A wounded spirit and an angry God in a broken law will bring down the loftiest looks, abase the proudest and haughtiest heart, and bring the poor sinner to the feet of the Lord Jesus Christ with the cry of the publican, "God, be merciful to me a sinner."

Beloved, do you know anything of a burdened conscience and a wounded spirit? Have you ever had the feelings of the poet, when he said,

"Here on my heart the burden lies,
And past offences pain my eyes?"

My friends, the burden of sin felt on the conscience of a poor sinner makes him to hang down his head like a bulrush. It makes him weary, heavy-laden, oppressed and sorrowful. His former companions and relations cannot tell what is the matter with him, or what to do with him; some will say he is insane, others that he is becoming melancholy, and a third will advise him to be taken into good company and amusements to divert and cheer him. Thus many things are done in order to heal his wounded spirit; but it is all to no avail. He will never get ease to his sorrowful soul till he is able to obey the exhortation, "Cast thy burden upon the Lord, and he shall sustain thee; he will never suffer the righteous to be moved."

Beloved, as sure as the poor soul is brought into these circumstances, so sure will the Lord uphold, support and sustain him, and neither men nor devils will be able to keep him from coming to the throne of grace. He will get into some private and retired corner where he may pour out his soul to God in earnest cries and supplications. Like Isaac, he will take his walk at eventide, and wander solitarily in his gloom and sadness, moaning, crying and anxiously seeking for a revelation of pardoning mercy to his wounded spirit. Strangers are ignorant of what is going on in his soul, but the Lord is making him acquainted with the hidden evils of his heart. He is not merely unfolding to his view the guilt of outward sin, but he is discovering to him the hidden evils that dwell and lurk within, and leading him into the imagery in the hidden chambers of his soul. This makes him to cry out with David, "My wounds stink and are corrupt, because of my foolishness. I am troubled; I am bowed down greatly; I go mourning all the day long. For my loins are filled with a loathsome disease; and there is no soundness in my flesh. I am feeble and sore broken; I have roared by reason of the disquietness of my heart."

The poor soul when brought here is full of doubts and fears, and nearly overwhelmed with sighs and cries before the Lord, panting for deliverance. O, my friends, if there are no cries, no pantings, no longings to the Lord, there is great reason to fear such a person has never had any true and spiritual religion. But the poor, bowed down, burdened sinner groans and cries to the Lord for help; and he says, "Lord, all my desire is before thee, and my groaning is not hid from thee." And again, "Let the sighing of the prisoner come before thee." Such are not forgotten before the Lord; they are vessels of mercy afore prepared unto glory, and redeemed from among men by the blood of the covenant. The blessed Spirit takes possession of the heart of this poor soul, and brings him unto Jesus and his finished salvation. "The Lord looked down from the height of his sanctuary; from heaven did the Lord behold the earth; to hear the groaning of the prisoner; to loose those that are appointed to death." "He will regard the prayer of the destitute, and will not despise their cry."

The Lord says to the poor soul who is bowed down with sin outwardly and sin inwardly, who is troubled with it in the house of God and is a burden and a plague to himself, who knows not what to do, nor whither to flee, and who finds refuge to fail him on every hand – the Lord says to him, "Come, poor, burdened soul, bring your hard heart, your vain thoughts to me. Keep not anything back, but confess thy sins at the footstool of my grace. Tell me all thy griefs and sorrows arising from the workings within of thy carnal and wicked heart." "Cast thy burden upon the Lord, and he will sustain thee; he will never suffer the righteous to be moved."

Now I believe the exhortation to be good: it is blessed and precious, my friends. But something more is wanted in Christian experience. The poor soul bowed down with trials may hear these things set forth, and it may encourage him under his burdens; and he may go again and again and try to cast his burden upon the Lord; but he cannot. He would cast it upon, and leave it with the Lord, if he could; but he cannot. What is wanted then to enable him to do so? The influence of the blessed Spirit. When the Lord enables the poor sinner to come with a soft and feeling heart, with godly sorrow for sin, and with tears of contrition trickling down his cheeks to the feet of Jesus, to look by precious faith to him, and to see that Jehovah the Father, against whom he has sinned, has imputed his sins to the dear Redeemer, and cast them into the depths of the sea, this will sustain and support his burdened and sorrowful soul. "All we like sheep have gone astray, we have turned every one to his own way; and the Lord hath laid on him the iniquity of us all." Brethren, when this is seen by faith, and felt in the soul of the poor, burdened sinner, how it helps and sustains his spirit. "He that knew no sin" (a precious Christ), "was made sin for us, that we might be made the righteousness of God in him."

As the believing soul is led by the Spirit to the dear Redeemer, to see sin imputed to him; as he is led to the cross of Christ, and beholds Jesus putting away his sins by the sacrifice of himself, making an end of transgression, finishing sin, and bringing in everlasting righteousness – these immortal blessings are received by faith in his soul. The precious, atoning blood of the Lamb is felt in his conscience, and he is sustained and supported. But something yet more is experienced. What more then does he feel? The burden is removed! the burden is removed! When John Bunyan's pilgrim was brought to the foot of the cross, and by faith beheld the dear Redeemer bearing his sins in his own body on the tree, wounded for his iniquities and made a curse for him – while he looked upon the wondrous sight, joy and peace flowed into his conscience like a river. While he was gazing upon the cross, he lost his burden! he lost his burden! His heart melted with love, and tears of thanksgiving flowed down his cheeks. "Cast thy burden upon the Lord, and he shall sustain thee."

But nothing can support or sustain a precious soul which I have been describing but a precious Christ, the one Mediator between God and men, the Man Christ Jesus – the Rock of our salvation. The believer's soul is sustained and supported by the Person of Immanuel, the incarnate God; and when he finds he has this prop to rest upon, it feels so firm and precious to him, that he sings with a glad heart,

> "How can I sink with such a prop,
> That bears the world, and all things up?"

This is being sustained, my friends. When the poor sinner is led to see that his sins and iniquities are done away; that when they are sought for they shall not be found; that the curse due to sin fell upon a precious Christ; that he finished the work which the Father gave him to do; and that his precious salvation is made known to the conscience by the power of the Holy Ghost – it sustains and supports his mind, and the poor soul bowed down with fear bursts forth and sings, "Behold, God is my salvation; I will trust" (not in my own heart, nor lean to my own understanding) – "I will trust, and not be afraid" (that my sins will bring me under the curse of the law), "for the Lord Jehovah is my song; he also is become my salvation." These are the things that sustain and support the child of God. "Cast thy burden upon the Lord, and he shall sustain thee; he will never suffer the righteous to be moved."

Beloved, will anything short of a precious Christ, the incarnate God, his finished and complete salvation which is all of grace, support our souls and bear our spirits up? If it will, your heart is not right with God. The language of Paul, which I am going to cite, enters into the soul of the poor sinner upon this important point. He says, "I know whom I have believed (or trusted); and am persuaded that he (a precious Christ) is able to keep that which I have committed unto him against that day." As if the apostle had said, "I have been enabled through the gracious teachings of the blessed Spirit, to cast myself, with all I am, at my dear Redeemer's feet, and leave my case and soul in his precious hands. I have a blessed feeling wrought in my heart by the dear Comforter that a precious Jesus will bear me up, and land me safe in immortal glory. Here is my comfort and consolation; this sustains and supports my soul." And there is no comfort and consolation for a burdened soul anywhere else.

"But," says some poor child of God, "if I only knew I had an interest in a precious Christ, and that he was carrying on my cause in the high court of heaven, I should feel my mind supported and sustained amid my burdens." Well now, the Lord says (and if he should enable you to obtain a faith's view of it, it will do your soul good, as it has done mine many a time), "If any man sin, we have an Advocate with the Father, Jesus Christ the righteous, and he is the propitiation for our sins." Let me ask you, poor soul, have you been taught your lost, ruined and undone state as a sinner before God? Do you feel that you have no worth or worthiness of your own? Do you believe that Christ is able to save to the uttermost all that come unto God by him? The Lord enable you to look to a precious Jesus, to his atoning blood and his justifying righteousness for life and salvation. There is no righteousness but the righteousness of Immanuel, "the righteousness which is of God by faith," that will do for the burdened soul.

The Lord enable you to commit your cause into his blessed hands; you can never die while Jesus lives; and he says, "I give unto my sheep eternal life, and they shall never perish, neither shall any man pluck them out of my hand." The Lord enable us to cast our burden upon him; he will sustain us; he will never forsake us. "They that trust in the Lord shall never be ashamed nor confounded world without end." O no, my friends, the Lord will take care of those who trust in his grace and hope in his mercy; and those who fear and love him now shall in a little while dwell in his immediate presence, where there is fulness of joy, and at his right hand, where there are pleasures for evermore.

> "Those who in the Lord confide,
> And shelter in his wounded side;
> Shall see the danger overpast,
> Outride each storm, and live at last."

Now the dear children of God have many burdens and troubles to endure all the way through the wilderness. Nearly the whole of their threescore years and ten, or perhaps fourscore years, are consumed more or less in trouble and sorrow. I have known some good men greatly burdened with providential difficulties in trade; they have not known how to pay their bills, or to take them up when due, and this has been a sore burden and trial to their souls. Others, who fear the

Lord, have bad and undutiful children, who give them a great deal of trouble, causing them many sighs, groans and tears. Again, the Lord's family often experience trouble in the church of God; many crooked things arise among brethren, and sometimes angry words are used, which is a source of sorrow to the Lord's dear children, and which cause them frequently to sigh and cry to the Lord. But, my friends, whatever be the burden, sorrow or trouble that oppresses or sinks you, there is no other remedy for it than this blessed exhortation and promise, "Cast thy burden upon the Lord, and he shall sustain thee; he will never suffer the righteous to be moved." We cannot extricate ourselves from our burdens and sorrows by taking anxious thought. O no; I hear the Lord saying to his dear children in all their difficulties and trials, (it is a sweet voice; may the Lord speak the word with power to the heart of some poor, troubled child while the words drop from the lips of his poor dust), "Casting all your care upon him, for he careth for you." O, my friends, did he not care for the prophet Elijah in the wilderness? Did he not send the ravens to feed him? Did he not care for the poor woman of Sarepta in the time of famine? The devil and unbelief said she would be sure to be starved; but the Lord sent the prophet to sustain her and keep her alive. The Lord of Hosts still lives! Our heavenly Father knoweth our wants and necessities; the gold and the silver are his, and the cattle upon a thousand hills; and he has promised to satisfy "all our needs according to his riches in glory by Christ Jesus."

Some persons are ashamed that it should ever be known they were once poor, or to acknowledge the hole of the pit from whence they have been hewn. But I recollect one particular time in my own case, when I was young. I had been some time out of work, the family were without provision, and I had no money to procure any. I could not see my way; darkness and clouds rested on my path; the devil and unbelief began to work, and powerfully to assail me. But the Lord sustained my mind, and sweetly dropped into my soul this precious portion from the prophet Habakkuk. I shall never forget the time. "Although the fig-tree shall not blossom, neither shall fruit be in the vines; the labour of the olive shall fail, and the fields shall yield no meat; the flock shall be cut off from the fold, and there shall be no herd in the stalls; yet I will rejoice in the Lord, I will joy in the God of my salvation." The Lord enabled me to cast myself and family into the faithful care and kindness of a God of providence and grace, and to leave myself in his blessed hands.

O that we may be enabled to leave ourselves more with him, with all our troubles and sorrows, who maketh darkness light, crooked things straight, and rough places plain! When we are enabled to do so by the blessed Spirit, it brings us where the Apostle Paul was, when he said, "And not only so, but we glory in tribulations also; knowing that tribulation worketh patience; and patience, experience; and experience, hope; and hope maketh not ashamed, because the love of God is shed abroad in our hearts by the Holy Ghost which is given unto us." The Lord enable you, poor tried soul, to leave yourself, your cares, and your burdens at his blessed footstool. Thy God reigns as a God of providence as well as a God of grace; and he will make all thy difficulties and trials work together for thy good and the honour of his great name. As the dear child of God is led into these immortal truths, he is enabled to cast out the anchor of hope, and to sing,

> "Since all that I meet shall work for my good,
> The bitter is sweet, the medicine is food;
> Though painful at present, 'twill cease before long,
> And then, O how pleasant, the conqueror's song."

This is God's religion, my friends, and it supports the minds of his tried family and enables them to confide in him while surrounded with difficulties and sorrows.

Again. Are any of you burdened in reference to trade and the hardness of the times so that you do not know how to pay your way and act honestly and uprightly among men in the fear of God? The Lord enable you to bring your difficulties to him, and cast your burdens at his precious feet. He has all hearts in his hands; plead and wrestle with him, therefore, that he would give those to whom you are indebted a merciful and a kind spirit, that they may wait, and have a little patience with you, so that you may pay them all. Beloved, may the Lord enable thee by precious faith to "cast thy burden upon the Lord, and he will sustain thee."

I knew a poor tried child of God in the north in these circumstances. The person to whom he owed the debt came to him, and told him unless he paid the debt in so many days, he should put the bailiff in his house. The poor man thought his heart would break, but he went with his burden to the Lord and threw himself down at his blessed feet, and said, "Lord, thou seest how I am circumstanced; this man is coming upon me, with enmity in his heart because of my religion, to distress me. But thou hast all hearts in thy hand, and if it is for thy honour, let him not hurt me; for I know thou canst keep the man back." And the Lord heard and answered the poor man's cry; for he kept the man back, induced him to wait for his money, and the poor child of God was enabled to discharge the debt and pay all that he owed him. I bring this circumstance forward to encourage those of you who fear the Lord, and who may be in difficulties in providence, to "cast your burden upon the Lord, and he will sustain you; he will never suffer the righteous to be moved."

I knew a good woman, a mother in Israel, who lived to the honour of God and the glory of his name. She was well to do in the world. But all God's people must have a crook in the lot. She had a bad son, who had caused her much sorrow of heart; he had run away and enlisted for a soldier five or six times. But one day when I called upon her, she said to me, "I tell thee what, friend Kershaw, I have taken Richard to the Lord, but I cannot keep him there; I bring him back again."

This is our misery, my friends; we take our burdens to the Lord, but are unable to leave them with him. But someone will say, "Have we not the promise in the Bible that the Lord will sustain us? Ought we not to take him at his word?" I love my Bible, and the promise too; but, my friends, I find I have to wait for the fulfilment of the promise to my soul. It is my mercy that God's promise takes hold of me, and that it is not left to my taking hold of the promise. Sometimes, when we go to the throne of grace burdened, we see the promise in the Bible fits our case, but relief is not experienced. There is something more wanted. What is wanted? To have the precious promise dropped with power from heaven in the conscience. When the promise comes from the Lord, the soul is refreshed, so that it can sing with the poet,

> "O! I have seen the day,
> When with a single word,
> God helping me to say,
> My trust is in the Lord:
> My soul has quelled a thousand foes,
> Fearless of all that could oppose."

Thus when the promise is brought home by the blessed Remembrancer to the heart, it raises up the dear child of God. When he says, "Fear not, for I am with thee; be not dismayed, for I am thy God; I will strengthen thee; yea, I will help thee; yea, I will uphold thee with the right hand of my right-eousness;" and "I will be with thee in six troubles; yea, in seven there shall no evil befall thee" – it encourages and refreshes the poor soul. If he is called to pass through the fires of perse-cution, or the waters of affliction, the Lord says, "When thou passest through the waters I will be with thee; and through the rivers they shall not overflow thee: when thou walkest through the fire thou shalt not be burned, neither shall the flame kindle upon thee." Such a precious soul as this will not have to wait upon the Lord in vain; but he will arise for his help, and bring him to say to the praise and glory of his name,

"This God is my God for ever and ever; he will be my guide even unto death."

O, my friends, I feel a solemn pleasure in labouring as God's instrument to encourage you to cast all your burdens, trials and difficulties into his blessed hands. There is no peace or rest for the heaven-born soul anywhere else. Our blessed Lord has left us this legacy, and we prove its truth continually, "In the world ye shall have tribulation, but in me ye shall have peace." The Lord enable us to trust in him at all times; he is a refuge and strength for his people in every time of trouble. "Cast thy burden upon the Lord, and he will sustain thee; he will never suffer the righteous to be moved."

II. I have gone, my friends, through the first part of the subject, and as the time is nearly gone I feel in a strait whether I should close these remarks, or pass on to the second observation – the solemn declaration made, "He will not suffer the righteous to be moved." But, as I only come to you once a year, you must bear with me a few moments longer.

"He will not suffer the righteous to be moved." Upon this I need say but little tonight. There are none righteous in the sight of God, as we stand in relation to Adam. Such a man or woman cannot be found under the canopy of heaven. "The Lord looked down from heaven upon the children of men, to see if there were any that did understand, that did seek God. Every one of them is gone back; they are altogether become filthy; there is none that doeth good; no, not one" (Psalm 53. 2, 3). No person is righteous in God's sight, but he who stands in union to the dear Redeemer. The blessed Spirit discovers to the poor sinner his inward guilt and defilement; shows him that all his righteousnesses are as filthy rags; gives him to see that God's commandments are exceeding broad, extending to the thoughts and intents of the heart. He reveals to him that none are righteous or accepted before God but those who are in union to a precious Christ. Every heaven-born soul, made sick of self, pants after Christ's righteousness, for he is "the end

of the law for righteousness to every one that believeth."
Wherever the Lord dwells in the heart, there is implanted a
righteous principle within, not only to hate and oppose sin in
ourselves, and with Job to abhor ourselves and repent in dust
and ashes, but to hate and oppose it also in others. And
wherever this principle dwells, there is a longing desire to be
conformed to the image of Christ, to have the Spirit of Christ,
and to serve the Lord in our day and generation, and live to
the praise and honour of his great name.

But the text says, "He will never suffer the righteous to be
moved." Now in what sense is this to be understood? If we
were to endeavour to prove from this that the righteous were
always in one blessed state of feeling and enjoyment, and were
never moved away from it, it would not stand the test; it
would be neither in accordance with the Word of God nor
Christian experience. Were we to say that the righteous were
always rejoicing in the God of their salvation, always living
above doubts and fears, always enjoying the light of God's
countenance, then we should say what could not be proved. It
is not the province of the heaven-born soul to be always on
the mount of enjoyment in this time-state. The days of
darkness are many with God's family; but the Lord sometimes
indulges his dear children with his love-tokens, with a little of
his presence, and to have sweet and happy enjoyment for a few
moments at his dear footstool.

Methinks I hear someone ready to say, "Ah, Lord, this is
what I want."

> "My willing soul would stay
>   In such a frame as this,
> And sit and sing herself away,
>   To everlasting bliss."

Beloved, when my soul was first brought here, I thought
heaven was mine, a covenant God mine, and that I should go
to glory in silver slippers. But I have passed through many
changes since; long nights and dark seasons have intervened
between, with scarce a glimmering ray of hope. The Psalmist

says, in great enjoyment of soul, "Bless the Lord, O my soul; and all that is within me, bless his holy name." And, "Lord, by thy favour thou hast made my mountain to stand strong;" but in the next sentence, he says, "Thou didst hide thy face, and I was troubled." But he shall tell his own tale. He says, "Are his mercies clean gone for ever? Doth his promise fail for evermore? Will he be favourable no more? Hath he in anger shut up his tender mercies?" And at times he was cast down and dejected in his feelings, the same as you and I are. He was, as Berridge says,

"Sometimes hot, sometimes cold,
Sometimes down, and sometimes up."

"O thou afflicted, tossed with tempest, and not comforted!" There are many changes with the children of God in this vale of tears. But however tossed with tempests, and not comforted, however wretched and miserable in ourselves, the text stands, "He will never suffer the righteous to be moved."

Now then for the true sense of the passage. The righteous shall never be moved from the love of God, from the love of a Triune Jehovah. The election of grace, as they stand in the Lord Jesus Christ, can never be removed from him, through time and all eternity. Just look for a moment where they are fixed; they centre in Christ Jesus; they are chosen in Christ, loved in Christ, and blessed in Christ. The Father loves them with the same love wherewith he loves Christ; and Jesus says, "Thou hast loved them, as thou hast loved me." Now as Christ the Head was never removed from the love of the Father, neither shall the members of his body be ever removed from him;

"With Christ our Lord we share a part,
In the affections of his heart."

O what a mercy to realize this in soul experience! What a blessed standing is this! The righteous shall never be moved out of the heart of a covenant God; they stood there from eternity, are there through time, and shall continue there in eternity to come.

Again, he will never suffer the righteous to be moved from the finished salvation of the Lord Jesus Christ. The Lord is round the church like a brazen bulwark. The walls of salvation encompass them continually. Poor Zion thought she should be moved; but the Lord says, "Thou shalt never be forgotten of me." What did Zion's God say? "Can a woman forsake her sucking child that she should not have compassion on the son of her womb? yea, they may forget, yet will I not forget thee." "I will be a wall of fire round about thee to take care of thee: thou shalt never be moved from my dying love, my justifying righteousness; never be moved from my advocacy, I will plead thy cause; never be moved from my hands and my Father"s hands." O, my friends, the Lord encourage us to look to a precious Christ, to see that we are saved in him with an everlasting salvation.

"He will never suffer the righteous to be moved" from their right and title in Christ to immortal glory from before the foundations of the world. A victor's crown of glory is in reserve for those who love and fear the Lord. Blessed be his name! The thought of this does my soul good. He says, "Let not your heart be troubled; ye believe in God, believe also in me. In my Father's house are many mansions; if it were not so, I would have told you. I go to prepare a place for you: and if I go and prepare a place for you, I will come again and receive you unto myself, that where I am, there ye may be also." "I love you and cannot be happy without you: I must have you to reign with me in glory." " Father, I will that they also whom thou hast given me, be with me where I am; that they may behold my glory, which thou hast given me; for thou lovedst me before the foundation of the world."

The heaven-born soul says, "Blessed be the name of the Lord, that is just what I want; I never can be happy without it." "Then shall I be satisfied when I awake in thy likeness; for in thy presence is fulness of joy, and at thy right hand there are pleasures for evermore!"

15. GREAT THINGS THE LORD HAS DONE

Preached at Gower Street Chapel, London, on January 7th, 1855

Text: *"The Lord hath done great things for us, whereof we are glad." (Psalm 126. 3).*

[The chapel in Gower Street was built after the death of William Huntington for those who had left the chapel where he preached, not being satisfied with the ministry. William Gadsby preached at the opening services in 1820.

However, in 1842 there was a separation of those who were not satisfied with the pastor Edward Blackstock's position on strict communion, and a room was opened for worship by Mr. Kershaw in Gadsby's Yard, off Tottenham Court Road. This place proving too small, a chapel in Eden Street, Hampstead Road, was offered them, and a strict baptist church formed.

After some time, the congregation at Gower Street having dwindled, in 1855 the Eden Street people were able to buy the chapel and return. This is the sermon preached at the re-opening services.]

These words stand in inseparable connection with what is said in this Psalm of the return of the children of Israel out of the Babylonish captivity. Hence the Psalm begins, "When the Lord turned again the captivity of Zion, we were like them that dream." Observe! The return of the children of Israel out of the Babylonish captivity was the work of the Lord. "When *the Lord* turned again the captivity of Zion, we were like them that dream." The thing was so sudden and unexpected that they could not for a time conclude that it was a reality. It was with them as with Peter, whom the angel of the Lord was dispatched to bring out of prison, when locked fast between two soldiers; and he marches after the angel to one gate and another. He thought it was a vision, that it was a dream; but when the angel left him in the street of the city, he knew that it was a reality and that the thing was entirely of the

Lord. So when the Lord turned again the captivity of Zion, they were as those that were dreaming; but yet, as in Peter's case, it was a solemn reality.

"Then was our mouth filled with laughter, and our tongue with singing." Not carnal laughter. O, no! They had a glad and a merry heart. The joy of their heart was like that of Sarah when she heard the angel proclaim that she should still bring forth the promised one, through whom all the families of the earth should be blessed. Sarah, in the joy of her heart, laughed. And so the children of Israel, feeling great joy and gladness, laughed, and their tongue was filled with singing – praise and thanksgiving to that God who had made bare his arm for their signal and unexpected deliverance. "Then was our mouth filled with laughter, and our tongue with singing: then said they among the heathen, The Lord hath done great things for them."

Heathen nations were looking on and beholding the various deliverances of heaven towards the children of Israel; and when it was made known to them that the Lord had delivered the Israelites in such a conspicuous manner, and had brought them out of the Babylonish captivity, then were the heathen constrained to say, "The Lord hath done great things for them." The Lord hath done great things for those Israelites; he brought them out of the land of Egypt; he divided the waters of the Red Sea; he led them through the wilderness and put them in possession of the land that was promised to Abraham; and he has again made bare his arm on their behalf: "Then said they among the heathen, The Lord hath done great things for them."

And then comes our text: "The Lord hath done great things for us." The children of Israel could appropriate the language to themselves. They did not say the Lord had done great things for them; but the Lord hath in reality done great things for us, whereof we are glad.

I know for a certainty that there are many glad hearts now within these hallowed walls. What occasions your present joy and gladness? The kind interposition of our divine Lord and Master, in his providential leadings with us, in bringing us back again to wait upon him and to worship him in this place. Give to the Lord the honour and the glory that is due unto his name: "Not unto us, O Lord, not unto us," but unto the name of our covenant God be all the praise for every token of his manifold goodness toward us.

When I heard in my own place that the people at Eden Street were uniting together to raise funds, with the design to buy ground and to build a new chapel, a gloom was ever on my mind, when thinking on the subject, except when I looked to this place. When I was with you in September last, at Eden Street, it was said that a very eligible spot of ground had presented itself; and you remember I said this to you, "Watch the hand of the Lord!" Well, in the morning I could not rest, and pondering these things I got up early and took my walks; and many times I went into Gower Street, paced in front of the chapel, and then went across the road and looked up at it, while my heart and soul went up to the Lord that he would, if consistent with his sovereign pleasure, put that place into the hands of the people that had originally worshipped in it. And from the nearness that I felt to the Lord in my prayer, I knew that I had some reason to believe that such would be the result. But I did not expect the thing to come so suddenly. It has come, and we are glad in our hearts for it: "The Lord hath done great things for us, whereof we are glad."

I well remember, and I hope I ever shall, the circumstances under which I opened the cause in Gadsby's Yard, Tottenham Court Road. I came to London that time with my heart and eyes up to the Lord. My esteemed neighbour, Mr. Gadsby, and myself were of one heart and one soul in the business; and some of you may remember my first text: "Whatsoever ye do, do all to the glory of God." Now, my friends, let us pause here a moment. In all our ways it is our privilege to acknowledge the Lord, to ponder the path of our feet, and to be concerned that our steps should be ordered of the Lord and by his Word; that we may be guided by the unerring Spirit of the Lord. And, if this be the case, our ends will be the honour and glory of the Lord in the salvation of his church, the peace and prosperity of Zion.

There is one portion of God's Word which has been much impressed on my own mind, and I pray that my blessed Master may keep it more and more on my mind and yours also, so that we may never lose sight of it. You have to do with a faithful God. The portion is this: "Them that honour me I will honour, but they that despise me shall be lightly esteemed." Have we not seen the fulfilment of that portion of God's Word in reference to both declarations? Where God has been honoured and glorified, honour has been put upon instrumentality; and where there has been a forsaking of the simplicity of the gospel, there has been a dishonouring of God; and have such as dishonoured the Lord, either in principle or practice, been highly esteemed? I trow not. He cannot esteem other instrumentality than that which is employed in seeking the honour, and peace, and prosperity of Zion.

But, my friends, the Lord has brought you back, and the Lord keep you humble, watchful, prayerful, and striving together for the faith of the gospel, in the unity of the spirit and in the bond of peace, and grant that you may be increased in your own souls with the increase of God; that you may be increased with men and women as a flock; and that the Lord will ride forth among you in the chariot of the gospel, that his arrows may be swift to pierce the hearts of the king's enemies; and that the Lord may appear in his power from time to time and seal up the souls of his chosen ones in this place.

Now for the text: "The Lord hath done great things for us, whereof we are glad."

I.   We may observe, first, that the appellation of the honoured name, Lord, is given to the Triune Jehovah – the Three that bear record in heaven, the Father, the Word and the Holy Ghost. In the first place, Jehovah the Father is called Lord in that memorable, important and blessed portion of his Word, the 53rd of Isaiah: "All we like sheep have gone astray; but the Lord (the Lord Jehovah) hath laid on him (Christ) the iniquity of us all." And again, when the psalmist took his prophetic view of the resurrection and ascension of Christ and his entrance into the realms of bliss, he spoke in this wise in the 110th Psalm: "The Lord said unto my Lord, Sit thou on my right hand, until I make thine enemies thy footstool." Jehovah the Father, Lord of all, welcomed his beloved Son, our Elder Brother, the Captain of our salvation, our Great High Priest, our Advocate. He welcomes him to the realms of bliss and to take his seat at the right hand of the majesty on high with that solemn declaration.

And now, in the second place, my friends, is not the Lord Jesus Christ, in various portions of the Scriptures, called Lord? Speaking of himself, he says, "Ye call me Master and Lord, and ye say well, for so I am. If I, your Lord and Master, am with you as one that serveth, ought ye not to serve one another?" Our Jesus is the Captain of our salvation. See the lordly character of our Redeemer – the King of kings, and Lord of lords – the Lord and Master in the church. There is that glory, that beauty, that blessed reality, that the apostle says, "No man, save those who speak by the Spirit, can call him Lord." A man may call him Lord in his judgment and acknowledge him Lord with his tongue; but no man can enter sweetly and feelingly into the mystery, into the power or the glory of the dear Redeemer, as the Lord of lords, but by the Holy Ghost; to recognize him as possessing all power in heaven and upon earth in his hands, and all events under his control. O that our minds may be sweetly stayed upon the Lord our Master, who is the same yesterday, today, and for ever.

But, further, the appellation of Lord is given to the ever-blessed Spirit, for the Eternal Spirit is one with the

Immortal Word and our covenant God and Father in every attribute and perfection of Deity. Paul, in writing to the church at Corinth, says: "There are diversities of gifts, but the same Spirit." The same Lord, the same Spirit, the same God that dwells in the hearts of his people, and teaches and guides them into the truth as it is in the Lord Jesus Christ. So that the Spirit is by Paul emphatically called *Lord*. And, my friends, the apostle makes use of this beautiful mode of expression in reference to the Holy Ghost: "The Lord (the Spirit) direct your hearts into the love of God, and into the patient waiting for Christ."

Thus we see that the appellation of "the Lord," is given to our covenant God and Father, that it is given to the Lord Jesus Christ, and that it is also applied to the blessed and eternal Spirit. Then we come again to the text: "The Lord (Jehovah in his Trinity of Persons) hath done great things for us, whereof we are glad." Whenever there is a deviation from this cardinal doctrine of the gospel – the Trinity in Unity, and the Unity in Trinity, as engaged in covenant for the salvation of the church – there is a swerving from the purity and simplicity of the gospel; and, as my esteemed brother Gadsby used to say, "I never like men who begin nibbling at the doctrine of the Trinity, or at the Personality of the Holy Ghost; this trying to comprehend, by human reason, the incomprehensible Jehovah. This ought never to be done." No, my friends; the doctrine of the Trinity is not a doctrine of reason, but of revelation. It is the glorious mystery of godliness that is revealed by the blessed Spirit made known to the church, and it rejoices our heart.

Now, in the first place, what has our covenant God and Father done for us, whereof we are glad? In reference to this we must trace all our blessings of grace and salvation up to what the apostle calls his eternal purposes of love and mercy that he purposed in Christ Jesus before the world was. Jehovah purposed and determined in his own mind to glorify the riches of his grace and mercy in the salvation of countless millions of Adam's fallen race, in, through and by the blood-shedding of the incarnate God. This is called "the purpose of God, according to election," which must stand, "not of works," but according to the riches of his grace and mercy, who said to Moses, "I will have mercy on whom I will have mercy; I will have compassion on whom I will have compassion." God's predestination and election are the first links in the golden chain of our salvation. Everlasting, electing love is the spring and source from whence every blessing of grace and salvation flows, through the precious blood of Christ, to poor guilty sinners.

We cannot stop to dwell on this, beloved, as a doctrine. I hope it is an article in the faith of most who are now congregated together within these walls. But did we always receive it? Did it always gladden our hearts? O, no! The first view I had of it – soon after grace had taken possession of my heart – was such a gloomy view that, instead of joy and gladness, O the bitterness, O the opposition and the carnal workings that I felt in my own soul against God's sovereignty! No Arminian ever reasoned in substance more powerfully against it. I never wonder at men, merely professing Christianity, fighting against the sovereignty of Jehovah the Father in the eternal choice of his people in Christ Jesus to salvation from the beginning. But when the Lord has brought the poor sinner to lie passively under his hand, like clay in the hands of the potter, and has taught him his lost, guilty, filthy, polluted state and condition as a sinner, and led him to see God's holiness, justice and righteousness in his law, and the way whereby God can be just and yet the justifier of the poor, guilty sinner, how different are his views! At one time the poor wretch feels the deepest anguish at the thought of God's marking his iniquity and sending him to hell; but when he has sunk down under the thought of this great condemnation and the Lord says, by his Word and his Holy Spirit, "I have loved thee, poor soul, with an everlasting love; I had thoughts of love, mercy and peace towards thee before all worlds" – as the blessed Spirit leads the soul into the covenant love and mercy of Jehovah the Father, I know it will make him glad. O how it will cheer and animate his spirit!

"We love him because he first loved us." Ah, my friends, I can look back to the morning when I stood in a solitary place before the Lord, and when his sweet covenant love was manifested to my soul, and it was revealed to me so blessedly that tears of joy and contrition, in an abundant measure, trickled down my cheeks; tears of contrition for sin, and of joy to think that the God and Father of all should have cared for such a guilty and worthless worm as I felt myself to be.

I have often heard my late old friend tell of a circumstance which occurred at his ordination, as some call it. Some of the ministers were afraid that when called upon to make his confession of faith, he might go on too far, or get rather too humoursome on so solemn an occasion; so they put a very staid old minister into the pulpit to ask him the questions. When Mr. Gadsby came to speak upon the doctrine of God's election and the great things that a covenant God had done for his people, in their choice before all worlds, he remarked, "Some folks say this doctrine of election and predestination makes their stomachs ache; but God knows it does my heart and soul good." The old man in the pulpit, who was to have stopped him if he rambled too much, caught the fire, and exclaimed, "Aye, my lad, and so it does mine." And I know that if God blesses you with a sweet taste of his covenant love, it will gladden your hearts also. It cheers the faint, it enlarges the heart; the more we enjoy of it the more we want to enjoy, and to live under its blessed influence to the honour of our covenant God and Father.

I do not wish to leave the weaklings behind. It may be that some of my hearers can say, "I believe the doctrine, but then the question with me is, Am I one of them? Has he loved and chosen me? Am I elected?" Very solemn and important inquiries. God loves the inquirer; and I delight to speak a word of encouragement to the heart of the child of God. How many of us can solemnly say we believe and are satisfied that our names are written in heaven? Perhaps not many of us. But I know that many of us can respond to a mode of expression like this:

"In thy fair book of life and grace,
    O may I find my name
  Recorded in some humble place,
    Beneath my Lord, the Lamb."

"Ah!" says the poor child of God. "That is my desire, that is my feeling." That desire was not put into your heart that it might be disappointed. O no; thy record is on high.

Again, my friends, many of us would scruple to say, fearing we should be saying too much, that we firmly believe and are satisfied that we are the objects of Jehovah's electing love. But can we use these words – and we put them together as God has put them together in his Word, because I would buoy up your minds with the girdle of eternal truth – and say that we love God? Do you feel any concern for his honour and glory? Do you love the prosperity of Zion? Do you love the brethren? Is the desire of your soul in your solitary moments towards the name of the Lord and that you may be found in him? The poor child of God says it is God who knows my heart, knows that I can say with Peter, "Thou knowest that I love thee;" and I want to love him better, to live nearer to him and more to his honour and glory. Well, then, what does God say? "I love them that love me." We love God, and God loves us. Your loving the Lord is an evidence that he loves you, seeing that our love is the result of his own. "We love him because he first loved us." May we not say, therefore, with this manifested love of Jehovah in our souls, "The Lord hath done great things for us, whereof we are glad?"

II.   The Lord Jesus Christ "hath done great things for us, whereof we are glad." And what has he done? In the first place, beloved, let us direct our attention to his covenant engagements. My mind feels solemnly awed as I reflect upon the subject before we enter upon it. The covenant engagement of the immortal Word! Never was such an engagement entered upon before. What was it? Christ engaged in covenant council with the Father (for the covenant was between them both) to raise the objects of the Father's love from their state of sin, guilt and condemnation, to deliver them from the curse of the law and the wrath of God, to bring them from all their degradation, and shame, and wretchedness, and to present them without blemish before the Father's glorious presence, "with joys divinely great."

The covenant engagement of our dear Redeemer, O, it is a blessed, cheering, gladdening doctrine in the midst of affliction and trial. You remember how it sustained David's heart: "Though my house be not so with God (as I could wish), yet He hath made with me an everlasting covenant, ordered in all things and sure." He saw the covenant Head, and it gladdened his heart many a time. And has it not gladdened my heart, has it not rejoiced my soul, and yours too, brethren, to see that the cause of the church is in such glorious, noble and powerful hands as in those of the dear Redeemer? Surely it has. It cannot be in better hands. May we say feelingly with the apostle, "I know whom I have believed" – Christ, our covenant Head; and in his covenant engagement "he is able to keep that which I have committed unto him against that day."

But, secondly, the Lord Jesus Christ "hath done great things for us, whereof we are glad." Behold the greatness of his condescension and humiliation in his incarnation. He had a glory with the Father before the world was; but at the appointed time he threw his glory by and descended from the shining courts of bliss and blessedness. The apostle contrasts the humiliation and exaltation of Christ in these memorable words: "Let this mind be in you which was also in Jesus." That text applies most gloriously to Christ: "Before honour is humility." "He was rich" – the Most High God, possessor of the heavens and the earth – "yet for our sakes became poor, that we, through his poverty, might be made rich."

There was an absolute necessity for the incarnation of Jesus. Whence did that necessity arise? God's just and holy law had been violated and trampled on in human nature, and it was necessary that sin should be punished and condemned and law and justice satisfied in the very nature in which it had been violated. Forasmuch as his brethren "were partakers of flesh and blood, he also himself took part of the same; that through death he might destroy him that had the power of death, that is, the devil." So, my friends, the incarnation of Christ is a doctrine which gladdened the hearts of thousands now in glory. It does mine also; and does it not yours? Hark! "It is a faithful saying, and worthy of all acceptation, that Christ Jesus came into the world to save sinners," even the chief. We believe the doctrine, and not only believe it; it is the joy and rejoicing of our souls. Reason upon it for a moment experimentally.

I am now addressing a company of attentive hearers. If the Holy Ghost dwells in your hearts, you know and feel that you are poor sinners; you are sick of yourselves, your sinfulness and vileness. You have tried to save yourselves, but you could not. Has it never cheered and gladdened your heart to behold by faith, according to God's Word, the condescension of the immortal Word in consenting to become flesh, that he might suffer, bleed and die for our sins, and bring us rebels to God? And what gladness this must always be to the souls of the Lord's coming family.

But again, thirdly, the Lord Jesus "hath done great things for us, whereof we are glad." He was made under the law, he began at the beginning and fulfilled every precept of the divine law, down to its jots and tittles; in the thoughts of his heart, in the expressions of his lips, and in all his acts. The eye of the law and of justice was upon him from the manger to the cross and was divinely satisfied; for God himself declares, "who is glorious in holiness," "I am well pleased for his righteousness' sake." "He hath magnified the law, and made it honourable." Now what is that? Is it not well calculated to gladden the hearts of such as you and I? Nothing but real experience in the soul can teach us the real sweetness and joy which arise out of the glorious doctrine of the imputation of the righteousness of an incarnate God to a poor guilty sinner.

Now, my friends, let conscience testify what is your feeling. Can you say with the prophet Isaiah, "We are all as an unclean thing; all our righteousnesses is as filthy rags"? Until you feel this you will know nothing experimentally of the righteousness of Christ. We must be brought where Paul was brought when be exclaimed, "What things were gain to me, those I counted loss for Christ." What little value does the apostle put upon everything when compared with the dear Redeemer! Have we been brought there? Have we ever joyfully responded from the bottom of our hearts to the sentiment of this song:

> "Yes, I must and will esteem
> All things but loss, for Jesus' name?"

Every earthly thing must fall and Christ alone be exalted. The poor child of God is brought to renounce everything in himself; and he is dead to all hope of justification and salvation by works of righteousness done by himself. He hears the Lord Jesus Christ saying to him, "Look unto me. I am the end of the law for righteousness to thy poor soul." A covenant God speaks and says (O blessed language to every one that is in Christ Jesus!), "Christ is of God made unto us" – poor, guilty, filthy, polluted worms as we are – "wisdom and righteousness, sanctification and redemption." Does it do you good, friends? Can you rejoice in it? Have you been enabled to realize the language: "Surely shall one say, In the Lord have

I righteousness and strength," in whom all the seed of Israel are justified?

This glorious Christ has a perfect robe of righteousness. It gladdened the heart of the church of old. Hark! "I will greatly rejoice in the Lord, and my soul shall be joyful in my God; for he hath clothed me with the garments of salvation." Does your joy, comfort and consolation arise from yourself, your good name, your good heart, your good deeds, your excellent character? If so, my friends, you are not far off where Simon Magus was: "In the gall of bitterness, and in the bond of iniquity." But I know there are many precious souls here who can respond and say, "Instead of my joy and comfort arising from myself, when I look to my own soul I see that it is vile and sinful, and I have no joy at all; but when I see Jesus doing away with sin and bringing in a glorious righteousness for me then I feel, as David did, the blessedness of the man to whom the Lord imputeth not iniquity."

But look for a moment at the passive obedience of Jesus. See Christ bearing all the weight of our sin and iniquity in his own body in the garden of Gethsemane and on the cross of Calvary. What a wonderful statement that is of the prophet: "He was wounded for our transgressions, he was bruised for our iniquities," he trod the winepress of the wrath of God, due to sin, himself alone, and made an offering for sin. "It pleased the Lord to bruise him; he hath put him to grief," that had never sinned. It is one of the greatest mysteries to my soul that it should please the covenant God to bruise his beloved Son, who never sinned, and make him the victim and sacrifice for our transgressions – for us, who had insulted him, trampled upon his laws and despised him in our hearts, that we might be delivered from our sin, from the curse of the divine law, and be admitted into the divine presence and for ever surround his throne in the better world. O what a glorious view did the beloved Daniel take of the subject, when he foresaw that Christ was to make an end of all sin on the cross, and make reconciliation for all our iniquities, by the shedding of his blood, and to bring in an everlasting righteousness.

This is a salvation which has in many ages gladdened the hearts of God's living family. Has it ever gladdened yours? I remember the time when I could not see how I could be saved. I felt that I could not save myself; and I could not understand the way which God had revealed in the Bible until the Holy Spirit instructed me. But O! how it made me glad when I was led to see that Christ had done the whole work of salvation and had not left me one jot or tittle to do. Ah! it is a blessed way for a poor, guilty sinner to fall into the hands of Jesus, who says, "Come unto me, all ye that labour and are heavy laden, and I will give you rest." The burden of sin is then removed; and nothing can gladden and comfort the poor sinner more than a realization of salvation in the soul.

III. But we must go a little into the third part of the subject; namely, that the Holy Ghost is the Lord; and see that he also "hath done great things for us, whereof we are glad." What has the blessed Spirit done? We cannot say of his work as we did of Christ's – that it is finished. The Holy Ghost's work is not; and it never will be wholly accomplished until the top-stone of the spiritual temple shall be brought, with shoutings of "Grace, grace unto it." God's elect, with the rest of mankind, where are they? Dead in trespasses and sins. But, saith the apostle of the Holy Ghost, "You hath he quickened, who were dead in trespasses and sins." We were "by nature children of wrath, even as others," and saying in our hearts, "We will not have this man to reign over us." "Look unto the rock whence ye are hewn, and to the hole of the pit whence ye are digged." What a state of enmity, what a state of carnality and stubbornness we were in!

It humbles my mind to remember the condition I was in before the Holy Spirit took my soul in hand. What power was it that brought down my lofty looks? What made my heart willing to forsake sin? The power of the Eternal Spirit. The

Lord, according to covenant engagement, by his Holy Spirit creates a godly fear in the soul of the poor sinner. "I will, and they shall," is the language of Jehovah. "I will be to them a God, and they shall be to me a people." The Holy Ghost brings down lofty looks and abases the proud, that the Lord alone may be exalted in the salvation of his chosen people. There is no heart so hard and no will so stubborn but that the Holy Ghost can subdue and soften it.

Some few years ago the Lord, by his great and mighty power, laid hold of an influential man* in our town and neighbourhood and brought him to me. Many and many a time he spoke of the dealings of the Lord with his soul and, with his fist clenched, he would say, "Friend Kershaw! I don't care who they are; however proud and high-minded – however bent and determined on their way – if the same mighty power lay hold of their soul that laid hold of mine, it will bring them down, humble their hearts, and sicken them of all self-trust." Is there a soul here that has been arrested in his sins, and brought to the feet of Jesus, and made to say, "God be merciful to me a sinner?" I know, if there be such an one, that that soul is glad and quite ready to acknowledge that it is the work of the Holy Spirit to reveal a precious Christ to his soul.

Again, the Holy Ghost hath done great things for us in the revelation which he makes to us of Christ. He takes of the things of Christ and shows them to us, as Christ himself had said, shedding his love abroad in the soul of the poor, believing sinner; for Christ shall be our "All and in all."

Once more. We are glad in this, that the Holy Ghost is not only the beginner, but the carrier on of the work of grace in the soul. He will complete the work; not set it going and then leave the sinner to carry it on, "to cultivate grace," as some people say. My soul loathes the term! Cultivate grace!

* John Roby. John Kershaw's autobiography gives a most interesting account of him (pages 285-297, 1994 edition)

It is wrong. God's grace takes possession of the soul and God himself carries on the work which he has begun. "As thy days, so shall thy strength be," is the promise; and "My grace is sufficient for thee." And that grace shall land every elect vessel of mercy in immortal glory.

> "The feeblest saint shall win the day,
> Though death and hell obstruct the way."

So we are glad; and we rejoice in the work of the Father, of the Son, and of the Blessed Spirit; and we would sing with rapture, "Crown Jehovah Lord of all, for ever and for ever!"

16. THE NEW BIRTH

Preached at Zoar Chapel, Great Alie Street, London, on May 6th, 1855.

Text: *"Which were born, not of blood, nor of the will of the flesh, nor of the will of man, but of God" (John 1. 13).*

We had these words under consideration this morning, and promised, as it should please the Lord to assist, first, to take notice of the threefold negative in reference to being born again: that it is not of blood, nor of the will of the flesh, nor of the will of man, secondly, the positive declaration concerning the new birth – it is solemnly declared to be "of God"; and in the third place, we promised to point out some of the scriptural marks and evidences of a poor sinner being born of God.

It is not our design to take up much time in recapitulating what has already been said. Suffice it to say that religion does not run in the blood from the parent to the child. This we showed from sundry parts of the Scriptures, and proved to a demonstration from observation and experience. In the second place, we have shown that being born again is not of the will of the flesh; because poor, corrupt and depraved nature, which is what we are to understand by the flesh, stands directly opposed to regeneration in its commencement, and that flesh is said to lust against the Spirit, to fight and war against the grace of God in the heart all the way through, so that it is not of the will of the flesh that we are born of God, but it is contrary to it. In the third place, it is said that it is not of the will of man. Man's corrupt, depraved will ever was, is now, and ever will be in opposition to God's work of grace in the soul of a poor sinner; so that man, neither in reference to his blood, nor his flesh, nor his will, has anything to do with the work of regeneration, as regards the effecting of it. As our text declares, we are "born of God." We have dwelt upon the positive declaration, showing that it is God's work to create a poor sinner anew in Christ Jesus, to quicken the sinner dead in trespasses and sins, to call him by his efficacious and all-conquering grace, to open the heart, to open the blind eyes, and to unstop the deaf ear. Whatever metaphor is used, it implies that the work is exclusively effected by God. Though the Lord does and will honour instrumentality, that instrumentality is nothing without the power and gracious influence of the Holy Spirit. Paul plants and Apollos waters, but there is no increase in the conversion of sinners, no lofty looks are brought down, no haughty head abased, but as the power of God is made manifest in the Word. No soul is truly humbled and brought into the liberty of the sons of God but as the power of the Lord is displayed, not by creature might but by the power of the great Creator of the heavens, the mighty God of Jacob.

We now come to the evidence you and I have that we are, or are not, born of God. This is a very solemn subject. O that the preacher may be under the guidance and direction of the unerring Spirit of God in entering upon it! The Lord grant you the hearing ear and the understanding heart, and a spirit of serious examination. Let there be great searchings of heart among us, that we may see how matters stand between God and our precious, never-dying souls. We may have a form of godliness, a name to live, and make a great show in the flesh, and yet not be born of God; and what will it avail us in a dying hour, in the swellings of Jordan, if we are destitute of a good hope through grace of interest in the finished work of the Redeemer? If we are born and taught of God, we have Christ formed in our hearts by the Holy Spirit of God, the hope of immortal glory, which hope to the heaven-born soul is an anchor sure and steadfast.

But to the subject in hand – the evidences of being born again adduced from the Word of God. Now what is the evidence of a child being born into the world and that it is a living child? As sure as the child is born and is alive, so sure the child will cry. So it is in a spiritual point of view. As soon as God's work in regeneration takes place in the soul of a poor sinner, he will, like a new-born child, begin to cry; for *crying or prayer is the very breath of the soul that is born of the Spirit of God.* No one of Adam's fallen race ever could or ever can cry and pray to God spiritually until the Lord has commenced the work of regeneration and of grace in his soul. He may indeed pray, but not spiritually. Devils prayed, and the Lord answered and granted their request that they might go into the herd of swine. A natural man may pray, and it is right he should, for those natural favours and mercies which he feels he stands in need of, and he should be thankful to his great Creator and Benefactor for them. It was Nebuchadnezzar's great sin that he did not acknowledge God in whose hand his breath was. There neither is nor can be spiritual prayer without regenerating grace.

Now we must have proof from God's own Word for every statement that we bring forward; and in reference to this subject we shall refer to Saul of Tarsus. Before he was born of God and called by God's grace he was a Pharisee of the Pharisees, one of those that made long prayers and used "vain repetitions" and loved to be heard for their much speaking. No doubt he was a very fine prayer-maker and much admired for his talent and ability, but he never spiritually cried to God till God regenerated his soul. When Jesus met him in the way to Damascus and took possession of his soul and said, "Saul, Saul, why persecutest thou me? It is hard for thee to kick against the pricks," then the Word of the Lord, that is quick and powerful and sharper than any two-edged sword, entered into his very heart and soul. Jesus pulled down the strong man armed that had been keeping his palace in safety, and set up his own kingdom in his soul. "Lord," said Saul, "what wilt thou have me to do? I am in thy hand like clay in the hand of the potter" – an evidence that grace had taken possession of his soul. He was made willing in the day of the Lord's power. The Lord directed him where to go and said it should be told

him what he should do and suffer for his name's sake. And
the Lord appeared to Ananias and bade him go to this Saul of
Tarsus. Ananias was alarmed and raised objections. "Ah
Lord," he said, "we know what evil he has done to the saints
in Jerusalem, and he is come with authority to persecute us
and put us into prison. Do not send me into the paw of this
Benjamite who is coming like a wolf against thy people." But
the Lord settled all his scruples by informing him that after all
Saul's persecution, he was a vessel of mercy, and he said,
"*Behold, he prayeth*." He was truly converted. He was like the
new-born babe or the sucking lamb; so that when Ananias
understood his character and knew that he was a vessel of
mercy, he felt soul-union to him, entered into his house, called
him brother, and spoke to him the words of eternal life.

We have something here, my friends, to test ourselves by.
Are we living without heart-felt prayer to God? If so, there is
no evidence that we are born of God. We may read and pray,
drawing near to God with our lips, but having our hearts far
from him. Prayers may be repeated in words, but yet not felt
in the soul of the poor sinner. The preparation of the heart for
real spiritual prayer is from the Lord alone. As sure as a sinner
is born of God, God convinces him of sin and lays death, the
judgment day, and eternal realities with a solemn weight upon
his mind. Many before God have been made, like the
Philippian jailor, to tremble in their souls and to answer to the
character of whom the Lord has said: "To this man will I look,
even to him that is poor and of a contrite spirit, and that
trembleth at my Word." The poor sinner trembles not only in
body, but in soul, and cries out with the publican, "God be
merciful to me a sinner"; and that will be his prayer all
through the wilderness, and on a dying bed. The poor publican was born of God when he was bowed down with sin and
guilt and dared not lift up so much as his eyes to heaven, but
smote upon his breast while he exclaimed with his whole heart
and soul: "God be merciful to me a sinner." Ah, my friends,

if we are born of God and feel ourselves sinking with a guilty conscience, with the burden of our sins – sins more in number than the hairs of our head and too heavy for us to bear – we shall cry to the Lord, and our prayer will be: "Lord, save me, or I perish."

I do not think that the prayer of those that are born of God is very long. It is more in broken accents and heartfelt breathings and longings: "Lord, help me. O Lord, I am oppressed, undertake for me!" David was born of God when he felt himself sinking in the miry clay and the horrible pit. He cried unto the Lord, and the Lord heard him and raised him up and fixed him upon the Rock of Ages and established his goings. Beloved, can you give any account of the Lord so working in your soul to will and to do of his own good pleasure, so that you are necessitated to go into some quiet, secluded place for self-examination, to kneel down before the Lord and confess your sin and sinfulness; to tell the Lord that if he were to mark iniquity and deal with you according to your transgressions, you could not stand before him; to pray with earnestness and fervency that he would save you, teach you, guide you, and make you what he would have you to be? If you are born of God, there will be a heartfelt sighing, groaning, lamentation and woe in your souls because of the discoveries you have made of the depravity of your nature, of the evil of your heart, and of your manifold transgressions. If you are born and taught of God, you will be arraigned at God's bar in the court of your conscience, and tried by God's law. All hope of saving and helping yourselves will be cut off, and you will be brought in guilty and condemned, and lying at the feet of the dear Redeemer you will say, "I am resolved, and that is my last defence, if I perish, to perish at the footstool of mercy."

These are some of the evidences that a poor sinner is born of God. Those who are born of God no more live without prayer, without crying to God and panting, than they can live without food. Those who are born of God have their hungerings and thirstings after him: "Blessed are they which do hunger and thirst after righteousness, for they shall be filled." Nature, like water, can rise no higher than to its own level – natural and worldly things. Grace, like spiritual water, will rise to its own level – spiritual realities. "The water that I shall give him" – regeneration, my Holy Spirit, and my grace – "shall be in him a well of water springing up into everlasting life." The springing well is felt in the heaven-born soul who feels and says with David, "As the hart panteth after the water-brooks, so panteth my soul after thee, O God." In the soul that is born of God there is a going out in meditation, in prayer, sighs, groans, pantings, breathings and longings after the Lord that we may know him feelingly and experimentally for ourselves, and that we may have his sweet love shed abroad in our hearts. Man in a state of nature never wants to feel the love of Christ. The heaven-born soul cries to the Lord that he may have a knowledge of and interest in redeeming love and blood; that living or dying he may be found clothed in Immanuel's robe of righteousness; that he may stand complete and accepted in the Beloved; that he may be conformed to his image and live to his honour and glory. This is the evidence of life in the souls of God's living and regenerated family. Do you know anything of it? I hope many of you can say: "My soul responds to these Bible statements and these experimental evidences of being born of God."

But again, another experience of those born again we have in our Lord's own words: "*Except ye be converted and become as little children*, ye shall not enter into the kingdom of heaven." In what sense of the word are we to become as a little child? Nicodemus could not make this out; he was amazed at the doctrine. "Can a man," he said, "enter a second time into his mother's womb and be born?" O no; "That which is born of the flesh is flesh, and that which is born of the Spirit is spirit." Yet the metaphor holds good. If we are born of God, we are converted and experimentally become as little children. We have the emblem described more fully by the Lord himself in Ezekiel 16, under the form of a new-born child cast out into the open field to the loathing of itself, in its blood, unwashed, unsuckled, unclothed, destitute, indigent and forlorn, the very picture of helplessness, unable to do the least thing for itself; it can do nothing but cry. Now there is not a man that is born of God and truly taught his weakness and helplessness, his depravity, nakedness and inability even to think a good thought, who does not see in this child an emblem of himself. More than forty years have I seen myself described as a poor sinner in the new-born babe under these very circumstances. If any of you think you have a good heart and can do anything for yourselves towards your salvation, either in whole or in part, you are not true-born babes, you are not truly and spiritually born and taught of God and made acquainted with indigence and helplessness. This emblem will not only fit the new-born babe in grace; but the child, the young man, the father and mother in Israel will find themselves as weak and helpless and as dependent upon the Lord as the new-born babe was.

Before I left the vestry tonight and entered the pulpit, though I have long been in the work of the ministry and long known the Lord, I think I felt my own weakness, inability and insufficiency to do anything spiritually good, to preach the Word of life to comfort, profit and edification, as much as I ever did in my life. If we are born of God, like this little child we feel our weakness and helplessness. And we cannot, my friends, be too sensible of our own weakness, helplessness and sinfulness, nor lie too humble in the dust before the Lord. Paul says, "When I am weak, then am I strong"; and the Lord says he gives power to the faint, and to them that have no might he increases strength.

See the regard that the Lord has for a poor sinner that is truly born of God, converted, and become as a little child. In the very case under consideration we read that the Lord passed by and saw the new-born babe, looked upon it with compassion and love, and spread his skirt over it – typical of his glorious robe of righteousness with which he adorns the heaven-born family, the heirs of immortal bliss. He washed the child, emblematical not only of the washing of regeneration and the renewing of the Holy Ghost, but of all our sin and pollution being washed away in the atoning blood of the Lamb. Heaven-born souls cannot do without blood, the atoning blood of Christ, the precious fountain open for the house of David and the inhabitants of Jerusalem. The Lord adorned and decorated the child, and so the time was a time of love. Thus we see the evidences of being born again and becoming as little children, seeing and feeling our helplessness, weakness, insufficiency, inability, and our real spiritual poverty and destitution. All we can do is to add sin to sin and to bewail our wretchedness. But the Lord will have mercy and compassion upon the poor sinner thus born of his blessed Spirit and will do everything for him that he stands in need of.

I have no doubt there is many a precious soul here tonight that says, "Well, the emblem of a new-born babe sets forth my case. I am as weak and helpless and as dependent and indigent as the new-born babe. I am nothing but sin and weakness. I can do nothing but make the rent worse. The Lord must do all or I am undone." Do you really feel thus? Are you brought to the point that you really and solemnly feel that you are nothing and that you can do nothing, and that all must be done for you? Have you really learned that solemn truth that dropped from the Master's lips: "Without me ye can do nothing"? And that if Christ strengthens you, you can do all things? These are scriptural marks and evidences of a child being born of God.

Again, Peter illustrates this by a metaphor similar to that which we have just had under consideration, only he directs our attention in another channel: "As new-born babes, desire the sincere milk of the Word, that ye may grow thereby, if so be that ye have tasted that the Lord is gracious." Now, first to the emblem and then to the illustration of its spirituality. The God of nature has implanted in the very constitution of the new-born babe a craving desire for the breast and milk of its mother, that it may grow thereby. The affectionate mother takes the babe in her arms and puts it to the breast, and how naturally does the child begin to suck, while the mother looks down upon it with the greatest love and affection; and if she is a gracious, God-fearing woman she looks higher and prays that ten thousand blessings may rest upon it. Then come to the reality of the subject. The God of grace has implanted in the very constitution of a regenerated child of God *a fervent, earnest, craving desire for the sincere milk of the Word*, the Word of God's grace, the sacred Scriptures, and a desire for the ministration of the Word by his sent servants. As sure as a poor sinner is born of God he will be led to obey the Word of God: "Search the Scriptures, for in them ye think ye have eternal life, and they are they which testify of me."

I have seen many who have been born of God, and before that time they could not read a chapter, and some of them did not know even their letters; but a thirst came upon them, such a desire for the Word of God, that they have got some friends to teach them their letters. Then they have been able to put two or three words together and read little sentences; and then they have got into the New Testament, and could read the sermon on the mount: "Blessed are the poor in spirit; for theirs is the kingdom of heaven." Afterwards they have got some books and some hymns that they found good to their souls. O how fast they learn! They are the best learners, because they have the Spirit and grace of God dwelling in them and creating a fervent desire to know the sacred Scriptures, to have them written upon the fleshy tables of their heart by the Spirit of the living God, that they may be the living epistles of our Lord Jesus Christ, known and read of all men, written not with ink, but by the Spirit of God, not upon tables of stone, but upon the fleshy tables of their hearts.

We had some years ago a singular incident illustrating this. There lived in a village an old grey-headed sinner, bordering upon fourscore years old. There were two God-fearing men in the village, who felt for the old man, and one of them said to him, "Our minister is going to preach at a friend's house on such a night; I will call for you. Will you go with me?" "No," he said, "I won't. I will have nothing to do with you dissenters. I am a churchman. All my ancestors were church people. I was christened, confirmed and married at church, and I intend to be buried there; and it is enough for me." "Well," said the other, "you and I have been good friends. I have several times done you a kindness, and I should take it as a kindness if you would come with me and hear our minister preach the Word of eternal life." "Well," said the old man, "you certainly have been a good neighbour and have done me many kindnesses, and if it will oblige you, I will go."

The time came, and the God-fearing man called for the grey-headed sinner and poured out his heart in prayer that the Holy Ghost would wound the conscience of the old man. The minister drew the bow at a venture, the Holy Ghost directed the arrow, and the man felt a wounded conscience. He went home, and, sitting by the fire, he reflected, and looked into the grate, but he said not a word for a considerable time. His old wife, an ignorant woman, said to him in the Lancashire dialect, "What's to do?" "I cannot tell," said the old man; "but yonder minister said words that sank deeper into my soul than any that ever dropped from the lips of man in all my born days." "Ah!" she said, "I thought how it would be. They'll make us as bad as themselves. We'll not desert our religion. Thou shalt go no more." So much for her ignorance. But when the word of the Lord is rivetted in the conscience like a nail in a sure place, it cannot be erased.

The next time the old man did not need to be called for;

he longed for the time to come, and he went again, and the Lord wrought more powerfully and effectually than before. He returned with greater exercises and soul-concern about eternal realities than ever he felt before. He sat in the same position before the fire as he did on the previous occasion, and as a new-born babe this man of fourscore years desired the sincere milk of the Word. "I wish," he said to his wife, "you would find me our old Bible." It needed to be found, for it had not been used for months, or perhaps for years. The Bible was found. The wife takes her apron and rubs off the dust, and gives the Book to her husband. He reads a little here and there, and ponders it over in his mind, and then he says, "I say, wife, is this our right old Bible that we had ever since we were married?" "Yes," she said; "you know we never had any other." Then he reads again, and after thinking, with greater earnestness he says, "I say, is this our right old Bible?" "Yes," she says; "why, can't you believe me? We never had another." "Well, then," says he, "if it's our right old Bible, I've got new een" – that is, new eyes. Yes, the eyes of his understanding were opened; the veil of ignorance was rent off; he had a new heart, new desires, and he began to see the wonders recorded in the sacred Scriptures.

As sure, my friends, as a soul is born of God, so sure will that soul have a desire for the Word of God, and though it condemns and reproves him, he must come to the light. "Search me, O God, and know my heart, try me and know my thoughts, and see if there be any wicked way in me, and lead me in the way everlasting." "O Lord, teach me! I am dark and ignorant; instruct me." If we are born of God we shall be glad that we have the Scriptures in our own mother tongue, and we shall read them for edification, comfort and profit and say as Jeremiah did: "Thy words were found and I did eat them, and thy Word was unto me the joy and rejoicing of my heart." "How sweet," said David, "are thy words to my taste! yea, sweeter than honey to my mouth!" The soul that is not born of God does not enjoy this sweetness; he does not eat the Word of God and inwardly digest it and live upon it by precious faith.

But more on this branch of the subject. A man born of God, prior to that birth may have been spending his Sabbaths in carnal pleasures and amusements, as thousands have been doing in your great metropolis this day, neglecting the means of grace and turning their backs upon the preached gospel; and when I look at that class I have no stones to throw at them. I see the day in the eye of my mind when I hated the means of grace and fled from them as much as I could. The people of God were to me a people of no pleasure and enjoyment. I remember saying when my father and his associates used to meet in prayer, "Poor moping fools, men of no pleasure and enjoyment!" And I said within myself, when my father would compel me to attend prayer-meetings, for I did not like this exercise of his authority though I revered him as a natural father, "The day will come when I shall be my own master, when I shall be from under your authority, and then I will go with my companions and have my enjoyment." But O! I have blessed the Lord a thousand times that before I came to that age, my soul was born of God. God's grace and kingdom were set up in my heart, and the result was that old things passed away, old companions were forsaken, old practices left off, and new feelings and desires filled my soul.

Where there is a thirst for the Word of God's grace the soul will go to the house of God and love to hear the character of the poor sinner described, delight to hear the way of salvation pointed out through the precious blood of the Son of God. Where there is a desire for the sincere milk of the Word as recorded in the Bible, where there is a desire for the ministration of the Word and a delight to hear the silver trumpet of the gospel blown, that soul is born of God. The tabernacles of the Lord became amiable. O what an amazing change regenerating grace produces! The soul that is born of God can say, "How amiable are thy tabernacles, O Lord! I had rather be a doorkeeper in the house of my God" – where prayer is offered, praise is sung, the everlasting gospel preached, and where the saints of the most high God meet – "than dwell in the tents of wickedness." O how amiable is the place where the Lord condescends to meet with and bless his family! These are tokens, undeniable scriptural evidences that we are born again, and if we are born of God we are the sons of God and joint-heirs of God, heirs with the Lord of life and glory.

But in connection with this subject we observe again that if we are born of God and blessed with spirituality, the new man is created in righteousness and true holiness. O let us pause here and seriously examine ourselves by the rule laid down. If we are born again of God, we have a spiritual appetite, a spiritual palate, and nothing can satisfy our longing desires but God, the living God of grace, the God of salvation. If a soul is born of God, let him have all the gold and silver and lands and tenements heaped upon him, let him have all the honours and titles that can be given among men; will they satisfy him? Will they bring peace and rest and joy into his soul? No; the heaven-born soul in such circumstances will feel: "All is vanity below the sun and vexation of spirit," and will exclaim:

> "Were I possessor of the earth,
>   And called the stars my own,
>   Without thy graces and thyself,
>   I were a wretch undone!"

The heaven-born soul can never be satisfied with the world, but must aspire to nobler, more glorious and substantial things.

Again, if we are born of God we shall *never be satisfied with ourselves and our efforts.* Other men are pleased and delighted with what they do and have a good opinion of themselves. They are pure in their own eyes and never see their need of being washed from their filthiness. If you and I were to test ourselves by this principle, if we are born of God, the longer we live the more dissatisfied shall we be with our depraved nature and our evil hearts, our vain thoughts, our sinful inclinations, our evil tempers, and our murmurings and repinings. A heaven-born soul exclaims, "O wretched man that I am! who shall deliver me from the body of this death?" "In me, that is in my flesh, dwelleth no good thing." Thus if we are born of God we have humiliating views and feelings concerning ourselves, and a minister of Jesus Christ, lifting up his voice like a trumpet, can never lay a heaven-born soul too low. The soul that is thus laid in the dust and on the dunghill of self-abasement responds inwardly and says, "O wretched man! Unprofitable, hell-deserving sinner that I am! I never can be laid too low." The ever-blessed Spirit of God always brings down lofty looks, abases proud hearts, and lays them as beggars in the dust, and according to Hannah's song such shall be regarded of the Lord and set among princes; they shall inherit the throne of glory, for the pillars of the earth are the Lord's.

If we are born of God nothing will satisfy our appetite but what is embodied in that blessed declaration: "I will abundantly bless her provision; I will satisfy her poor with bread." Here, heaven-born soul, are the Lord's hungry poor, and here is the provision of the Father's house that satisfies the Father's children. The poor prodigal was born of God when he began to be in want and to feel a craving appetite for the bread of his father's house: "In my father's house there is bread enough and to spare. I will arise and go to my father." He does not say, "I will tell him what a good lad I have been." There is not a word about goodness or worthiness, but he says: "I will tell him that I have sinned against heaven and in his sight, and am no more worthy to be called his son." O brethren, nothing will satisfy the heaven-born soul but Jesus Christ in his glorified Person, Immanuel, God with us; Jesus in his covenant engagement, the precious Christ in his incarnation. Christ in his glorious robe of righteousness who has finished transgression, made an end of sin, and reconciled us unto God; Christ and him crucified; Jesus bearing our sins in his own body and carrying them into the land of forgetfulness, dying for our sins, being made a curse for us; salvation finished by the incarnate God on the cross exclaiming with his last expiring breath, "It is finished!" Heaven-born souls are *never satisfied, never happy, never comfortable, but as they seek and enjoy their dear Redeemer*, their All in all. What is your comfort, friends? What is the joy and rejoicing of your soul? If you are born of God and know anything of his love, your answer is: "Christ Jesus is precious to my soul; he is the joy of my heart. O that he would but shed abroad his sweet love in my soul and constrain me to love and serve him better, more acceptably, with reverence and godly fear!"

Again, the heaven-born soul, like Paul, *renounces everything in himself, counts all but dross for the excellency of the knowledge of Christ Jesus his Lord*, for whom Paul suffered the loss of all things and counted everything but dung that he might win Christ. Then the heaven-born soul says, "O that I may be found in Christ, not having on my own righteousness which is of the law, but the righteousness of God by faith; that I may be found built on the Rock of Ages, against which the gates of hell shall never prevail; that all my sins may be washed away in the blood of the Lamb and my conscience be sprinkled with that blood of atonement which speaketh better things than that of Abel; that I may be conformed to the image of Christ, have the mind of Christ, the Spirit of Christ; and that I may honour and glorify him with my body and spirit which are his; that I may hold on and endure to the end, be kept by his power, upheld by his mighty hand, and landed safe in immortal glory!" The prayer of the heaven-born soul is: "Guide me with thy counsel, and afterward receive me to glory." The song of exaltation of the heaven-born soul is: "This God is our God for ever and ever; he will be our Guide even unto death."

But the strength of my body fails. Glad I am of your attention to these solemn realities. Let me ask how many of us have reason to believe from these statements, founded upon the Word of God, that we are born again? Some dear child of God may say, "I can scarcely tell what to reply. I hope and trust I have some of the marks. I do love the brethren. I revere the place where God's honour dwells. But I have such a hard heart, and with me the great difficulty is, *I cannot tell when the work was begun.* Paul, for instance, could tell. Lydia could tell about God opening her heart to attend to the things spoken by Paul. Zaccheus could tell when the Lord called him down from the tree. The woman at Jacob's well could tell. I could tell sundry times when my conscience has been wounded, when the power of God has laid fast hold upon me and broken my soul down, so that my eyes have flowed with tears." But there are others of the Lord's family who, I believe, if their salvation depended upon it, could not tell when they were first called by divine grace and born of God. They have had convictions, their conscience has been wounded; but those convictions wore off and they sank back again for a time into sin. The Lord followed them, by grace hunted them out, sickened them of the world and themselves, and eventually brought them, lost and ruined and miserable in their feelings, to the feet of Jesus and enabled them to rest their soul's eternal all upon the dear Redeemer.

We read in God's Word: "The wind bloweth where it listeth, and thou hearest the sound thereof, but *canst not tell whence it cometh and whither it goeth*; so is everyone that is born of the Spirit." The Spirit is compared to wind which bloweth where it listeth. It is in the hand of God and under his direction. And when divine grace comes into the soul of the poor sinner, in some more gently and in others more powerfully, when the conscience is alarmed, the sinner cannot tell whence it comes nor where it will end. He begins to feel a concern for his soul and is separated from the world. He is

convinced of sin by the Holy Ghost, of God's righteousness
and justice, and of the certainty of the day of judgment. If you
are truly taught of God, *your mouth will be stopped and you will
acknowledge yourself guilty before God.* This text shall be fulfilled in the most extensive sense of the word. But there is
discrimination in it. Every elect vessel of mercy that is born of
God has his mouth stopped while in this life; that is, when he
comes before God he is dumb, inasmuch as he has neither a
good thought nor a good action to make mention of concerning himself. He is dumb. God says to his minister, "Open
thy mouth for the dumb and speak to the comfort and consolation of the dear child of God." Now if you have been
brought dumb before the Lord, it is grace that has brought
you. God's work is in you; and when the Lord opens his truth
in your heart and leads you into it by his Spirit and puts peace
and pardon into your soul, then the tongue of the dumb shall
speak plainly and shall bless the Lord and glorify him, saying,
"Bless the Lord, O my soul; and all that is within me bless his
holy name. Forget not all his benefits, who redeemeth thy life
from destruction and crowneth thee with lovingkindness and
tender mercies." The sword of the Spirit cuts two ways. O
that it may do so tonight, and that such of you as have reason
to believe that you are born of God may be thankful to the
Lord and say with the apostle, "By the grace of God I am what
I am."

And you, my friends, *whose consciences bear testimony that
you are strangers to heartfelt experimental prayer, strangers to your
weakness and helplessness;* you that neither see nor feel your
need of grace and the blessings of salvation treasured up in
Christ, who see no form nor comeliness in him that you
should desire him; you are in the gall of bitterness and the
bond of iniquity; and if you die in that state you will die in
your sins under the curse of God's law, and lift up your eyes
amid the horrors of the damned. O that the Lord would
awaken the careless sinner, that the thoughtless would con-

sider his latter end, that it may be said in the day of God, that this and that man was born here! O that a good work of grace may be wrought in your souls this night! Lord, grant it, if it be thy sovereign pleasure. Amen.

17. THE NAME OF JESUS

Preached at the opening of Rehoboth Chapel, Lower Ford Street, Coventry, on December 25th, 1857.

Text: *"And thou shalt call his name Jesus; for he shall save his people from their sins"* (Matt. 1. 21).

We have an account just before the text of the circumstances in which Joseph found Mary his espoused wife. Not willing to make an example of her, he would have put her away privily. He was a just man, considering the poor woman would have trouble enough; and while he thought on these things, the angel of the Lord appeared unto him, and said, "Joseph, thou son of David, fear not to take unto thee Mary thy wife; for that which is conceived in her is of the Holy Ghost. And she shall bring forth a son." And then comes in the text: "And thou shalt call his name Jesus; for he shall save his people from their sins."

I. In the first place I will, as the Lord shall help me, notice the reference to *the name* of Jesus.

II. *Who is* this Jesus?

III. His *people*.

IV. *What he shall do for them*.

I. In reference to the *name* of Jesus. There is no name to be found like it in any other book on earth, no names in any that are brought forth in comparison with it; but all must tremble before it.

In the greatness of his exaltation, the name of our Lord Jesus Christ is pre-eminent. We cannot illustrate it more strikingly and more beautifully than the apostle has done in Philippians 2. The exaltation of a precious Christ must shine more splendidly in contrast with his humiliation. "Let this mind be in you which was also in Christ Jesus, who, being in the form of God, thought it not robbery to be equal with God; but made himself of no reputation, and took on him the form of a servant, and was made in the likeness of men; and being found in fashion as a man, he humbled himself, and became obedient unto death, even the death of the cross."

Time would not allow us to dwell on the humiliation scene, that which our blessed Jesus had to pass through. Then said the apostle, "Wherefore God also hath highly exalted him, and given him a name which is above every name, that at the name of Jesus every knee should bow, of things in heaven, and things in earth, and things under the earth; and that every tongue should confess that Jesus Christ is Lord, to the glory of God the Father."

Observe here, my friends, Jesus has a name above every name, of things in heaven. There the innumerable company of angels, the patriarchs, prophets, apostles and confessors have left a great name on earth; but the name of Jesus, as Creator of the world and a Saviour, stands far above all. There the church triumphant, aided by angels, bows before his solemn, divine Majesty, ascribing all might, majesty, power and dominion to Jesus. He who stood condemned at Pilate's bar, crowned with thorns, and crucified, died for his people and was raised again for their justification, entered heaven, and is at the right hand of God to plead, intercede and manage the affairs of his church. He is the Head over all things to his body the church. Whatever they want will be supplied out of the fulness of this precious Jesus.

The apostle, in Ephesians 1, has this gracious declaration respecting the Lord Jesus: "According to the working of his mighty power, which he wrought in Christ when he raised him from the dead and set him at his own right hand in the heavenly places, far above all principality, and power, and might, and dominion, and every name that is named, not only in this world, but that which is to come; and hath put all things under his feet, and gave him to be Head over all things to the church, which is his body, the fulness of him that filleth all in all."

Mark again, my friends, that at the name of Jesus every knee should bow, not only of things in heaven, but of things that are on earth. This shall be solemnly fulfilled at the last day, when everyone shall be constrained to acknowledge him. Now, beloved, there is this discriminating difference. Every elect vessel of mercy, redeemed by the blood of Jesus, called by efficacious grace, convinced of his sin and his need of Jesus, is constrained from the indwelling and working of the Holy Spirit and the grace of God in his soul to bow the knee to Jesus here, and confess his sins and his need of him as his Saviour; and this absolutely and certainly flows from the working of his Spirit. He bows the knee, has godly sorrow for sin, calls upon his name for mercy, peace and pardon with shame and confusion of face; so that every knee shall bow, every tongue shall confess, either here or at the great day, that he is the Lord God Omnipotent, Zion's God.

He triumphs and reigns over all kings. He is King of kings and Lord of lords; for all things in heaven and in earth are in his hand. He is the confidence of the soul of every dear child of God, when led by the blessed Spirit to see the pre-eminence Christ has over every other name, every other power. Both men and devils are under his control. He says, "Hitherto shalt thou go, and no farther, and here shall thy proud waves be stayed."

The devils confessed and bowed to his power. We read of the seven sons of one Sceva, a Jew, who commanded the evil spirit to come out. The evil spirit said, "Jesus I know, and Paul I know; but who are you?" And the man in whom the evil spirit was leaped upon them and overcame them, and prevailed against them; so that they fled out of that house naked and wounded.

The name, the authority and power of the Lord Jesus is the same to this day. He is pre-eminent above all in heaven, and has the pre-eminence in his church upon earth. Say to Zion, "Thy God, thy Jesus, thy Saviour, thy Redeemer reigneth." In the song it is, "Hallelujah! The Lord God Omnipotent reigneth and triumphs over all." His name is above all names and most precious. The reason why it is so precious is because he shall save his people from their sins. There is not another name given under heaven or among men whereby poor sinners can be saved. How feelingly, powerfully and graciously Peter spoke in reference to this name, when before the Sanhedrim! Neither the Jewish council nor the Sanhedrim could interdict the power by which the lame man that sat at the Beautiful gate had been healed. Bold was Peter in his answer. He felt the name of Jesus precious. It warmed his heart. He said, "Be it known unto you all, and to all the people of Israel, that by the name of Jesus Christ of Nazareth, whom ye crucified, whom God raised from the dead, even by him doth this man stand here before you whole; neither is there salvation in any other; for there is none other name under heaven given among men whereby we must be saved." Precious name of Jesus! He is able to save to the uttermost all them that come unto God by him. It is in his heart to save; for the prophet Zephaniah says, "He *will* save." The sweetness and preciousness of the name of Jesus is because it is the only name whereby poor guilty sinners can be saved. "A just God and a Saviour." The prophet says, "Look unto me, and be ye saved, all the ends of the earth; for I am God, and there is none else." No Saviour, poor sinner, but Jesus. "Thou shalt call his name Jesus; for he shall save his people from their sins."

God's chosen and redeemed people, those taught by his blessed Spirit, are brought into that state of soul-feeling before the Lord that all the men on earth or angels in heaven cannot save them. As it respects saving themselves, they have tried that old covenant ground, and have felt completely sick at heart at this work. Having been brought in guilty, lost and ruined, weak and helpless, to the footstool of Jesus, pleading for mercy, they have feelingly said, "O Lord, my help must come from thee. Help is laid upon thee; and as there is no other name given under heaven whereby one so vile can be saved, O Lord, thou Son of David, have mercy on me!"

Thus the heart of the dear child of God is set upon Christ. His hope centres in him, hanging and cleaving to him with full purpose of heart. The Lord, by his blessed Spirit, brings his own family to feel the necessity of mercy.

Jesus is the Saviour of his people in that he saves them with an everlasting salvation. They are brought to give all into his hands, to lie at his blessed feet, saying, "If I must perish, I will perish at the feet of Jesus, clinging, cleaving to Jesus." Bless his name, he never gives a poor sinner to feel his need of him and puts a cry in his heart, and then disappoints the expectation of that precious soul. No, no! "He will fulfil the desire of them that fear him; he will hear their cry, and will save them."

Another reference to the name of Jesus is: there is confidence wrought in the soul of the believer by the Holy Spirit in the name of Jesus, above every other name. It is in this way, beloved, the Holy Spirit, whose prerogative it is to take of the things of Christ and show them to the poor sinner, convincing of sin and his need of Jesus, takes of the things of Christ and makes them known to the poor sinner, showing him the power, the ability, and all-sufficiency and the willingness of Jesus to save poor, lost, guilty sinners. The blessed Spirit works such confidence in the soul of the dear child of God in the very name, the power and the suitability of Jesus to save, that he does, under the holy anointing of the Spirit, name the name of Jesus.

Here let me observe that no man can call Jesus Lord but by the Holy Ghost. A man may by his mouth do so; but that is not the point. No man will worship Jesus with divine authority but by the Holy Ghost. No man knows his name fully and experimentally as Jesus, that he has confidence in, only as wrought in the soul by the Holy Spirit. Hence the desire of his soul is to the remembrance of his name. Blessed

Jesus, that I may be found in thee, the desire of my soul is to thy name, above every other name in heaven and earth.

Brethren and sisters in the Lord, how do matters stand? If your desires are to any other name, you are looking to a broken cistern, you are relying upon a false foundation.

It is also said in reference to the name of Jesus, as the ground and confidence of the soul's support, "They that know thy name," which is Jesus, that feel the preciousness and power of that name, "will put their trust in thee." Such is really the case; for wherever there is a revelation of that name, of the ability and the all-sufficiency of Christ to save, that soul will place all his confidence and dependence in the name, Person, blood, righteousness and power of Jesus. And no living soul, previous to this state, can be under any real gospel rest. No; until brought in this way to know the name of Jesus, to commit the care of our precious souls into his hand, as in the language of the apostle upon a vital point of experimental religion. There is no doubt of the genuine nature and reality of what is here expressed in the following portion of the Word of God. It bears the stamp of divine inspiration: "I know whom I have believed." I have believed in Jesus to the saving of my soul. "He that believes in him and is baptized shall be saved; he that believeth not shall be damned." "I know in whom I have believed, and am persuaded of his power, ability, sufficiency and willingness to save my soul. I am confident that he will keep that which I have committed into his hands against that day. I have committed my soul's salvation into his keeping, committed all into his hand – into the hand of the Lord Jesus the Saviour – with such sweet, solemn, blessed confidence and safety that I can sing with the prophet, 'Behold, God is my salvation. I will trust, and not be afraid; for the Lord Jehovah is my strength and my song. He also is become my salvation.'"

One of the songs that we sing in reference to this important subject among the friends, when we assemble for proposing or receiving members – and I believe that it is often the experimental feeling of their souls – is:

> "Jesus, my God, I know his name;
>   His name is all my trust."

Not a part; but *all* my trust:

> "Nor will he put my soul to shame,
>   Nor let my hope be lost."

And so on.

We find confidence in the name of Jesus because there is no name given on earth that is so sweet, so precious, so soul-animating to the Christian, taught by the Spirit of God, as that name. The name of the Lord Jesus is a good name, which is as ointment poured forth. Yes, my friends, a divine savour and odour is connected with the sweet and precious name of Jesus. When that name is revealed that Jesus makes known by the blessed Spirit in the soul of a poor sinner, that confidence wrought in the soul in the name of him of whom we have been speaking, the heart of the sinner is warmed within. His confidence in Jesus is strengthened. He feels such love to him, that he is so precious, so sweet, that his name is such a savour to him, that neither men nor devils can stop him from expressing his feelings in scriptural language: "Whom have I in heaven but thee? And there is none upon earth that I desire beside thee." Precious Jesus! Thou art to my soul the Chief among ten thousand, and the altogether lovely!

This name of Jesus has the pre-eminence in the souls of his dear children upon earth; so that, under the ministry of the Word, when the minister has been exalting the Lamb of God, under the blessed teaching of the Spirit, they have been laid low at his feet, and emptied of self. Their language and felt experience has been: "Let me be emptied, abased and laid low at his feet, in the dust of self-abasement." The language of our hearts is: "Let the Lamb of God, the sin-atoning Lamb, be exalted. Let me speak well of his name. Let me triumph in Christ and in the power of his resurrection." There is here complete salvation. When you have heard him set forth, in his death, resurrection, ascension and entrance into heaven, while the preacher has been exalting a precious Christ, the Lamb of God, the sin-atoning Lamb, there has been a secret something dwelling in the heart which has warmed and animated your spirit, filling your soul with gratitude, and setting you rejoicing inwardly; and you have placed the crown upon the head of a precious Christ, and said, "Crown him, Lord of all!" The name of Jesus, therefore, has the pre-eminence.

To close this branch of the subject, I will just mention this anecdote. More than forty years ago I was speaking of the preciousness of Christ at Halifax. The Lord blessed me with enlargement of heart in speaking of the name, Person and work of a precious Christ. When I descended from the pulpit, an old man was sitting at the foot of the stairs. He put his walking-stick under his arm, got fast hold of my hand in his, and looked me full in the face for a moment. I was at a loss to know whether he was going to condemn or express his approbation, when he burst forth with,

> "Join all the glorious names
> Of wisdom, love and power,
> That ever mortals knew,
> Or angels ever bore;
> All are too mean to speak his worth,
> Too mean to set my Saviour forth,"

at the same time giving my hand a hearty shake. You cannot tell what a response there was in my soul to what he said. It suited my spirit. The pre-eminence, the majesty, glory, strength, consolation and truth in the name of a precious Jesus is to be found in no other.

II. Speak of this *Person* who is to do this great work – "save his people." Who is he? There is a general sense in which it may be said scripturally that he is the Lord; and in his complex character of God and man he is the Lord, the adorable and ever-blessed God-Man. "There are Three that bear record in heaven, the Father, the Word, and the Holy Ghost; and these Three are One." The immortal Word is our Jesus. By him all things were created that are named. He became flesh and dwelt among us, and we beheld his glory as the only-begotten Son of God, full of grace and truth. Here we have the mystery of godliness set forth in our text. It is the incarnation of the immortal Word – "made of a woman, made under the law," to redeem his people from the curse of the law; our Immanuel, God with us.

Speaking of Jesus, he really is God over all, blessed for evermore. He is the Most High God, possessor of heaven and earth. All things are his. He is the great Creator and Bene-factor. His mercy and compassion are over all his works as the God of nature, causing the rain to descend and the sun to rise and shine on the evil and on the good, upon the just and unjust. But this is not the sense in which the angel is to be understood in addressing Joseph: "Thou shalt call his name Jesus; for he shall save his people from their sins."

III. Who are *his people*? Why, my friends, without any controversy, his people are they who were loved in him by a covenant God and Father with an everlasting love, chosen in him unto salvation from the beginning; not because of their being any better than others, or of any worth or worthiness in them more than others. O no, no! But it is all according to the good will of that God who anciently dwelt in the bush. We are, my friends, quite aware those old-fashioned doctrines of salvation and predestination are not popular in the age in which it has pleased God that we should live. Many persons who profess to believe them keep them in the background. And this brings a circumstance to my mind. Some time ago, one afternoon, going to visit a sick friend, on my way I passed the house of a very influential man, whom I had known from a youth [the famous Victorian statesman, John Bright]. I was familiar with his father. I saw him. He said, "Friend Kershaw,

I was at your chapel yesterday afternoon." I replied, "I thought you Friends" (called Quakers) "kept to your own meetings." He said, "Generally so; but the fact is I went to see a person, and he was gone to chapel, so I concluded to go and wait for him. I perceived the man who was preaching held the doctrines the same as thee; but he did not bring them out; he kept them in the background. Now, how was that?" How was that? He dared not come out with it, for fear of giving offence. "He that hath my Word let him speak my Word faithfully. What is the chaff to the wheat? saith the Lord."

One objection brought against this doctrine is that, knowing we are chosen and certain of salvation, it is apt to make us lifted up, to boast, be proud, despise others, and be high-minded. Now let me tell these objectors they know nothing about it. They are out of the secret. If ever God by his Spirit shows a man what a sinner he is, what he has merited at his hands, and that the great and gracious God should in his covenant love have mercy and compassion upon him, the effect will be to humble him in the dust of self-abasement, and to admire that love that first fixed upon one so unworthy. Instead of despising others, his song will be of God's free mercy and sovereign grace. How abundantly his mercy is set forth in his own words in John 17: "Thine they were and thou gavest them me. All mine are thine and thine are mine." No man shall pluck them out of his hand. "My Father that gave them me put them into my hands, secured them in me. My Father is greater than all, and no man shall ever be able to pluck them out my Father's hands."

These people are his inheritance, his portion. "The Lord's portion is his people; Jacob is the lot of his inheritance. He found him in a desert land, in a waste howling wilderness; he led him about, he instructed him, he kept him as the apple of his eye." But, as Berridge says,

> "Good doctrines can do me no good,
>   While floating in the brain;

Unless they yield my heart some food
They bring no real gain."
It is only as they are made manifest in my heart and soul by the
power of the Holy Ghost. There it is, and it does my soul
good. Berridge dwells more particularly on the experimental
part of the Father's love, chosen by him, given into the hands
of Jesus as the covenant Head and Representative of his
people, their Saviour and Redeemer. Then the question
arises, "Are you among that happy number? Am I one of
those whom the Father hath chosen, and given my cause into
the hand of Christ my covenant Head? Have I placed all my
confidence and dependence in him?" That is a sweet portion
of our Lord's on this point, that sweet declaration: "All that
the Father giveth me *shall come* to me." Not have offers and
proffers merely; he tells them they *shall* come. "Thy people
shall be willing in the day of thy power." As Bunyan says,
"When *shall come* gets hold of them, he brings down their lofty
looks; the proud heart is abased, and brought to the feet of
Jesus."

Now, the question is, "Has the Lord laid hold of us?" For
myself, I can say, when the Lord first began with me, when the
arrow of conviction first laid hold of my conscience, when the
hidden sorrow for sin caused me to separate from my worldly
companions by the power of divine grace, I was brought out of
this world and brought to the feet of Christ.

"All that the Father giveth me shall come" – the lost to be
saved, the guilty to be pardoned, the naked to be clothed, the
filthy to be washed in atoning blood, the weak to be
strengthened, the ignorant to be instructed. All Christ's
people were given to him by his Father. Being brought into
that state that they know they cannot do without him, they
are therefore compelled to come to him.

A word here to the dear child of God. When the Lord
Jesus put that question to his disciples, when many of them
went back and walked no more with him, "Will ye also go

away?" Peter did not say, "We will not"; but puts another question: "To whom shall we go but unto thee? For thou hast the words of eternal life. None can save us but thou, none can help us but thou. There is no joy or consolation only in thee." The dear children given by the Father into the hand of Christ, they are brought to him.

IV. *What Christ shall do for his people.* He shall save them from their sins. "Thou shalt call his name Jesus, for he shall save his people from their sins."

Now all the Lord's people are by God the Father kept and preserved in the Lord Jesus, the great Head of the church, sanctified and set apart, preserved in Christ Jesus, and called; and they shall be presented faultless before the presence of his glory with exceeding joy.

One experimental mark of the people given by the Father into the hand of the Lord Jesus is they are all taught by the blessed Spirit of God to commit the keeping of the salvation of their precious and never-dying souls into the hands of Jesus. If you and I, through grace, are enabled to believe on Jesus, make a humble, solemn surrender of ourselves to Jesus, begging that we may be his, and his only, that he would make it manifest we are his jewels, bound up in the bundle of life with him, a seed to serve him, a generation to call him blessed, vessels of honour, vessels of mercy afore prepared for the Master's use for immortal glory; if this feeling, these desires, are wrought in the soul by the Holy Ghost, this will make our souls joyful in God.

Speaking of the confidence of the church in our Lord Jesus Christ brings another interesting circumstance to my mind. About twenty-five years ago I was in London. One Lord's day I preached in Bury Street chapel. Dr. Watts used to speak there. There was a large and attentive congregation. My text was: "All that the Father giveth me shall come to me, and him that cometh to me I will in no wise cast out." I spoke of the sovereignty of God in bringing his own people from all parts, and referred to the case of John Newton, how the Lord brought him from being a blasphemer to be a preacher of his grace, and what a blessing he was made to the church of God. When the service was over, a very old gentleman said, "Friend, I was very glad to hear you make mention of my old pastor. I sat under him for many years; and what I have heard this morning has been blessed to my soul." A very short time after this the dear old man died. Two or three of the friends called to see him. He was very happy. He said he was going to heaven upon two crutches. His right-hand crutch was, "All that the Father giveth me shall come to me." "Shall come laid hold of me a long time ago; shall come brought me; shall come has kept me ready for my dismissal. My left-hand crutch is, 'And him that cometh I will in no wise cast out.'" This is resting on a good foundation. Two better crutches we never can have in the Jordan of death.

God Almighty command his blessing on these truths.

18. A FAREWELL

Fragment from the Last Sermon preached by Mr. Kershaw in Sunderland, July 27th, 1868

I must draw to a close; for my strength fails me; but I must first express my deep gratitude for the solemn attention with which you have listened to me this evening. I am an aged man, nearly 77, and I am expecting sickness and death; for I cannot be long here; but I know that "to live is Christ, to die is gain," and I trust and believe that to die will be my gain. Whether or not I shall ever see you again God only knows; but I am visiting my various friends with the feeling that it is for the last time. But, my friends, if I should never see you more, I pray God that the words which he has enabled me to speak this evening may bear fruit in days to come. God has said, "Cast thy bread upon the waters, and thou shalt find it after many days." God grant it may be so in this case, and that his word may not return unto him void.

But I have spoken of the rich inheritance of God's children, those whom he blesses collectively, individually and eternally. This has called up some solemn thoughts. God's saints! What a blessed lot is theirs, when the judgment day arrives, and they shall be received into heaven, a palm of victory and crown of glory be given them, and placed at the right hand of God, to sing the eternal praises of him who is their Saviour and Redeemer, who died for them that they might live, who has redeemed them from all sin in his own atoning blood. There they will stand for ever and for ever, singing songs of praises to God and the Lamb. But O! solemn thought! What is the case of those who live and die in their sins, never pardoned through a precious Saviour's blood? O! solemn thought! God shall turn to those, and say, "Depart from me, ye cursed, into everlasting fire, prepared for the devil and his angels, where there shall be weeping and gnashing of teeth." Pause and think, beloved, of the fearful fate awaiting those who are not cleansed from all sin and pollution in the precious atoning blood of Jesus Christ!

19. DIFFERENT STAGES OF GRACIOUS EXPERIENCE

A Fragment of a Sermon

Text: *"One shall say, I am the Lord's; and another shall call himself by the name of Jacob; and another shall subscribe with his hand unto the Lord, and surname himself by the name of Israel"* *(Isaiah 44. 5).*

The three characters spoken of in my text were children of God in different stages of experience: the first, in the full assurance of faith, with the enjoyment of peace and pardon in the soul; the second seemed to embrace by far the largest number of God's family – poor, fearful, staggering, doubting sinners, yet spiritual Jacobs; and the third, those who possessed some good degree of confidence, whose desire was unto the Lord, to serve him with purpose of heart.

I. *"One shall say, I am the Lord's."* Highly favoured and greatly blessed is the soul that can feelingly, honestly and, with the Spirit of God testifying to the conscience, humbly say, "I am the Lord's." How many are there of my hearers in the chapel this morning who can thus unhesitatingly declare, "I am the Lord's"? "My Beloved is mine, and I am his"? I do not think there are many who without a doubt or without fear could say so. Now, if we were in private conversation together, there would be many, doubtless, who would say, "I hope and trust I am the Lord's; but I fear to be presumptuous." But there are some here, I dare venture to say, who can well remember the time when the Lord appeared so graciously, and manifested himself so sweetly to the soul, that they were enabled in all holy confidence to say, "I am the Lord's"; "I am my Beloved's, and my beloved is mine." "Lord, I am thine," said one, "save me." And again: "For there stood by me this night," said the apostle, "the angel of God, whose I am."

II. *"And another shall call himself by the name of Jacob."* Now, I think I have before me many Jacobs this morning. But what do we understand by Jacob? What does Jacob say of himself? For if the account he gives, and the confession he makes to the Lord, do not agree in some measure with our case and feelings, we have no right to call ourselves by the name of Jacob. But what does Jacob say on that memorable occasion when he was about to meet his brother Esau, armed with four hundred men? I need not go into the history; but let us just see what Jacob says to the Lord: "O God of my father Abraham, and God of my father Isaac, I am not worthy of the least of all the mercies, and of all the truth, which thou hast shewed unto thy servant." "Ah," says some poor soul, "then I am a Jacob: I am not worthy of the least of God's mercies; I am the greatest sinner, the vilest wretch, a worthless worm."

And what does the Lord say to these poor things? Why, "Fear not, thou worm Jacob." For what was spoken to Jacob of old – these very promises were made to all and every one of the seeking seed of Jacob down to the end of time. In Hosea we find a remarkable passage: "He took his brother by the heel in the womb, and by his strength he had power with God: yea, he had power over the angel, and prevailed: he wept, and made supplication unto him: he found him in Bethel, and there he spake with us" – *with us*. So that what the Lord said to Jacob, he said to all his spiritual seed in him. And why does the Lord say, "Fear not, worm Jacob"? Because they are often so full of fears: they fear sin, fear Satan, fear themselves, fear various things as they pass along. But the Lord says, "Fear not, thou worm Jacob."

I have often thought and said, there is a verse of one of our poets that describes the substance of all my religion. You will say, "It must be very little, then, for a single verse of a hymn to contain it all." Well, but it does. And what is that? Why –

> "A guilty, weak, and helpless worm,
>   On thy kind arms I fall;
> Be thou my strength and righteousness,
>   My Jesus and my all."

There, my dear friends, is the sum and substance of my religion. And again:

> "Great God! how infinite art thou!
> What *worthless worms* are we!"

III. "*Another shall subscribe with his hand unto the Lord, and surname himself by the name of Israel.*" Jacob was the first name of every true Israelite. The name of Israel was given to Jacob on the occasion before referred to, when he wrestled with a man until the breaking of the day. Who was this man? Why, the Angel of the Covenant – God and Man – Emmanuel: God with us. And he said, "Let me go, for the day breaketh." But Jacob said, "I will not let thee go, except thou bless me." O, the power of faith! that this poor worm should be enabled to wrestle with the Lord, the God of heaven and earth! to hold him so firmly by the arms of faith and prayer, as for God himself to say "Let me go"! But no, "I will not," cannot, "let thee go, except thou bless me." And he said unto him, "What is thy name?" And he said, "Jacob." And he said, "Thou shalt be no more called Jacob, but Israel: for as a prince hast thou power with God and with men, and hast prevailed."

What a mercy for poor sinners, when enabled to wrestle with the Lord in times of trouble. How many times have I gone to my closet, in real earnest prayer to God, when I should never have gone there but for trouble! So that I bless God for trials and troubles which have brought me to him, wherein I have seen the goodness of God in hearing and answering my prayers and working deliverances for me. There is no real crying to the Lord until we are brought into trouble and necessity of some kind or in some measure; though the Lord, in his sovereignty, does not deal with all his people just alike. O, no; though all must be brought at length to be nothing that the Lord may be all in all.

God says, by his prophet Hosea, "I will be unto them as a lion." This is his way of working with some. He stops them at once; causes them to feel such deep and cutting convictions –

so terrible, it may be, that there appears to be no way of escape; nothing before them but destruction: and this may be for weeks or months, and even years, before they are enabled to lay hold of the Lord Jesus Christ.

There was a wealthy banker* in our town some years ago, a man of education and standing in life, whom the Lord met with in this way: "met him as a lion," cut his soul in pieces, and brought him down into the very dust. He would come down to my house sometimes and, with a countenance expressive of the real earnestness with which he spake and felt, would clench one hand and beat it on the palm of the other, saying to me, "I don't care how proud a man may be; let him be as stubborn, hard-hearted and determined in sin as he may, let the Lord meet with him as he met with *me*, he will be *brought down*." Nothing else may be able to do it; but when the Lord meets the soul like a lion, this will be sure to humble the proud, rebellious heart of any sinner.

But this is not the Lord's way with all. In some cases he brings them to a knowledge of themselves and of their sins in a more gradual, gentle way, according to his word: "I will be to Ephraim as a moth." Yes, my dear friends, the Lord works with some of his children as a moth. Now, there is a great difference between a moth and a lion. But what does the moth effect, literally? Why, when it gets into a garment, it begins fretting it into small holes; and as soon as we discover it, if we wish to preserve the garment, we try this remedy and the other, but the work of destruction goes on till at length the garment is cast aside as useless and worthless. So it is with the sinner: let the Lord come in this manner and enter the heart of a proud, self-righteous Pharisee, and begin fretting his garments into holes, discover to him the evil of his nature, make him sick of himself, even of his good works, and thus go on fretting and fretting his garments, till he is led to cast them

* John Roby. John Kershaw's autobiography gives a most interesting account of him (pages 285-297, 1994 edition).

all entirely away as filthy rags. Then, and not till then, feeling stripped and emptied, will he at last be brought down to seek help and righteousness alone from the Lord, whose work it is to save sinners, and to stop them at the first. Who stopped me in my mad career, going in the broad way of sin and death? Did I stop myself? O, no!

"And another shall subscribe with his hand, and surname himself by the name of Israel." But Paul says, "They are not all Israel who are of Israel." "But we," he says, "are the true circumcision, which worship God in the spirit, rejoice in Christ Jesus, and have no confidence in the flesh." Circumcision was a type; and though it is now done away literally, yet every spiritual Israelite must be circumcised in his heart.

Some poor souls – poor dear children of God – are so afraid of their sins, they think they are so great that they never can be pardoned; that there can be no mercy for such wretches as they feel themselves to be. But, poor soul, you need not in reality fear. O, no! Well, but some will say, "Then you encourage sin, and the doctrines you preach lead to licentiousness." No, my dear friends, not for a moment. But sin shall not have dominion over God's children; it is for ever put away, and buried in the sea of forgiving love and mercy, which

"Rises high, and drowns the hills,
Has neither shore nor bound;
Now, if we search to find our sins,
Our sins can ne'er be found."

In connection with the worm Jacob, I will just quote a portion of a verse by dear Berridge:

"Such a worm of nothing worth,
Crawling out and in the earth."

Yes, these poor worms come out of their holes sometimes. And what brings them out? Why, the rain and dew of heaven distilled on their precious souls; this will make them come forth to the light.

20. THE JUSTIFICATION OF A SINNER BEFORE GOD

Substance of two sermons preached at Gower Street Chapel, London
on November 14th and November 21st, 1841

[On Lord's Day morning, November 14th, 1841, Mr. Kershaw spoke on the doctrine of justification, taking for his text the 4th verse of the 25th chapter of the Book of Job. It appeared to have been his intention of taking it up – first, as a Bible doctrine; secondly, as manifested in the believer's conscience; and, thirdly, as productive of all those spiritual fruits and that moral deportment which adorn the Christian character. An outline of this sermon follows.

The whole of his time, however, being occupied with the first branch of the subject, he promised, God willing, to enter upon the remaining two on the next Sabbath morning. The second sermon is the fulfilment of his promise.]

Sermon 1

Text: *"How then can man be justified with God?"* (Job 25. 4.)

The doctrine of justification is clearly and strikingly revealed in the sacred oracles of truth, and is by God the Holy Ghost made manifest in the souls of all the election of grace. Hence, Paul speaks of it as one of the links in the chain of our salvation. "Moreover," says he, "whom God did predestinate, them he also called; and whom he called, them he also justified; and whom he justified, them he also glorified." Here is a precious chain of gospel truths, which neither men, nor sin, nor devils can ever break. No, blessed be God, all our sins, temptations, pollutions, harrassings and unbelievings can never break one link in this precious, golden chain. If our souls are established in this one truth by the teaching of God the Spirit, we shall never err very far from any of the other branches of divine truth connected with it; but if we are wrong here, we shall be wrong altogether.

In this great and glorious doctrine of justification lies the church's standing, the church's safety and the Redeemer's glory. In attempting to illustrate this doctrine, I shall endeavour:

I. To speak of it in a doctrinal point of view.

II. To show how the Eternal Spirit leads the election of grace into an experimental acquaintance with it.

III. To point out the practical effects produced thereby. And, my Christian friends, may the Lord give us his blessing and assistance, that we may be enabled faithfully to speak out the truth; and may he also give the hearing ear, that we may be comforted and enabled to rejoice together in this most precious and essential part of the revealed will of God.

First, then, we have to take notice of justification as a Bible doctrine. And our text, you will perceive, exhibits two parties to our view – man and God. It is requisite, therefore, that we take notice of these two parties, and of the circumstances in which they each stand. And first, as regards man. That is an important inquiry, "Lord, what is man?" I might detain you a long time in showing what man *was* in his primeval state, but I will not dwell here. It is said, "God made man upright." Now, as he declared all the workmanship of his hands to be very good, man being the great masterpiece of his workmanship, it follows that, in his first condition, he was included in that declaration: he was very good. But did he continue there? No; for by the disobedience of one many were made sinners. Adam being the federal Head, all his posterity lay in his loins; so that when he fell, all who lay in his loins fell and died with him. Even so all in Christ shall, by virtue of his death and resurrection, be made alive.

The doctrine of human depravity is a doctrine clearly revealed in the Word of God. Sin, that cursed and abominable thing which God hates, is in our natures – we are conceived in sin and shapen in iniquity. Sin, that cursed and abominable thing which a holy God hates, is in our hearts – they are carnal, deceitful, full of enmity, like unto a cage of unclean birds; and the Saviour, who knew what was in man's heart, said that murders, adulteries, and all manner of abominations, proceed from the heart. And not only the heart, but every faculty of the mind, every member of the body, and every action of the life, all are sinful; so that we stand guilty and condemned in our natures, and to them that are under the law it pronounces the most awful curses and condemnation. This is a very brief but scriptural account of what man is – so guilty, so contaminated, polluted and unholy that Job cries out, "How should man be just with God?"

With reference to the other party, God, he is represented as being glorious in holiness, righteous in all his ways, doing wonders. Such is the holiness and purity of God that the angels are continually exclaiming, "Holy, holy, holy is the Lord God Almighty." Holiness and perfection, righteousness and justice are the attributes, yea they are the very nature and essence of Deity itself; God is of purer eyes than to behold iniquity. The solemn voice of his Majesty has declared he "can in no wise clear the guilty"; his holy attributes of justice and righteousness bind him to say that sin shall not go unpunished. O beloved, what an awful breach has sin made in God's most holy law; such a breach that it never could have been made up but in the way in which it has been made up. There is one God of holiness, and one Mediator between God and man, and by his perfect obedience, his spotless righteousness, by his atoning sacrifice, he has made peace and effected reconciliation.

Having briefly taken notice of the state into which man sank by reason of sin, and of the holiness, justice and righteousness of God, we come now more immediately to the solemn inquiry in the text: "How can man be justified with God?" And, in the first place, there are two propositions in the subject to which I desire especially to call your attention.

On the part of man, there must be the *absence of sin*, and on the part of God there must be *the presence of righteousness*. Sin must be for ever removed out of the way, and such a righteousness wrought out and brought in as shall magnify the God of glory.

But how is sin to be removed? Can the poor sinner ever remove it of himself? The whole of the Lord's family have striven to do it, but the more they have striven, the more have they proved their own weakness and the utter impossibility of accomplishing it of themselves. But sin *must* be removed; and how can it be done? Beloved, the God of love has taken all the sins of the vessels of mercy away. And what has he done with them? Why, he laid them of the head of his dear Son. I would be very particular on this point because this is a doctrine that is sadly abused by some, and strongly denied by many. But, sirs, I say all the sins of the election of grace – sins of omission and commission – sins before calling and sins after calling – yea, *all* their sins are removed and laid on the Lord Jesus Christ, who is the Daysman between God and their souls.

Hearken to the voice of inspiration: "All we like sheep have gone astray, we have turned every one to his own way, and the Lord hath laid on him the iniquity of us all." And, beloved, if it were possible that one sin was left on you or me, not transferred to Christ, that one sin would for ever damn our souls. The apostle is exceedingly clear in this matter. He says, "He that knew no sin" – I pause on this important sentence – "He that knew no sin." Dr. Crisp* has an expression in one of his sermons which I cannot justify. His works were put into my hands some years ago, and I was much benefitted by them, and I believe them calculated exceedingly to comfort the Lord's tried, tempted and afflicted family in the wilderness. But he says, "All the sins of the elect being laid upon Christ, he must have been the greatest sinner in the

* Tobias Crisp (1600-1642)

world." I don't like the word "sin" to be applied to the immaculate Jesus, for "He knew no sin, neither was guile found in his mouth."

Yet it pleased the Lord to bruise him, to put him to grief, and to make his soul an offering for sin, because all his people's sins were laid upon him. And what did Jesus do with them? Ah! let us first inquire, What did these sins do with Christ? O, beloved, they caused him to sweat great drops of blood – to travail in sorrow and grief, and to hang and bleed and die on the accursed tree. "He was wounded for our transgressions, he was bruised for our iniquities, the chastisement of our peace was upon him, and by his stripes we are healed." We have this removal or transfer of sin typified in the scape-goat under the law. The high priest laid his hand on the head of the goat, and there he confessed the sins of Israel. The goat was then sent away into the land of forgetfulness, never more to return – typical of the removal, carrying and bearing away of sin by the holy Lamb of God. Daniel speaks very blessedly on this subject. Speaking of the Lord Jesus, he says, "He shall make an *end of sin*, and bring in everlasting righteousness." And to the same effect speaks the great apostle when he says, "God was in Christ, reconciling the world unto himself, not imputing their trespasses unto them."

We see, then, how it is that sin is removed out of the way. Poor quickened and awakened sinners, are you reconciled to God? God is reconciled to you; for "once in the end of the world hath he appeared to put away sin by the sacrifice of himself." Beloved, when Jesus gave himself up as a sacrifice to God for the sins of his people, all their sins sank for ever into the bottom of the grave. Yes, all the sins of his mystical body were buried with him – they were all eternally carried away by that fountain of blood which he opened and poured out, so that, though they may be sought for, they shall never be found. I once heard a good old man make use of an expression on this subject which at first rather struck me with surprise.

"Beloved," said he, "in point of fact you never had any sin." What? thought I, I feel sin to be in me now, my daily plague and sorrow. But he followed it up and proved from the Scriptures that, as all the sins of the elect were removed from them to Christ, in the eye of a holy and heart-searching God they never had any sin. God did not behold iniquity in Jacob, nor transgression in Israel. I know not, my friends, what this doctrine of eternal justification is to your hearts, but it is that which bears *my* spirit up amid all the changes, sorrows and sins of this wilderness world. Yes, beloved, the comfort arising from this doctrine is this, that however sin may plague, it cannot damn me.

Lift up your heads, ye poor souls – the blood, the redeeming blood of Emmanuel has carried away your sins, and they can never more be found. They are cast behind the back of Jehovah, where they can never more be seen. Here, then, is the absence of sin; and well might the apostle be determined to know nothing amongst men but a slaughtered Lamb.

Beloved, here is another point which, although it is not in the text, yet would I just put you in remembrance of it. It is a comfort to my soul that, as our sin has been borne away, we stand as pure and perfect before God as Christ himself – because we stand in him, are represented by him, covered over with his righteousness; as Watts has it, when he says:

"And, lest the shadow of a spot
    Should on my soul be found,
  He took the robe the Saviour wrought,
    And cast it all around."

Sermon 2

Text: *"And by him all that believe are justified from all things, from which ye could not be justified by the law of Moses" (Acts 13. 39).*

Some present will remember that last Lord's day morning I spoke of the ground upon which a poor sinner stands justified in the sight of God, and promised this morning to treat of justification as made manifest in the court of a sinner's conscience. The words which I have read appear more appropriate to this part of the subject than those of Job; for this reason I have changed the text – the subject is the same. I shall take up no time in recapitulating those things already entered into, or I shall not be able to go into the experimental part. But doctrine and experience must be mingled together – there must be an experimental acquaintance with, as well as a doctrinal knowledge of, divine truth. We must ever remember that it is God's predestinated people, and God's predestinated people only, who stand justified in his sight. It is God's predestinated people only that are called by special grace; and every one of these shall, in his own time, be brought to an experimental acquaintance of their own justification by an application of the atoning blood of Christ unto their consciences.

None can tell who the vessels of mercy, whom God hath chosen, are while in their Adam nature; or, as the Scriptures express it, while "they lie among the pots of the earth." There is no difference whatever between the election of grace and the rest of mankind (who are righteously left to fill up the measure of their iniquity that they might be damned) while they stand in their federal head Adam. Did I say there was no difference between the election of grace and the rest of mankind? I did; but I feel constrained in my mind, in a measure, to retract the expression. Where is the difference? It is here: many of the vessels of mercy are suffered to go to greater lengths of wickedness and abominable sin than others. Beloved, the poor worm who now stands before you is a living witness of this solemn truth. In the days of my unregeneracy and youth, I went into all the most abominable sins that it is possible for man to enter into; and while many of the companions of my youth and iniquities are left still to continue in that course, God, in the exercise of his sovereign grace, has been pleased to pluck me as a brand from the burning. O, beloved, see the great, the matchless, the unmerited mercy of God! See it in the poor dust now before you – see it in Saul of Tarsus, whose heart was filled with malice and rage against the Lord of life and glory – see it in a bloody Manasseh, who made the very streets of the city to flow with the blood of the slain – see it in a filthy Mary Magdalene, yea, see it in all the election of grace.

So, you see, God's choice of his people is not on account of any goodness in themselves. O no, there is a sweetness in that blessed scripture which says, "It is of grace" – salvation "is of grace, that the promise might be sure to all the (spiritual) seed." Hence it is written, "He shall see of the travail of his soul, and shall be satisfied. He shall see his seed; he shall prolong his days; and the pleasure of the Lord shall prosper in his hands."

The psalmist David speaks of "a set time to favour Zion"; and there is a set time when every one of the spiritual seed shall not only be called by grace, but shall be brought to know his justification in his own conscience. God works by rule. And what is his rule? Why, his own eternal counsel, his unalterable purpose. You read of the calling of Zacchæus down from the tree. Now this was in the Lord's time. Zacchæus had heard of the person of Christ. Some said he was a good man; others said nay. So Zacchæus thought he would see this person himself; and being thus prompted by curiosity, he climbed up into a tree where he thought he was comfortable enough, little thinking of what was coming to pass. The Lord did not see him with his bodily eyes until he came to the bottom of the tree; but it was fixed and settled in his eternal purpose that down from this very tree he should be called by Christ himself, and at this very time. I know assertions prove no argument; but we will come to argument. Who called Zacchæus? Was it not the Lord? Yes, I feel pleasure in declaring it was the omnipotent Jehovah, in the person of Jesus, that called Zacchæus. Now the Lord does nothing, either in providence or grace, but what is in strict accordance with his own sovereign will and eternal purpose.

But I proceed. All the vessels of mercy, then, must be brought to an experimental acquaintance with the fact of their justification in the sight of God; or, to use the language of Scripture, they must be apprehended of God, as Paul speaks when he says, "I follow after, if that I may apprehend that for which also I am apprehended of Christ Jesus." You know persons may go on for a long time violating and breaking the statutes of their country and plundering their neighbours' property without being apprehended or made to suffer for their crimes; but there is a time when they are stopped and visited for their transgressions. So is it with the Lord's people. They go on for a season violating the statutes of heaven and having their conversation among the ungodly, and are apparently the children of wrath even as others. But the time comes when the Lord lays hold of them, when he stops them and apprehends them, constraining then to bow before him and to cry out for mercy. They are his covenant people, and every one of his covenant people must and shall be made willing in the day of his power to turn away from their ungodliness unto him.

Now when God apprehends a poor sinner, his conscience is wounded; his heart is opened; the eyes of his understanding are enlightened; a solemn fear is implanted, and he begins to see that the way he has been treading is the broad way to perdition; and like David, he is made to feel the weight of his iniquities, and the awful condition in which his sins have placed him. He not only sees, but he *feels* that the course he has been pursuing is that which leads to eternal destruction, and he quakes and trembles in his conscience. He begins to rehearse within himself what he shall do; he says, "I will forsake my sins, and I will begin to be religious. I will read and pray and meditate and go to the house of God," and so on. He has a secret thought that by this means he shall obtain forgiveness and heaven.

Now this is the old covenant ground of standing; and I do not wonder at there being so many Arminians as there are, for the old covenant ground is the very foundation and rule of all natural and fleshly religion. It is that which just suits the natural feelings of man. This was the error of the Jews who "went about to establish their own righteousness, not submitting to the righteousness of God." This was the very error of Saul of Tarsus, who persecuted the saints unto death and thought he had not need for any other righteousness than what he himself could work out. It is thus with many a poor sinner. He is permitted to make clean the outside of the platter; sin is forsaken; a form of godliness is taken up; he becomes exceedingly devout – and the change is so manifest that even many of the saints begin to say he must be a good man.

I recollect being in this state of outward godliness myself – and I thought if I were not saved, what would become of thousands whom I saw around me? While in this state I went to a prayer meeting, where a good old man read a chapter out of Matthew's Gospel, and took occasion from a part of it to describe the character, religion and real condition of the scribes and pharisees. I had not the slightest idea at this time of a justification through the atoning blood and imputed righteousness of the Lord Jesus Christ. I was building upon my own; but when the old man came to lay open the state of the pharisees, he met my case, he described my character, and his word came with such power into my soul that I fell into the most dreadful confusion. All my fancied righteousness came tumbling about my ears, and I saw that it was nothing but filthy rags and could never be a standing for me before God. O what a sinking of soul I then experienced! I had about a mile and a half to go home, which distance I walked in the greatest distress and misery, counting myself one of the most unhappy wretches on the face of the earth. And from that day guilt laid so heavy on my conscience that I could not so much as look at anything I had done as a ground of hope.

Now in this work of quickening the soul and in making it alive to its real condition, the Holy Ghost makes use of the law; as Paul says, "The commandment which was ordained to life, I found to be unto death." Now there is a great difference between the poor sinner going to the law and the law going to the sinner. When the sinner goes to the law, he sees what is expected of him. He sees wherein he has violated its enactments, and he resolves to do better. But when the law comes home to the sinner's conscience, and when the voice of God thunders in his soul, "Cursed is every one that continueth not in all things written in the book of the law to do them," and when it declares again, that "he who offendeth in one point is guilty of all" – why then the poor creature is filled with the greatest horror; his soul is shaken to its very centre. He trembles and quakes for fear, and often does he think God will stretch forth his hand and cut him down as a cumberer of the ground. He now discovers that the law requires purity in the nature, purity in the thoughts, and purity in the action. He sees, instead of "loving the Lord with all his heart and soul and strength," he has a carnal heart, full of pride and envy and rebellion, and that he can by no means work up this perfect love within him.

Now this so powerfully alarms him; he becomes so distressed and wounded that the people say he is crazy; and he himself expects, poor soul, that the mad-house will be the only place for which he will be fit. He hangs down his head like a bulrush. A heavy weight of condemnation and a dark cloud of sorrow lies upon his mind, and he knows not where to go, nor what to do. I admit, all the Lord's people are not brought to such a depth of mental misery as this. But all of them must have their self-righteousness burnt up by the fire of God's law, and in a measure be stripped and emptied of self and shut up as a poor prisoner, being bound in his soul, and sighing and crying for pardon and liberty, though he scarcely dare hope he shall obtain it. I would not give the value of my old silk handkerchief for a man's religion if he has not been shut up in soul prison.

You find David crying out, "Let the sighing of the prisoner come up before thee, and deliver thou them that are appointed to die." Here you see, then, is a prisoner, and he feels as though he is appointed unto death, and all he can do is to sigh and groan; and therefore he says, "Let the sighing of the prisoner come up before thee." And if I have a poor soul here this morning who is in this "Slough of Despond," as John Bunyan terms it, one who has all his sins set in battle array before him; I say, if the Lord had a mind to destroy thee, he would never have shown thee these things. The Lord wounds in order that he may heal. He pulls down that he may build up. The Lord makes the poor sinner feel his filthiness in order that he may wash him. The Lord strips him, cuts him off from every false confidence, in order to clothe him and lead him to trust alone in him.

This is God's way of religion, but we know it is not the religion of the present day – the generality of professors are "imperceptibly drawn by love"; and being trained up in a profession, they love the form and they love the respectability of religion, and many of them in trade say they find it very advantageous. But this is not the way in which the Holy Ghost brings a vessel of mercy into religion. No, no! He deeply wounds, he breaks up the fallow ground of the heart, he lays the soul in the dust of humility, makes him to loathe himself and his sins and all creature doings.

But you will say, "You don't come to the doctrine of justification." I am paving my way to it, my friends. Now, the poor soul in this condition can do nothing with that justification that depends on his own doings. I have made a profession of religion for seven and thirty years*, twenty-three of which I have been in the ministry; and I was never more at

* Either Mr. Kershaw or the reporter got these dates wrong. They should be 32 and 27.

a point in this matter than I am this morning, that if my profession of religion, my preaching of the gospel, my visiting of the sick, my reading, my meditation and my prayers; if, I say, these things constituted the ground on which my hope of justification was founded, I am certain I must be eternally damned. When the poor quickened and convinced soul is brought into the state I have been describing, he solemnly feels the truth of those words of Watts, who says:

> "The best obedience of my hands,
> Dares not appear before thy throne;
> 'Tis faith must answer thy demands,
> By pleading what my Lord has done."

Yes, it is "*what my Lord has done*" – not what I have done – that is the ground of a poor sinner's plea and hope and confidence. Now then, man's extremity, you must observe, is God's opportunity. When the poor soul has been brought down so low that it can stand on nothing, nor in nothing but the almighty power of God, then is the time when the Lord will begin to discover himself as one pardoning iniquity, and passing by the transgressions of the remnant of his chosen heritage.

While I am speaking to you, I am looking back to the night when God made known unto me the pardon of my sins, and the justification of my soul. God's ministers ought to speak of the way in which it pleased God to teach them the things concerning their eternal peace. I would not give you a "thank you" for to hear any man preach who cannot tell how he learned Christ himself. As respects my own deliverance, then you shall have it my friends; but very briefly. I had been, one Lord's Day, to three services, and had heard our old friend Warburton*; after which, as I was returning home at night, I began to be most powerfully wrought upon in my mind. The first thing that struck me was that expression of the Apostle, "O, wretched man that I am, who shall deliver me

* John Warburton (1776 - 1857). At this time he was pastor at Hope Chapel, Rochdale.

from the body of this death?" I felt myself to be a miserable and wretched sinner; I felt I had indeed a body of sin and death, and a carnal mind, and a heart deceitful and desperately wicked. I got home as well as I could, when the next word that came to me was, "There is therefore now no condemnation to them that are in Christ Jesus." I took out my little Testament and I read the eighth chapter of the Romans; and most powerfully did it please the Lord to bless it to my soul. I felt thatI was indeed loved of God in Christ; that I was chosen in Christ; that I was redeemed by Christ; that I was saved through the precious blood-shedding of Christ; and peace rolled into soul like a river and I had joy and comfort in the Holy Ghost. O! what a solemn night of jubilee that was to my soul. I never had a wink of sleep; all that I could do was to look on, like one of old, at what God had done, and by faith to believe that it was done for me.

You will remember that last Sunday morning, I contended most earnestly for two points connected with this great doctrine of justification. I particularly dwelt on these two things – first, that there must be the *absence of sin*; and, secondly, there must be the *presence of righteousness*. Now my beloved, depend on it, that when God the Holy Ghost comes into the sinner's conscience with the blood of Christ, all his sins are taken away. This was as I found it myself: all my sins appeared to be gone, so that it came to my mind, "Why, where are your sins?" They were gone, I could not find one; they were all sunk as into the bottom of the sea. And though I have had many seasons dark and distressing since that time, yet on that night I could do nothing but rejoice and praise the Lord for the mercies he had bestowed upon and wrought within me. Yes, there must be, then, *the absence of sin*. And where, I ask, were all the sins of the vessels of mercy? Why, they were cast for ever behind our Heavenly Father's back; and he says, "They shall be sought for, and they shall not be found." God is reconciled to the redeemed by his Son, and they have pardon and peace for evermore.

But there was another point that I contended for last
Lord's day morning. There must not only be the absence of
sin but there must also be *the presence of righteousness.*

You see from the description I have given of the convinced sinner that he has no righteousness of his own. God
has burnt it all up; but the Holy Ghost brings near the
righteousness of Jesus. And how is this? Well, he is brought
to see that God has wrought it out and brought in everlasting
righteousness, and he sees that, "Blessed is the man unto
whom the Lord imputeth not iniquity." By the anointing and
sanctifying teachings of the Holy Spirit, he now feels that
"Christ is made of God unto him, wisdom, righteousness,
sanctification, and redemption." He sees, by faith, that he is
washed in the blood of Christ, stands clothed in the righteousness of Christ, and his holy song of triumph is,

> "Jesus my Lord and beauty is,
> My glorious robe of righteousness;
> Midst flaming worlds in this arrayed,
> With joy shall I lift up my head."

It is, then, by the blood-shedding of the Son of Godand
the working out and the bringing in of an everlasting righteousness by him that poor sinners are saved. It is by the
quickening, soul-humbling, life-giving operations of the
Eternal Spirit; by the application of Jesus' precious blood; by
the clothing of the soul in his spotless righteousness; by the
shedding abroad in the heart of his divine love; by the removal of guilt from the conscience, and the peace of God
implanted, that the poor soul feels and knows and enjoys his
acceptance in the Beloved. Now you shall have the language
of the church expressive of all this. Speaking of herself she
says: "We are altogether as an unclean thing; and all our
righteousnesses are as filthy rags." But what is her language
respecting her standing in Christ? "Surely shall one say, In the
Lord have I righteousness and strength." Again the spouse
says, "The Lord hath clothed me with the robe of right-

eousness, he hath covered me with the garments of salvation."
Here is the glorious dress; here is the sure foundation of the
poor believer; so that the apostle exclaims, "Who shall lay
anything to the charge of God's elect?" God says, "I have no
charge to bring"; justice says, "I am satisfied." So the Holy
Ghost, by the apostle, declares, "There is therefore now no
condemnation to them that are in Christ Jesus, who walk not
after the flesh, but after the Spirit."

The blessedness of this justification in the soul is realized
by faith. Paul has a very striking mode of expression when
speaking of this grace of faith. He says, "To him that worketh
not, but believeth on him that justifieth the ungodly, his faith
is counted for righteousness." And again he says, "Being
justified by faith, we have peace with God through our Lord
Jesus Christ." Are we, from these, to understand that faith
becomes a ground of justification? Certainly not: it is not the
actings of faith, but the *object* of faith, which is the Lord Jesus
Christ himself. One text sometimes throws a deal of light
upon another, and that account in the gospel of the poor
woman who pressed her way through the crowd, crying out,
"If I may but touch the hem of his garment, I shall be whole,"
appears to me to explain the apostle's meaning. After the
woman had touched "the border of his garment," Jesus said,
"Who touched me? for I perceive that virtue hath gone out of
me." Was it the woman's faith, or the virtue that flowed from
Christ himself that made her whole? It was not her faith, but
it was the precious virtue which came from Jesus; so that the
language of the thirsty soul is, "O that I may be found in him,
not having on mine own righteousness which is of the law, but
that which is through the faith of Christ, the righteousness
which is of God by faith." Faith is a grace of the blessed Spirit,
the first actings of which, as well as its growth and continu-
ance, are all the sovereign work of God the Holy Ghost. I feel
that of myself I have no more power to believe or to bring
home one promise to my soul now than I had before I was
made a partaker of divine grace.

But I must come to the last part of the subject, which is to show what justification is in an evidential or practical point of view. And if we come to practical godliness, the Apostle James will furnish us with some information respecting the fruits that it produces, wherein it may appear to some that he contradicts all I have been saying, and upsets even the doctrine as preached by Paul himself. But we know there can be no contradiction or schism in the revealed will of God. The truth is, Paul sinks the sinner down to the very lowest, and lifts up the Saviour; but James speaks of a present, a manifest justification in the sight of men. I am sick of those professors who have justification as a doctrine in the head, but who know nothing of it experimentally in the heart. I am satisfied of this, that if we enjoy justification in our consciences, we love the Lord Jesus Christ and all his holy commands. Real saints love to make it manifest that they are saints by a walk and conversation becoming the gospel. Religion without faith is a dead and filthy carcase; and faith without works is unprofitable either for time or eternity. You observe the Apostle James shows the nature and purity of genuine faith by the obedience which it renders unto God. The obedience of faith was strikingly manifested in Abraham's taking the knife, and lifting up his hand to strike the fatal blow. Thereby God proved the genuineness of Abraham's faith; and the true Israel of God can be distinguished from others only by their obedience and conformity to him.